PARTY COMPETITION IN ARGENTINA AND CHILE

PARTY COMPETITION IN ARGENTINA AND CHILE

Political Recruitment and Public Policy, 1890–1930

Karen L. Remmer

UNIVERSITY OF NEBRASKA PRESS
Lincoln and London

Material previously published in "The Timing, Pace, and Sequence of
Political Change in Chile, 1891–1925," by Karen L. Remmer, pp. 205–230
of the *Hispanic American Historical Review*, vol. 57, no. 2 (May 1977), copy-
right 1977 by Duke University Press.

Library of Congress Cataloging in Publication Data
Remmer, Karen L.
  Party competition in Argentina and Chile.
  Bibliography: p.
  Includes index.
  1. Political parties—Argentina—History. 2. Political
parties—Chile—History. 3. Political planning—
Argentina—History. 4. Political planning—Chile—
History. 5. Elite (Social sciences)—Argentina—History.
6. Elite (Social sciences)—Chile—History. I. Title.
JL2098.A1R44   1984   324'.0982   84–13119
ISBN 0-8032-3871-1 (alk. paper)

In the interests of timeliness and economy, this book was printed from
camera-ready copy supplied by the author.

CONTENTS

LIST OF TABLES

LIST OF TABLES

PREFACE

This book attempts to address issues of importance to scholars in two separate disciplines. Such "trespassing," as Albert O. Hirschman has called it, inevitably entails certain risks. Nevertheless, it is hoped that this book will appeal to both political scientists and historians. It deals with questions that are central to the theoretical concerns of political science, and it attempts to provide answers by comparing critically important periods in Argentine and Chilean history.

Between 1890 and 1930 Argentina and Chile both made the difficult transition from closed oligarchical rule to competitive party politics. In the case of Chile, this development has received little attention; indeed, historical research in general on the period between the civil war of 1891 and the election of Arturo Alessandri remains limited. Students of Argentine history have shown greater interest in the 1890-1930 period, but the events of those years rarely have been placed in comparative perspective.

This study also attempts to fill a gap in the scholarly literature by systematically analyzing the impact of party competition on the basis of a historical comparison. Efforts to understand the consequences of party competition typically have relied on comparisons among contemporary regimes. By turning instead to comparative diachronic data, this study challenges conventional wisdom and offers a basis for understanding why the results of party competition may vary greatly over time and across cases.

The present study began life more than a decade ago as a comparative analysis of party development and regime transformation in Argentina and Chile. With time the study expanded to include a detailed examination of the consequences of party competition in the two countries. In the process numerous debts have been incurred to teachers, friends, colleagues, and library staffs in Britain, Latin America, and the United States. Special thanks are reserved for Philippe Schmitter, who shaped my understanding of comparative politics and Latin America and who offered kindly advice and useful criticism at an early stage of my research; Lloyd Rudolph, who brought insights drawn from development processes in other regions of the world to bear upon a preliminary version of this study; Arnold J. Bauer, who generously shared information about

large estate owners in Chilean society; Simon Collier, whose
knowledgeable criticism helped me through several historical
thickets; Gilbert W. Merkx, who commented perceptively upon
multiple drafts of this work; and Mary Kay Day, whose skill and
good humor were invaluable in the final stages of the publication
process. I am also grateful to the Research Allocations Committee
of the University of New Mexico, which provided important
financial assistance, and to my children, Andrea and Peter, who
mounted useful diversionary activities and thereby helped in their
own way to move this book along toward publication.

INTRODUCTION

A regime without parties is, of necessity, a conservative regime.

Maurice Duverger

Political parties . . . are the only devices thus far invented by the wit of Western man which with some effectiveness can generate countervailing collective power on behalf of the many individually powerless against the relatively few who are individually—or organizationally—powerful.

Walter Dean Burnham

Assumptions about the importance of political parties and electoral competition pervade modern normative conceptions of democracy as well as empirical research in the field of comparative politics. In the case of Latin America, research for more than three decades has centered on the problems of explaining the breakdown of competitive party politics and the emergence of military rule. The sheer volume of scholarly interest in these questions suggests that regime changes affect not only *how* a country is ruled, but *for whom* and *for what* it is ruled. Yet, despite a growing literature on the relationship between political variables and public policy, the consequences of the political structures, rules, and procedures that define competitive regimes remain very much open to question.[1]

Similarly, great importance has been ascribed to political parties, even in those parts of the world where they are relatively fragile institutions. Political systems with parties are almost universally regarded as more "advanced," "modern," or "developed" than those without them.[2] The implication is that party development does not merely reflect socioeconomic change; it fundamentally alters the operation of the political system and shapes political outcomes. Again, the comparative evidence is rather weak.[3]

This study attempts to fill these gaps by exploring the consequences of regime changes in the Latin American context. Its central concern is the impact of party development and electoral competition on the struggle for political power in Chile and Argentina between 1890 and 1930.

Chile and Argentina were chosen for this study for several reasons. From a methodological standpoint these two countries are similar enough to allow for a manageable paired comparison, holding constant a number of significant variables: culture, religion, the nature and timing of independence, world political situation, and level of technology. Other factors, such as socioeconomic structure, vary within limited bounds. Perhaps even more important, it is possible to rule out cultural diffusion as a significant source of cross-national variation in the impact of party development and electoral competition.[4] The imitation of Western European programs provided an important impetus to policy change in both countries, especially in the field of social welfare; however, because of geographical propinquity and the near identity of time periods studied, cultural diffusion was a constant for the two nations.

Moreover, by Third World standards Chile and Argentina are "early developers."[5] For example, the two countries were more urbanized and had higher per capita incomes at the start of World War I than the majority of Latin American republics in 1950.[6] This point is of theoretical significance, because party structures and other political arrangements adopted by "late developers" in response to the diffusion of foreign ideas have been reshaped by situational conditions very different from those prevailing in the countries where these ideas originated. Hence concepts and theories based on the experience of the United States and Western Europe, including those related to party competition and public policy, are often inapplicable to a Third World context. Rough parametric similarities, however, exist between the "early developers" and Chile or Argentina. Indeed, except for the British "fragments,"[7] such as Australia, these two countries, which developed in a capitalist context with relatively homogeneous populations, close ties to Europe, and liberal political and economic orientations, probably came closest to fulfilling in a non-European context the conditions associated with the initial capitalist-pluralist wave of development.

Major contrasts also exist between the patterns of political development in Chile and Argentina since 1930 that make a study of the impact of party competition particularly interesting. The two countries are among the most modernized in Latin America, and in terms of such indices as literacy, urbanization, and per capita wealth they resemble one another fairly closely. Yet politically the two countries have differed considerably. The contrasts are familiar to most students of Latin American affairs: in the past five decades Argentine politics have been characterized by political instability and military intervention, whereas until 1973 a long series of constitutionally elected presidents ruled Chile. Likewise, parties have been at the center of power struggles in Chile, whereas their role in Argentina has been far less important.

These contrasts pose significant questions for theories about the origin and consolidation of political democracy. As one of the most stable constitutional democracies in the world since the turn of the century, Chile has stood out among other Latin American and Third World nations as a puzzling exception to generalizations about the relationship between socioeconomic development and democracy. Due to the failure of its experiments with democratic political institutions, Argentina likewise has represented a prominent deviant case that challenges attempts at explaining the incidence of democracy around the world.

The periods of party competition studied are 1891-1924 in the case of Chile and 1912-1930 for Argentina. The Chilean "parliamentary period," as it is conventionally called, was introduced by the civil war of 1891 and terminated by the military coup of 1924. In Argentina, the years 1912-1930 have been described as the "Radical era": the only extended period of party competition in the nation's history. The period began with the passage of the Saenz Peña law, which effected a fundamental reform of the Argentine electoral system, and ended with the military coup of 1930. Although not precisely coterminous, the overlap between the two periods is considerable, and a number of key similarities exist: economic prosperity based on foreign investment and external demand for primary products, the related growth of commercial and industrial activities, rapid urbanization, the rise of new political groups representing middle- and lower-class interests, the organization of political parties, the appearance of populist leaders, and the growth of electoral competition. Perhaps most significant, both periods were formative in the sense that they contributed to the long standing political contrasts between the two countries outlined above. Whereas in Chile the initial experiment with competitive political arrangements established the basis for the formation of a relatively well-institutionalized party system, in Argentina important groups failed to participate in or support a competitive regime almost from the outset. This contrast reflects the differing impact of regime change in the two countries. In Argentina party development and electoral competition entailed some loss of political control by established elites; in Chile the result was nearly the opposite.

THEORETICAL PERSPECTIVES

The argument that public policy and other political outcomes vary with regime type is based on the assumption that institutional arrangements differentially structure access to positions of political power in ways that favor some sectors of society at the expense of others. Different kinds of regimes not only should produce different kinds of political leaders; they also should confront decision makers with different sets of options, constraints, and incentives. Even though most empirical research on the relationship between regime type and policy performance has failed to support these propositions,[8] they are widely accepted. Hence scholars using very divergent theoretical frameworks continue to place questions about the causes of regime change and consolidation at the center of their research agenda on the assumption that the institutional structure of the state must influence who governs and who loses and benefits from government.[9]

In general the theoretical literature on the impact of political institutions suggests that party competition minimizes the autonomy of government authorities and maximizes the influence of subordinate groups; i.e., it creates a relatively broad distribution of political power.[10] Two closely related lines of argument are used to support this proposition. One is that party competition draws large numbers of people into political activity and provides channels for the expression and representation of their interests. Thus authorities are confronted not only with pressures from other elites, but also with demands from a wide range of social interests. Concomitantly, party competition expands political opportunities and broadens the base from which political leaders are drawn.[11] This line of argument is particularly prevalent in the literature on U.S. local government, which suggests that nonpartisan elections discourage lower-class political involvement, increase the tendency for political candidates to be recruited from the upper socioeconomic echelons, bias decision making in favor of middle- and upper-class interests, and generally contribute to a "politics of acquaintance."[12]

The second argument is that parties, by organizing electoral alternatives, place sanctions in the hands of non-elites, creating pressures and incentives for authorities to take the interests, opinions, and demands of subordinate groups into account when formulating public policy. As V.O. Key argued in his classic study of U.S. southern state politics, unless the electorate can distinguish between "ins" and "outs," it cannot make meaningful choices or hold elites responsible for public policy.[13]

In summary, these arguments imply that by expanding the scope of political participation and structuring political competition, the emergence of a competitive party regime will reduce inequalities in the access to political power and increase the number of interests taken into account in the formulation of public policy. It may be noted that this theoretical position does not suggest that a competitive regime is a *necessary* condition for the implementation of policies favorable to non-elites or the recruitment of leaders from a relatively broad social base. The achievements of revolutionary-authoritarian regimes in these areas are commonly accepted. Neither do the arguments outlined above imply that the introduction of a competitive regime will completely equalize the distribution of political power. As empirical research on countries such as the United States has demonstrated, political opportunities may remain somewhat stratified; likewise, government policy may not faithfully reflect public opinion.[14] Nevertheless, the arguments outlined above do imply that party competition shifts political outcomes in a more egalitarian direction, regardless of the distribution of resources in a society and regardless of specific institutional arrangements or other potentially important sources of political variation. Whether a competitive regime is parliamentary or presidential, based on proportional representation or a majority electoral system, characterized by two-party or multi-party competition, or elected by literate males rather than the entire adult population, the direction of change will be the same. *Ceteris paribus* party development and electoral competition will produce shifts in policies and recruitment practices beneficial to less privileged social groups.

In contrast, this study argues that (1) the impact of party competition is conditioned by two basic variables—the scope of popular participation and the structure of competition, and (2) under certain conditions, notably when the electorate is small and political competition is not structured along well-defined lines, the introduction of a competitive system may even have negative implications for subordinate social groups. Since these findings suggest that the impact of party competition may vary widely across cases, they provide a possible basis for explaining the failure of previous empirical studies to uncover any strong relationship between party competition and political outcomes.

Most comparative research on the impact of party competition has relied on statistical inferences drawn from cross-sectional comparisons among nations or sub-national political units. This study is based instead on a paired diachronic comparison, which offers some distinct advantages. Unlike large sample comparative studies, which achieve statistical reliability at the expense of limiting analysis to readily quantifiable variables and crude indicators of similarities and differences,[15] paired comparisons make it possible to bring extensive information to bear on the definition and measurement of critical variables. The result is a study of greater "depth" or validity. The chief limitation of a paired comparison is that it typically depends on descriptive evaluation and potentially controversial counter-factual assumptions. This limitation, however, is offset by the use of a diachronic or longitudinal approach. Important variables that differentiate nations and hence need to be taken into account in cross-national studies, such as geography and culture, are in effect held constant for the single nation studied through time. To the extent that two cases selected for diachronic comparison are similar in background characteristics, the sources of variation are likewise reduced, avoiding the proliferation of possible alternative explanations for observed relationships, as well as the "apples versus oranges" criticism often directed at studies with large samples.[16]

Perhaps most important, a time-oriented approach is both methodologically and substantively critical for the development of theory about processes occurring through time, such as party development, public policy, and political recruitment.[17] As the literature on political development emphasizes, relationships among variables are conditioned by time sequences, rates of change, and historical contexts—none of which can be analyzed on the basis of cross-sectional comparisons.[18] Moreover, a diachronic approach permits much more efficient and powerful assumptions about the nature of causal relationships, because inferences about causality can be drawn from the sequence of change through time. Ahistorical approaches, on the other hand, may lead to misleading inferences about causality. These advantages of a diachronic approach are well illustrated by the now discredited early literature on socioeconomic development and democracy, which drew unwarranted and erroneous conclusions about causal time-spanning processes within political units from cross-sectional comparisons.[19]

MAJOR CONCEPTS

Because much of the subsequent analysis hinges on the meaning of "political party" and "party competition," a few words should be said about how these terms are used in this book. Theoretical work on political parties has been severely hampered by conceptual problems. Some definitions of the term "party" are so broad that they include all political structures with a popular base, regardless of their characteristic form of activity; other definitions are so restrictive that they virtually apply only to the Conservative and Labour parties of Great Britain.

This study employs a concept of party falling between such extremes that is based on William N. Chambers' work on party origins in the United States.[20] Parties are distinguished from other groups seeking power within the political arena by four defining characteristics: (1) a set of consciously shared perspectives, opinions, or beliefs (as indicated by the use of a party label and the promulgation of a party platform); (2) continuing and regularized connections between political leaders at the center and local party activists (as indicated by the existence of party units at the local level and formal channels of coordination, such as national conventions); (3) a durable base of popular support (as indicated by persistence over a time period of several national elections and a minimal achievement in terms of national electoral support); and (4) coordinated efforts to win popular support in order to exercise control over the selection of government authorities and the formulation of public policy (as indicated by the nomination of candidates and active campaigning for electoral support).

Only political formations displaying all four of these characteristics are classified as political parties. It should be noted, however, that factions or cliques often resemble parties in one or more critical respects. During their early stages of organizational development parties are also likely to bear important similarities to nonparty formations. Loyalty to party, for example, may emerge as a compound of traditional *caudillismo* and modern sentiments of partisanship. The above definition is not intended to deny the existence of such similarities. It is proposed solely to facilitate classification, which requires that an analytical and operational distinction be drawn between parties and other phenomena. The concept offered here makes it possible to draw such a distinction, without violating a common sense understanding of the term "party." In addition, the concept does not define away a large number of interesting variables that may be theoretically related to parties; i.e., it makes few assumptions about the social and political conditions under which parties arise and persist, the functions they perform, or the consequences of parties for political systems.

With the above concept in mind, a competitive party regime may be defined simply as a structure of government in which individuals acquire positions of political authority by means of a competitive struggle between two or more parties for the popular vote.[21] This definition implies certain parametric conditions: regular and reasonably open elections; relative freedom of organization, expression, and suffrage; and official recognition of the right of political leaders to compete for popular support.

The first portion of this book examines the emergence of such a structure of government in Argentina and Chile near the turn of the century and attempts to explain major political similarities and differences between the two countries in terms of three general sets of factors: the previous pattern of development, the socioeconomic context, and the process of transition from semi-competitive oligarchical rule to competitive party politics. The second portion of the work analyzes the consequences of party development and electoral competition. It focuses specifically on changing patterns of leadership selection and public policy formation and relates variations in political outcomes in Argentina and Chile to the scope of participation and the structure of political conflict.

CHAPTER I

THE STRUCTURE OF POLITICAL CONFLICT BEFORE 1890

Historians have traditionally traced the origins of Argentine and Chilean political parties back to the early years of national independence. In both countries, however, the political cleavages that emerged in the wake of the disintegration of Spanish colonial authority involved loose coalitions of rival leaders, kinship networks, and local cliques rather than organized political structures.

In Chile factional strife centered around two conflicting ideological tendencies. The *pipiolos*—literally "novices"—favored a liberal form of government, while the *pelucones* or "bigwigs" opposed reforms in the name of order, authority, and tradition. The civil war of 1829-1830 settled the conflict in favor of the more conservative *pelucón* tendency, which dominated the government of Chile until 1851.[1]

In Argentina the conflict over national political organization gave rise to a prolonged dispute between federalists and centralists. The basis of this dispute varied considerably over time, but essentially the *federalistas* favored a federal constitutional structure that would release the provinces from the hegemony of Buenos Aires, while the *unitarios* sought a republic unified under a strong national government. Neither group was organized. Indeed the label *federalista* was applied to men both in Buenos Aires and the provinces who often found themselves working at cross purposes.[2]

Political conflicts in the two countries only assumed a more structured form in the last half of the nineteenth century. The first steps in this direction took place in Chile, where the period of chaos that succeeded independence throughout Latin America came to a very early end. Under the constitution of 1833, which established a centralized national government and powerful executive, a regular succession of elected presidents ruled Chile until 1891. The unifying effects of Chile's military victory over Peru and Bolivia in the 1830s, the economic prosperity associated with the expansion of mining and agricultural exports, and the country's geography all contributed to this record of political stability, which was exceptional by Latin American standards. In contrast, the struggle to consolidate national unity and governmental institutions was extremely protracted in Argentina, which was a far less homogeneous, prosperous, and geographically compact society. The first tentative success was marked by the constitution of 1853, but it took another three decades before a final solution was found to the problem of national organization.

Partially because of these contrasts, the process of party development in the two countries differed considerably. The stable national political structure established in Chile allowed for relatively early acceptance of the principle of the legitimacy of organized political opposition. By the 1870s a tradition of peaceful competition between rival political groups, which were organized around ideological rather than purely personal considerations, had developed. This tradition was unique in nineteenth-century Latin America, and it facilitated the transition to a system of political party competition after 1891. In Argentina, on the other hand, political parties did not grow out of an institutionalized system of competition at the elite level. Throughout most of the nineteenth century opposition groups were denied political representation, and political conflicts were not channelled through government institutions. In these circumstances, political parties developed as a challenge to government authority, and pressures for the introduction of a competitive regime met greater elite resistance than in Chile.

POLITICAL CONFLICT IN NINETEENTH-CENTURY CHILE

The structure of government established in Chile initially offered very little scope for the activities of independent political associations. It has with some accuracy been described as an "autocratic republic,"[3] because although the legislature developed some institutional autonomy, from 1831 to 1851 the Chilean president's power and authority were virtually unassailable. As divisions developed within the ruling elite, this situation began to change. The administration of Manuel Montt (1851-1861) marks a crucial turning point.

The Growth of Political Opposition

Montt's predecessor, Manuel Bulnes, had been forced to deal with a certain amount of opposition. The 1840s were a period of intellectual revival in Chile. Influenced by developments in Europe, particularly the revolutionary ferment of 1848, a new enthusiasm for liberal principles developed that found expression not only in the publication of books and periodicals, but in concrete political activity. The ranks of the liberal opposition were further swelled by the 1849 division of government forces that followed the dismissal of the Minister of the Interior, Manuel Camilo Vial, from Bulnes' cabinet. This opposition culminated in the months preceding the presidential election of 1851. President Bulnes' chosen successor, Montt, was anathema to almost all men of liberal sympathies, and a campaign of public agitation, led by the newly formed Sociedad de Igualdad,[4] was launched to combat his candidacy. In reaction the government declared a state of siege in two provinces, muffled the press, disbanded the Sociedad de Igualdad, and sent many of its leaders into exile. Regional interests with a variety of economic and political grievances against the central government combined with liberals in launching an unsuccessful military revolt.[5]

When Montt assumed office he thus already faced considerable opposition. Despite the relatively favorable economic conditions created by the growth of mining, railroads, and agricultural exports, discontent became so intense that by 1856 it took only a small and apparently trivial incident to split the ruling *pelucones* completely: the so-called "Affair of the Sacristan," which involved a jurisdictional dispute between ecclesiastical and civil tribunals.[6]

Until Montt's time religious issues had not played a major role in Chilean politics. Under the constitution of 1833 the country was officially Roman Catholic, and the president was empowered to exercise the *patronato*; i.e., subject to senate approval he named archbishops, bishops, and prebends from a list of names suggested by the Council of State. The president's prerogatives had never been seriously challenged, but in the 1850s the ultramontane argument, which was essentially that the *patronato* was spiritual in origin and not automatically transferred from the Spanish king, was suddenly revived. The religious conflict transformed the politics of the country. The *pelucones* split into two groups. One group sided with the clerical element led by Archbishop Valdivieso, while the other supported Montt. The liberals did not necessarily agree with the arguments put forth by the clerical sector, but most of them sympathized with the archbishop in the dispute because of their antagonism towards Montt. The president was thus left with a very reduced number of supporters to face an opposition alliance of clergy, liberals, and prochurch conservatives. Economic grievances and resentment against the increased centralization of government authority contributed to Montt's political difficulties.[7] According to Alberto Edwards Vives, one of Chile's most eminent political historians and the classic authority on party development, "It is an historical fact that after 1857 the government of Montt was far from being able to count on the support of the majority of the country."[8]

Montt used the very considerable array of powers at his disposal to circumscribe the activities of the opposition, but its sheer size and importance in the country meant that it could not be readily eliminated. Fusionists, as members of the opposition alliance were called, carried out a program of obstruction in the legislature and campaigned in the elections of 1858 in which they secured fourteen seats in the Chamber of Deputies. The following year Pedro León Gallo, a wealthy miner from Copiapó with liberal political orientations, led a disparate collection of regional forces in another armed rebellion against the central government.[9]

Following the breakdown of conservative unity under Montt, every Chilean president was faced with an opposition and was forced to search for partisan support to govern. Montt's successor, José Joaquín Pérez (1861-1871), recognized the untenability of

Montt's political position and chose to govern with the backing of
the Fusionists. The Montt-Varists or Nationals, as Montt's supporters were known, moved to the opposition. There they were
joined by the Radicals, who made up a new political group composed largely of liberals whose freemasonry views led them to
find the fusion with proclerical conservatives unacceptable.[10] The
Radicals and Nationals held similar ideas on the clerical issue, and
although the most advanced liberals apparently had little else
in common with their former opponents, the Nationals' position
on such issues as electoral freedom changed when they found
themselves in the opposition and vulnerable to repressive government activity. In any case the relationship between church and
state remained a leading political issue, and the church did not
differentiate among its opponents. From the clerical perspective
the Nationals and Radicals were equally heretical groups, and they
were denounced as such from pulpits throughout the country.[11]

The tensions inherent in the liberal-conservative fusion came
to the surface during the administration of Federico Errázuriz
Zañartu (1871-1875), when liberals pressed for a number of
reforms that threatened the position of the church.[12] As a result
the government coalition collapsed and was replaced by one
composed of *liberales, radicales,* and *nacionales*, which persisted,
with few modifications, until 1891.

Protoparty Competition, 1870-1891

During the "Liberal Republic" (1870-1891) a system of competition between legislative groups or "protoparties" became firmly
established in Chile. In certain respects the groups that participated
in this system resembled political parties. First, they were relatively
durable groups in the sense that they persisted over an extended
period of time. The conservatives who opposed Montt, their liberal
allies, Montt's supporters, and the Radicals who appeared as a discrete political group under President Pérez could all be identified
on the eve of the civil war of 1891 as, respectively, the Conservatives, Liberals, Nationals, and Radicals. Second, these groups were
more than just cliques bound together by personal loyalties, family
connections, or other particularistic considerations, although such

ties did play an important role in nineteenth-century Chile, as might be expected given the small number of men who participated in politics and the relatively traditional nature of the society. The members of the various political groupings shared certain political beliefs and developed a limited sense of partisan identity and loyalty. From Montt's time onward it is possible to classify most members of the Chilean legislature according to partisan affiliation.[13] The growth of partisanship can also be traced in the political press. By the end of the Liberal Republic two important dailies supported the Nationals: *El Mercurio* of Valparaíso and *La Epoca* of Santiago; the government Liberals' viewpoint was expressed by *La Tribuna* and *La Nación* of Santiago and *El Comercio* of Valparaíso; the Conservatives' by *El Independiente* and *El Estandarte Católico* in the capital and *La Unión* in Valparaíso; the Radicals' by *El Heraldo* in Valparaíso; while *La Libertad Electoral* in Santiago spoke in favor of the opposition or independent Liberals.[14] In contrast to the early 1800s politics had become very much a matter of partisan rather than individual or family orientation.

From a modern perspective it is difficult to understand the basis for this developing sense of partisanship, because underlying social or economic conflicts do not readily explain the political differences among the various political groups. The Radicals can be linked with northern mining interests, the Nationals with banking interests, or the Conservatives with the large estates of central Chile; yet all the groups represented a very narrow upper class and their members shared the same fundamental socioeconomic interests and outlook.[15] For this reason the divisions between them appear artificial; however, the Chilean upper class of the time, which could depend on the passivity and deference of subordinate groups, did not feel itself united by common interests but fragmented by differences of opinion and traditions of enmity.

The relationship between church and state remained a prominent political issue. During the 1871 to 1886 period a series of legislative measures abolished the ecclesiastical *fuero*, made civil marriage compulsory, secularized cemeteries, and deprived the church of its exclusive right to keep birth, death, and marriage statistics. This attack on the temporal powers of the church involved practical as well as ideological considerations. After the 1850s the church actively intervened in political affairs on the side of the opposition, so governments had a definite incentive to reduce clerical influence. Furthermore, the clerical issue could be used to unite the Liberals, Nationals, and Radicals, who otherwise had very little in common, in support of a government.

The church reacted strongly to the legislation. Archbishop Rafael Valentín Valdivieso actually excommunicated those who supported the anticlerical reforms under Errázuriz.[16] Tensions reached a peak under President Domingo Santa María (1881-1886) over the question of the appointment of a new archbishop to fill the vacancy left by Archbishop Valdivieso's death in 1878. At the request of the clergy a papal delegate travelled to Chile to settle the dispute. When he sided with the clergy, Santa María expelled him from the country, and normal diplomatic relations between Rome and Santiago were severed.[17]

The clerical issue isolated the Conservatives and provided them in a sense with their raison d'être. The issue of political reform divided the other groups. The Liberals, Nationals, and Radicals differed in their degree of attachment to traditional as opposed to parliamentary forms of government and also over the question of political freedom, especially with respect to elections. The Radicals and Nationals were united by their anticlericalism but had very different ideas on these other issues. The former favored a variety of reforms to limit the political power of the president, while the latter by tradition stood for a strong, energetic executive.[18] To some extent the issue of political reform also separated the Liberals and the Radicals, although it is difficult to generalize about the Liberals. During the second half of the Liberal Republic they divided into two separate factions: one, the *liberales disidentes*, tended to side with the Radicals, while the other, the *liberales de gobierno*, displayed less interest in curbing the power of the national administration. Traditional antipathies, rather than ideological differences, separated the latter from the Nationals. Both the Nationals and Liberals traced their origins back to the conflict of Montt's time, and they had subsequently confronted one another under both Pérez and Errázuriz.

While historians such as Francisco Antonio Encina have disparaged the importance of ideological differences in nineteenth-century Chile,[19] others have insisted that partisan conflict was essentially principled.[20] The truth lies somewhere between these extremes. Doctrines alone do not fully account for party solidarity in any political system. Positions of principle are adopted and altered for opportunistic reasons. Nineteenth-century Chile was no exception. When a group such as the Radicals joined the government its reformist zeal tended to wane. The basis for group loyalty also varied. Differences of opinion and principles were important to the Conservatives, Radicals, and *liberales disidentes*, while the Nationals and *liberales de gobierno* were held together more by practical considerations, including prospects of government employment and contracts.

Partisan positions on issues were only occasionally expressed as programs or formal statements of beliefs and goals.[21] Presidential and legislative candidates might articulate a program in the course of an electoral campaign, but they generally did so as individuals, rather than as spokesmen for their legislative group as a whole.[22] This tendency reflects the limited organization of political groups in Chile before 1891 as well as the restricted nature of their political activities.

Unlike political parties, none of the political groups competing for power in the 1870-1891 period formally existed outside the legislature. The Radicals were organized into *asambleas* in various localities, but until 1888, when they held their first national convention in Santiago, they had no national structure. Each *asamblea* acted autonomously, and consequently there were no leaders or central authorities who could formulate a national program or speak on behalf of the Radical grouping as a whole. The other groups were even less organized. Outside the legislature men of Conservative, Liberal, or National persuasions might meet on an informal basis, but local organization on the lines of the Radical *asamblea* was unknown.

Even within the legislature the different groups tended to be rather loosely consolidated. Factionalism affected them all, even the Conservatives, who were isolated from power by their views on the clerical issue. Prospects of ministerial posts and other perquisites which could be offered by the president in exchange for support tempted factions to break away from their correligionaries and join the governing alliance. In 1873, for example, the Radicals divided after one of their leaders made a personal alliance with President Errázuriz and joined the government.[23] The Liberals displayed the least cohesion. As indicated previously, they did not respond to a single core of leaders but generally divided into two groups: *liberales de gobierno* and *liberales disidentes*. Moreover, within each of these groups different *círculos* or factions could be identified.[24] The *disidentes* tended to be little more than an undisciplined collection of prominent individuals: poets and novelists such as Eusebio Lillo, eminent lawyers such as Júlio Zegers, and scholars such as Diego Barras Arana and Benjamín Vicuña Mackenna.[25] They opposed and even occasionally supported the government as individuals and cliques but did not act as a collectivity. More unity characterized the *liberales de gobierno*, although in many cases they were also prominent men whose support had to be won by the president on an individual basis.[26]

Under Presidents Santa María and José Manuel Balmaceda (1886-1891) the government liberals became more disciplined. Both presidents used the machinery of government to build up a large, effective, and national network of supporters: mainly public functionaries and persons directly dependent on the government, such as contractors. The two presidents also intervened in elections to increase their control over liberals in the legislature. Strictly speaking, however, the result was not a party structure. As the Radical leader Enrique Mac-Iver argued in a debate over the elections of 1888:

> I know that when one speaks of the government as an electoral factor or of the intervention of government agents and elements in elections, there are many who say: it is not the government that intervenes, it is the party that is in control of the government.
>
> This assertion is not accurate. The party that controls the government does not manage, contest, influence, and win. It is the government itself; it is the President of the Republic, the ministers, the intendants, the governors, the subdelegates and the inspectors who have the influence and the controlling and persuading resources of authority.[27]

Moreover, the *partido de gobierno* or government party was not a very durable structure; indeed, one should probably speak of *par-*

tidos de gobierno, because each president forged his own.

Government control over electoral outcomes tended to discourage the development of more durable and unified political structures. Unlike parties, political groups in nineteenth-century Chile did not control the nomination of candidates for public office, nor did they coordinate campaigns for popular electoral support on a national basis, mainly because the political system in which they operated offered them few incentives or opportunities to do so.

Prior to 1891 the national administration generally nominated and elected candidates for public office in Chile. After 1871 national political conventions theoretically nominated presidential candidates, but in reality presidents chose their successors as they had done since 1830. Public functionaries and presidential relatives and friends accounted for a healthy proportion of the delegates at the "official" or government conventions.[28] The composition of the opposition conventions is more obscure, but it is clear such conventions did not meet to choose but merely to ratify a candidate, in some cases the "official" one.[29]

More decentralization characterized the selection of congressional candidates, but the national administration still played a major role. Vicente Reyes, an eminent Liberal, described how he and two other young men entered the legislature at the end of Montt's terms: ". . . we were made deputies. I say made because in reality we were not elected but anointed by the government which controlled electoral affairs in those days."[30]

In his autobiography Abdón Cifuentes, a leading Conservative, offers a similar description of elections under Pérez. At that time, says Cifuentes, "The government named, the country did not elect, its representatives."[31] Cifuentes, however, goes on to provide an account of his own election to the legislature in 1867, which shows that large landholders also exercised influence over the selection of candidates. An informal meeting of Conservative landholders formulated a list of candidates for the Department of Rancagua, and Cifuentes' name was included at the insistence of Juan de Dios Correa, the largest landholder in the department. The list was then forwarded to the Minister of the Interior for approval. The account is particularly interesting, because Cifuentes, who was then an editor of *El Independiente* and a critic, albeit a friendly one, of the government, was not accepted as a candidate, and the national administration specifically instructed local officials to prevent his election. That probably would have been the end of the matter, but Juan de Dios Correa approached President Pérez on Cifuentes' behalf. The president intervened and Cifuentes was duly elected.[32]

Normally the Minister of the Interior had the last word. In 1873, for example, only six candidates not on the official list won a seat in the legislature.[33] Centralized control and blatant fraud prevented anything resembling genuine electoral competition. Again Cifuentes' frank accounts of political affairs are revealing. In 1876 he stood for reelection as a Conservative candidate in a district where most of the landholders were Conservatives. Of the 1,100 voters Cifuentes says they could count on 900. But on this occasion the Conservatives were no longer supporting the government, and the intendant was instructed to prevent Cifuentes' election. He performed his task so enthusiastically that Cifuentes failed to be credited with a single vote. When intimidation and ordinary electoral fraud failed, the intendant simply falsified the results.[34]

Electoral abuses of this type became increasingly unpopular, and by the end of the nineteenth century Chileans of all partisan persuasions sought a greater measure of electoral freedom. Beginning in the 1870s the legislature passed a series of constitutional reforms that, at least in principle, reduced the president's power and made the existing system more democratic. The following are among the most important innovations: (1) the administration of the electoral system was taken out of the hands of presidential appointees; (2) the president's power to suspend the constitution was restricted; (3) certain types of "parliamentary incompatibilities" were established that excluded judges, governors, and other public employees directly dependent on the president from the legislature; (4) the secret ballot was introduced; (5) senators were to be directly elected by province rather than from a single list for the whole country; (6) the cumulative vote, which theoretically favored the representation of minorities, replaced the complete list system in the election of deputies;[35] and (7) by the laws

of 1874 and 1888 property qualifications were removed and the
vote extended to all literate males over twenty-one years of
age.[36]

In spite of these political reforms, the government continued
to control elections until after the civil war of 1891. The assertion
of presidential control over electoral outcomes, however, increasingly required heavy-handed methods that generated intense
opposition and undermined the legitimacy of the established
regime. Presidents Santa María and Balmaceda both ignored these
political costs. In the elections of 1882 the administration of
Santa María reduced opposition representation in the national
legislature to its lowest point in more than two decades.[37] Under
President Balmaceda the control became, if anything, even more
systematic. The government formally had lost its authority over
the electoral machinery, since the largest taxpayers in each district
made up the committees that qualified voters, supervised the polls,
and counted the votes. But with the assistance of tax officials,
Balmaceda's administration created *mayores contribuyentes* with
pro-government sympathies on a vast scale and thereby obtained
de facto control over the electoral system throughout the whole
country. Balmaceda utilized this power to eliminate electoral
cacicazgos or independent bases of electoral power in an attempt
to create a disciplined block of Liberal supporters in the legislature.[38] His administration also attempted to gain control over the
opposition. The Conservatives received a guarantee of representation on the condition they would agree to support candidates
chosen by the administration. The Conservatives rejected the
government's list, but the only Conservative candidates who won
seats in the legislature were those nominated by the national
administration.[39]

The Radical leader Enrique Mac-Iver summed up the feelings
of many Chileans in a speech before the Chamber of Deputies on
July 7th, 1888:

  I think that hardly a trace of electoral freedom exists in Chile. Here we
  do not have assorted parties, groups, or men competing for the support
  and votes of the people with equal forces and on common ground.
  Instead we have a government that uses all the resources that the law has
  put into its hands for the common good to get its supporters elected; and
  we have parties, which are generally badly organized, disunited groups,

and individuals of varying degrees of influence who oppose it, almost always unsuccessfully. This is the general nature of our elections.[40]

Balmaceda sought to create a unified Liberal party that would be responsive to his leadership. Instead he created a vigorous opposition, which was sufficiently organized and powerful to overthrow his government and dismantle what remained of the centralized political system established by the *pelucones*.

The Chilean Civil War of 1891

On the surface the civil war of 1891 involved a constitutional conflict. Balmaceda attempted to defend the powers of his office against what he viewed as illegitimate legislative encroachment, while forces in the legislature sought to defend principles of cabinet responsibility and electoral freedom against what they regarded as arbitrary, authoritarian, and unconstitutional executive actions. Civil war broke out in January 1891 after Balmaceda announced that he would cope with legislative obstructionism by implementing his budgetary proposals without the usual enabling legislation.[41]

According to some interpretations, the roots of the civil war can be traced back to Balmaceda's nationalistic and interventionist economic policies.[42] The Marxist historian Julio César Jobet, for example, has argued that threats to landholding, plutocratic, and imperialist interests played a key role in the growth of opposition to Balmaceda.[43] This line of analysis remains questionable, not least because Balmaceda took a far from consistent position on many important issues. Indeed, it has been argued that Balmaceda aroused the opposition of the Chilean oligarchy both (1) because he favored metallic conversion and a stable currency that would have created financial difficulties for employers, exporters, and landowners;[44] and (2) because he favored inflationary issues of paper money.[45] But the most fundamental objection to economic interpretations of the civil war is that they do not really come to grips with the fact that the crisis of presidential authority preceded Balmaceda's assumption of office. Balmaceda himself has been quoted as saying that President Pinto was only saved from political revolt by the War of the Pacific.[46] Attempts to circumscribe the power of the executive had also created serious political difficulties for Santa María, Balmaceda's immediate predecessor. Santa María did not propose any revolutionary economic policies, but the situation in 1886 was similar to that of 1890: a powerful parliamentary opposition obstructed the president's revenue law in an attempt to obtain more parliamentary autonomy, increased electoral freedom, and greater control over the rapidly expanding resources of the Chilean state.

At the end of Balmaceda's term the opposition forces included Radicals, Conservatives, dissident Liberals, and Nationals. The issues of parliamentary control and electoral freedom provided these groups with a common platform around which they could unify in opposition to the president. The Conservatives extended support to this platform chiefly because of their lengthy exclusion from power during the Liberal Republic. A more decentralized system, based on the predominance of the parliament rather than the executive, offered them the opportunity to take advantage of the considerable influence large landholders and clergy wielded at the local level.[47] Similar considerations inspired the Nationals. Although the latter originally supported Balmaceda, a faction of the party led by Agustín Edwards Ross advocated electoral freedom and a parliamentary form of government.[48] The Radicals possessed fewer traditional political resources than the Conservatives, but they too could expect to gain a greater measure of influence through elections that were not centrally controlled, particularly since their organization had developed considerably between 1870 and 1890. It is difficult to generalize about the dissident Liberals, who had a variety of motives for opposing Balmaceda, some of them purely personal. Balmaceda's choice of successor, Enrique Salvador Sanfuentes, who apparently pleased none of the Liberal factions, provided one immediate reason for opposition.[49]

With the civil war of 1891 the locus of political power shifted from the executive to the legislature and to the assorted political groups that began to compete relatively freely for electoral support and control of the cabinet. The civil war thus marked the beginning of a new political era, the "Parliamentary Republic" (1891-1924), which witnessed the true emergence of political parties in Chile. The background of this development has been explored at some length, both to clarify the nature of the political groups that competed for influence in Chile prior to 1891 and to provide a basis for understanding important differences between the first Argentine and Chilean party systems. The political rivalries that developed in nineteenth-century Chile persisted over time and shaped the structure of political conflict after 1891.

POLITICAL CONFLICT IN NINETEENTH-CENTURY ARGENTINA

In contrast to Chile, the political conflicts of the early years of Argentine national independence were not resolved in favor of a defined constitutional framework. Instead, the early dispute between federalists and centralists came to an end with the dictatorship of Juan Manuel de Rosas, the *caudillo* par excellence of Argentine history. In 1829 Rosas became governor of the Province of Buenos Aires, and, under the guise of federalism, he gradually managed to extend his control over rival provincial *caudillos*. By 1835 he had achieved a fragile de facto unification of the fragmented country. When Rosas was overthrown in 1852 no centralized institutions remained, nor had the tendency towards provincial *caudillismo* been completely eliminated. Yet, paradoxically, Rosas had taken advantage of the spirit of localism to forge a basis for national organization.

His successors reached a consensus on a federal form of constitution in 1853, thereby legalizing the federal unity Rosas had imposed. The question of Buenos Aires' relationship to the rest of the provinces, however, remained a troublesome problem. Suspicious that its interests would not be protected by the new confederacy, the most prosperous and populous province resorted to arms to defend its autonomy. It was defeated by confederate forces led by General Urquiza in 1859, but in 1861 a new insurrection broke out. This time Buenos Aires, led by Bartolomé Mitre, triumphed.

In 1862 Mitre took office as the first president of the united Argentine Republic. The leadership of the country fell to liberal intellectuals, the so-called "Generation of '37," who consciously set out to transform the socioeconomic structure of the country through foreign immigration, education, and foreign investment. This program was carried forward under Presidents Mitre, Domingo Sarmiento (1868-1874), and Nicolás Avellaneda (1874-1880) with marked success. During these eighteen years national unity also became more of a reality, although tensions between the interior provinces and Buenos Aires and conflicts arising out of the ambitions of rival *caudillos* still continued to plague the republic.

Violence and personalism, rather than peaceful competition among rival legislative groups, characterized the struggle for control of the national government during this period. Groups calling themselves parties participated in the struggle, but their activities can best be explained in terms of the self-interest of their chiefs. Unlike Chile, the unity and very existence of political groups in Argentina owed very little to general principles or diffuse partisan feelings. Mitre, who played a prominent role in Argentine politics until the time of his death in 1906, led a group called the Nationalists whose political base was the Province of Buenos Aires. His chief rivals were Adolfo Alsina, a *porteño* whose followers were known as the Autonomists, and Avellaneda, who had the support of an alliance of provincial leaders referred to, somewhat confusingly, as the Nationals. Both the Nationalists and Autonomists acquired popular followings; however, neither group extended its influence outside the Province of Buenos Aires, and neither proved very durable.

The presidential elections of 1874 and 1880 provide insights into the nature of political conflict in Argentina during these years. Avellaneda won the election of 1874 with the support of President Sarmiento, provincial leaders, and Alsina's Autonomists. He was a compromise candidate in the sense that he was a native of Tucumán, and hence acceptable to men of the interior, as well as an established resident of Buenos Aires who had held important posts in both the national and Buenos Aires governments. Nonetheless, Mitre led an unsuccessful revolt against the federal government following his electoral defeat by a candidate whose roots were in the interior.

The prospect that a more peaceful solution could be found to the problem of choosing Avellaneda's successor emerged in 1877 when Mitre and Alsina, who were ostensibly implacable opponents, made an agreement to cooperate in the forthcoming elections in the Province of Buenos Aires.[50] Control of the province was important to the presidential contest, and Alsina was evidently inspired by presidential ambitions. Strong opposition to the *acuerdo*, however, developed among Alsina's own followers. A youthful faction led by Aristóbulo del Valle denounced the pact and broke away to form a new association, the "Republican party," which was to be modelled on the lines of North American parties.[51] The faction included Leandro Alem, Carlos Pellegrini, Dardo Rocha, Roque Saenz Peña, and Hipólito Irigoyen: men who subsequently held positions of great political importance in Argentina and who shared at this stage of their careers a concern for municipal autonomy, effective federalism, electoral freedom, and principled politics.[52] The national political party they set out to establish did not prosper, but the Republicans' initiative did indicate that the highly personalistic and undemocratic style of politics, which was typified by the Mitre-Alsina *acuerdo*, was falling into disrepute.

Other circles received the *conciliación* more warmly, but the promise of peaceful presidential succession vanished with the death of Alsina. Several new presidential candidates appeared to fill the void, but none of them commanded the support of all the Autonomists or all of the Nationalists, much less a coalition of the two. The major candidates in 1878 were Julio Roca, the Minister of War and hero of the campaign against the Indians that had opened up sizeable new tracts of land for settlement; Carlos Tejedor, the Governor of Buenos Aires; and ex-president Sarmiento. Roca ranked as the main contender, because he had the support of the league of provincial leaders—the so-called National party— that had backed Avellaneda, plus the administration, many Autonomists and Republicans, and even some Nationalists. His strongest opponent, Tejedor, had the support of both Autonomists and Nationalists too. Sarmiento really had no solid base of support, but he hoped to succeed as a compromise candidate.[53] In short, the labels "Autonomist" or "Nationalist" offer little or no guidance. The electoral contest involved two contingent coalitions that were constructed to meet the occasion. The major political groups were all fragmented into a variety of factions, political clubs, and personalist circles. Even the Republicans failed to act as a unified group. While some supported Roca, others favored Sarmiento or Bernardo de Irigoyen.[54]

The backing of the national administration or that of the provincial government of Buenos Aires formed the essential basis for any serious candidature in Argentina at this time. Indeed the whole electoral struggle may be characterized as a conflict between the two governmental powers. When the national administration triumphed in 1880, as it had in 1874, Tejedor led what was to be the last provincially based insurrection against the federal government. By 1880 the prestige and resources of the national administration had grown sufficiently for it to defeat Tejedor and impose a national solution to the old problem of the City of Buenos Aires. The nation's largest city and its valuable port revenues were placed directly under national control through the territorial device of a separate federal district. Thus deprived of its greatest political and financial resource, the Province of Buenos Aires became incapable of single-handedly challenging and even dominating the national government as it had in the past. The process of Argentine national unification was finally completed.

The Development of PAN

The settlement imposed on Buenos Aires significantly enhanced the power of the national government, and this change immediately affected the structure of political conflict in Argentina. When Roca assumed the presidency he set about organizing the political forces that had supported him into a new powerful political machine: the Partido Autonomista Nacional or PAN, which resembled the "official party" put together by Santa María and Balmaceda in Chile.

The foundations of PAN were established in 1874 with the union of Autonomists and Nationals, but it was Roca who welded these two forces into an effective national political structure. PAN not only won the support of the large cattle-raising oligarchy of Buenos Aires, which had up to this time dominated the national government, but it integrated provincial elites as well. Moreover, the attempt to create a national party initially received enthusiastic support from other social elements, including university students, members of the Buenos Aires petty bourgeoisie, and intellectuals such as Sarmiento, who felt the time had come to replace factions and personalistic parties with more enduring national structures.[55] Former Republicans, who had been involved in an earlier attempt to create a new type of political organization, also lent Roca their support. Both Alem and Del Valle, for example, belonged to the first national governing board of PAN.[56]

Basically PAN represented a league or alliance of provincial governors. Gradually it developed into a centralizing instrument of government, and the relationships of dependence that existed between the president and governors were partially reversed; however, neither Roca nor his successors altered PAN's fundamental character. Provincial governors remained the key structural element.[57]

Disenchantment with PAN soon developed, as it functioned as an organization of public officials dedicated to the perpetuation of their own power. At the local level its chief agents were the tax assessor, municipal intendant, police commissioner, and justice of the peace. In some provinces one or more of these posts were theoretically elective, but in practice governors ceded the power to appoint these officials to local *caudillos*, who in return ensured that the governor's partisans succeeded in all elections.[58] A similar relationship prevailed between the president and provincial governors. Governors supported PAN's presidential candidate and made certain that he won the election. In return they considered themselves entitled to choose provincial legislators, national legislators, and their own successors.[59] These arrangements put governors in a particularly good position to secure prestigious posts for their friends and families as well as to provide for their own future. The result in many interior provinces was a stable oligarchic system. For example, in a speech before the Chamber of Deputies in 1912 Vicente Gallo described the situation in Salta:

> A purely oligarchic government exists in Salta. For many years the executive power has been transferred within the same family, from uncle to nephew, from nephew to cousin, from cousin to uncle, in an uninterrupted succession . . .[60]

There was nothing particularly new about this system of succession, but under Roca control became more systematic and centralized.[61] One important development was the abolition of the provincial militia in 1879.[62] Thereafter governors had to depend on the national administration for military support. Its withdrawal amounted to an open invitation to domestic violence that gave the president the opportunity to intervene under the constitution or to refrain from intervening if he favored the insurgents.[63] Other important presidential resources were economic: control over the distribution of national revenues, which grew considerably after 1880;[64] control over the distribution of public land; and influence over the new Banco Nacional and the distribution of credit.[65] Improved national communications also helped Roca and his successors to exercise greater command over the political situation throughout the country. In 1870 there were only 732 kilometers of railway in Argentina, which meant that most provinces were isolated from the capital. By 1880 2,313 kilometers of track had been built, and by 1890 the figure was 10,000.[66]

In Argentina, where the tradition of federalism was very strong, the formation of a national association that allowed the president to choose his successor, control the national legislature, and contain opposition represented a significant political development; and to many Argentines, it was an alarming one. Opponents of the *unicato*, as the regime that was based on PAN was called, viewed it as the complete antithesis of the federal and republican system that the constitution formally guaranteed, and they harshly condemned it as "unitarian" and "autocratic": an opinion with which certain modern writers have concurred.[67] Such an assessment, however, exaggerates the degree of national unity and presidential power. Compared to his Chilean counterpart, the Argentine president was not a very powerful figure. Although he could influence the choice of provincial authorities, he did not as a matter of routine appoint them, nor was he constitutionally entitled to do so. The provincial governors generally retained independent bases of political power, and to secure their support the president could not go too far in violating their autonomy.

Yet while the *unicato* was not strictly speaking an autocracy, it was certainly anything but republican, except in the most restricted sense. The whole orientation of the regime was profoundly undemocratic. The massive immigration and economic expansion that transformed Argentine society after 1880 affected the outlook of the native elite, which by virtue of its ownership of land became increasingly prosperous, conscious of its social superiority, and concerned with protecting its privileged position. This outlook was reflected in the structure and activities of PAN. As indicated previously, PAN was not organized on a popular basis. Its leaders made little effort to recruit popular support; indeed, in functional terms PAN might be described as a mechanism for ensuring that economic progress would not be jeopardized by democratic politics. Elections were so meaningless that opposition candidates rarely appeared. PAN had little need even to bribe voters; they were almost irrelevant.

Partially as a result, popular participation and interest in Argentine politics were negligible.[68] At this time the Chilean system also presented few opportunities for genuine electoral competition and widespread political participation; yet a Chilean, Abraham König, travelling in Argentina in 1890 was struck by the tremendous civic indifference to elections and politics that he found there:

> Everyone is preoccupied with making money, in attaining the easy life, and only those who have some interest to safeguard or something to gain take an active part in politics; the rest abstain or at most act languidly and diffidently . . .
> The result of all this is a general apathy, a coolness, and indifference to public life . . .[69]

König was in Córdoba in February 1890 when elections for the national legislature took place.

> Having nothing else to do except look around, walk about, and observe, I covered the city in all directions. Nowhere, at any time, during the whole day did I see popular activity, assemblies of voters, voting places: in short, any sign which would indicate that the people on this day were going to exercise their most sacred and important right. I learned later, however, that the election had taken place. . . .[70]

PAN was particularly strong in Córdoba, the province from which both Roca and his successor Miguel Juárez Celman were drawn, but the situation differed little in the rest of Argentina.

These same elections were described on February 4, 1890 as "farcical" in *La Nación*, which observed:

> The first magistrate of the country, whose election was marked by fraud, has promoted violence as a system of government, gradually annulling public intervention in the management of public affairs. . . .
>
> The political vision of the president of the republic is realized: in the congress of 1890 not a single discordant voice will be heard. The fourteen governors adhere unconditionally to the policy of the *jefe único* of PAN. . . .
>
> Sunday one could observe the complete absence of the public in all of the polling places. . . .[71]

Not only did the leaders of PAN not bother to recruit popular support, but they never developed a set of beliefs or ideas that could be identified as a partisan perspective. Apart from Roca's succinct and pragmatic formula, "peace and administration," and Juárez' similar theme, "peace, toleration, and conciliation," PAN had no political program. Political life consequently appeared to consist of little more than naked personal conflicts for power. The personalism of Argentine politics also struck the Chilean König, who travelled in Argentina in 1890:

> In the Argentine Republic there are no parties with organized ideas. When the time comes for a general or provincial election, the voters group themselves around one man, not around a party label [*bandera*] represented by a man.[72]

Even the question of relations between church and state failed to generate enduring ideological cleavages in Argentina. Under Roca and Juárez various pieces of anticlerical legislation were passed, among the most notable of which were the laws of 1884 and 1888, which ended religious instruction in public schools and provided for civil registration of marriages. Although the reforms met with a certain amount of opposition from the clergy and its supporters, they did not lead to the organization of a clerical grouping on the lines of the Chilean Conservatives. The deep and widely shared concern for the material progress of the country apparently left no room for one.[73]

PAN then was not a political party in the usual sense of the term. It had no distinctive partisan ideology or popular following, and it made no attempt to acquire either. It was, as *La Nación* bluntly stated in 1886, "a party invented by official phraseology."[74]

The Growth of Organized Opposition

During the administrations of both Roca and Juárez the national government confronted little organized opposition.[75] If control of a provincial government changed hands, peacefully or violently, both the outgoing governor and his successor were likely to claim they supported PAN. Political struggles, which were predominantly local and personal in character, all took place within PAN's broad umbrella. After 1890 the situation began to change as a new political force, the Unión Cívica, was organized in violent opposition to the government. Originally an unstructured collection of opposition elements, between 1890 and 1910 the Unión Cívica developed into a full-fledged political party whose intense pressures for electoral reform and popular democracy shattered the unity and confidence of Argentina's ruling elite and eventually destroyed the *unicato*.

The history of the organization of the Unión Cívica has been explored in great detail elsewhere, and only a brief account of its origins needs to be presented here.[76] It developed out of a formation called the Unión Cívica de la Juventud, which was formally organized at a large public meeting in 1889 around a program emphasizing electoral freedom, political morality, and provincial autonomy. To achieve greater prestige and influence, the new organization drew in prominent opposition figures such as Mitre, Alem, and del Valle, and within a short space of time the "Juventud" was dropped. In 1890 the Unión Cívica thus appeared as the union of a new political generation with two traditional and rival groups: the Mitristas and the pre-1880 Autonomists who had found the Alsina-Mitre alliance of 1877 unacceptable. These elements united solely on the basis of their common opposition to the existing administration.

The new organization spread rapidly in 1890. Almost sixty Unión Cívica clubs were founded in Buenos Aires, and although the other provinces did not respond with the same degree of enthusiasm, clubs also emerged in Salta, Santa Fe, Tucumán, Río Cuarto, Mendoza, Corrientes, San Luis, and Córdoba.[77] Under the leadership of Alem the activities of the Unión Cívica centered around the organization of a revolt against the national government. Plans for an uprising began to develop as early as December 1889,[78] and in subsequent months Alem entered into communication with men in the interior. From the beginning, however, the plan was to concentrate on Buenos Aires. Sympathetic officers in the military were contacted, and the military leadership entrusted to a supporter of Mitre, General Manuel J. Campos. Leaders of the Asociación Católica, who opposed the *unicato* because of its attack on the church, and prestigious representatives of Buenos Aires' landholding and financial elite, such as Manuel A. Ocampo, a former governor of Buenos Aires and president of the provincial bank, also extended support.

The revolt broke out in July of 1890 and collapsed within three days, partially because the plans were betrayed in advance to the government, but also because the quality of the military leadership was poor and the size of the revolutionary force altogether inadequate.[79] The uprising, however, did return control over the national government to the landholding and commercial interests of Buenos Aires and permit Roca to recapture the leadership of PAN. The serious financial crisis that had precipitated the revolt had thoroughly discredited the national administration, and Juárez Celman was forced to resign in favor of Vice-President Carlos Pellegrini.

The revolt of 1890 marks the initial stage of political party organization in Argentina. Hence, like the Chilean civil war of 1891, it represented something of a watershed. In the Argentine case, however, it took another twenty years before a competitive regime comparable to that introduced by the Chilean civil war finally emerged. This delay reinforced the sharp polarization between government and opposition elements that had characterized nineteenth-century Argentine politics. Regional rivalries and the tendency for political loyalties to be cemented on the basis of personal ties and patronage persisted over time as well. The structure of political conflict established in nineteenth-century Argentina thus contributed to the formation of a party system very different from the Chilean one, which developed out of a multi-polar and relatively well-institutionalized system of ideological oppositions at the elite level.

CHAPTER II

THE SOCIAL AND ECONOMIC CONTEXT

The emergence of political parties in Chile and Argentina at the turn of the century reflected social and economic developments. After 1880 both countries experienced a period of rapid economic growth and social change that increased the variety of social groups competing for political influence, expanded the number of potential political participants, and thereby created new incentives and opportunities for the formation of political parties. Together with the diffusion of democratic ideas from Western Europe and North America, these changes contributed to the pressures for political reform that surfaced in the 1891 Chilean civil war and the abortive Argentine revolt of 1890. Increased literacy, social diversification, and urbanization all played a major role in this process.

THE PATTERN OF SOCIOECONOMIC DEVELOPMENT IN CHILE

The main impetus to socioeconomic change in Chile was the War of the Pacific (1879-1883), which led to the incorporation of the valuable northern nitrate territories. Between 1880 and 1890 Chilean exports rose from $88,036,053 to $144,381,805 pesos of 18 pence, largely because of the increased sale of nitrates.[1] By 1910 Chilean exports were valued at $328,827,176 pesos,[2] nearly 85 percent of which were mining products.[3] Almost overnight Chile found itself an unusually wealthy country by Latin American standards. In 1887 it is said to have enjoyed the highest per capita income on the continent.[4]

This new prosperity and the military victory over Peru and Bolivia were a great source of national pride. *El Mercurio* boasted: "Chile's greatness is now immense and all other nations acknowledge it . . . How could its glory be greater? Is there any other American nation that has accomplished so much?"[5] Chileans became tremendously optimistic about their country's economic future, and this optimism, perhaps as much as the boom in nitrates, sparked off a period of industrial and commercial development. Another economic stimulant was the successful completion of the campaign against the Araucanians in 1883, which opened up valuable lands for agricultural development in southern Chile.[6] The economic prospects did indeed look bright, and foreign investors and bankers, who were no doubt also impressed by the country's long record of political stability, provided funds that reinforced the boom conditions and spread them to other economic sectors.

Not all of the wealth derived from nitrates acted as a direct stimulant on the rest of the economy. In the first place, much of the nitrate wealth was used unproductively to finance imports (often of a luxury category), service the ever-mounting national debt, and alleviate direct domestic taxation. Second, because the nitrate industry was relatively primitive and its labor force poorly paid, it generated only limited demand for either capital or consumer goods, although the expansion of the industry's work force did open up a new internal market for agricultural producers. Finally, and most important, foreign investors purchased a high proportion of the industry in the years immediately following the War of the Pacific.[7] Markos J. Mamalakis estimates that one-third of the total wealth derived from nitrate exports in the 1880-1924 period was absorbed by the government in the form of export taxes, another third represented a return on capital, and the remainder was accounted for by production costs. Mamalakis also suggests that two-thirds of the profits were sent abroad: an enormous sum, roughly equivalent to 7 percent of Chile's GNP.[8]

Despite these limitations, the nitrate boom still had a very positive economic impact. No growth estimates are available for the 1880-1910 period as a whole, but between 1910 and 1924 national income expanded at an average rate of 4.3 percent or

2.7 percent per capita.[9] Not only does this rate of growth compare very favorably to that achieved by Chile since 1925,[10] but it is clear that the economy expanded even more rapidly in the three decades immediately following the War of the Pacific. After 1910 many of the economic imbalances and dangers associated with Chile's heavy dependence on nitrate exports became palpable. The outbreak of World War I, in particular, caused severe economic disruption.[11] Most Chilean industries required imports of fuel and materials, and the economy as a whole depended on nitrate exports. Between 1913 and 1916 the number of industrial establishments in Chile actually declined, and it took four years before the prewar level of industrial employment was reestablished.[12] After a brief period of revival, the nitrate market collapsed again in 1919, resulting in the smallest volume of exports since 1892, and in the next five years nitrate exports frequently failed to reach prewar levels.[13]

The subjective assessment of contemporaries also implies that the 1880-1910 period saw great economic progress. After 1910 the nation's former self-congratulatory attitude turned to one of despair, and Chileans became preoccupied with analyzing the reasons for their country's poor economic performance.[14] That contemporaries regarded the latter part of the parliamentary period as one of utter stagnation, even though it was not, suggests that they must have previously experienced rather substantial rates of economic growth.

Economic and Social Diversification

Export figures provide one concrete indication of the expansion of the Chilean economy in the 1880-1900 period. Import statistics are also revealing. As Table 1 shows, imports of metals, fuels, and other raw materials increased over 350 percent between 1880 and 1900, while consumer goods imports declined as a percentage of total imports. These trends reflect the rapid growth of national industry after the War of the Pacific, which created new economic interests and greater competition for control over the expanding resources of the Chilean state.

TABLE 1

CHILE: IMPORTS OF CONSUMER GOODS AND
RAW MATERIALS, 1870-1907

	Consumer Goods		Raw Materials	
	Millions of pesos of 18d	% Total Imports	Millions of pesos of 18d	% Total Imports
1870	53.4	89.6	2.7	4.5
1875	59.9	74.4	8.6	10.7
1880	47.6	75.9	7.8	12.4
1885	61.5	72.7	10.2	12.1
1890	87.1	60.8	20.4	14.3
1900	74.4	57.9	36.3	28.3
1907	142.4	48.5	99.9	34.0

SOURCE: Ricardo Lagos Escobar, *La industria en Chile: antecedentes estructurales* (Santiago, 1966), pp. 25-26.

By 1895 there were approximately 2,500 artisan and industrial firms in Chile, over 75 percent of which had been established after 1880.[15] Industry continued to expand rapidly in the years leading up to World War I. According to an industrial census taken in 1911, there were 5,722 industrial firms in Chile, employing a total of 74,618 workers.[16] The census takers in this case used a very generous definition of "industry," however, and included firms which were small and purely local in character and which in some cases employed only one or two workers. An industrial census taken in 1918 probably offers a more accurate picture of Chilean industry in this period.[17] This census separated small workshops, operating with a minimum of capital and an average of 1.7 employees, from larger establishments. The former numbered 4,661 and represented a total capital investment of only $9,848,270 pesos. The 2,820 larger firms employed an average of 25 workers each and had a total capital investment of $626,020,277 pesos, over half of which was invested in firms located in Santiago and Valparaíso. An analysis of ownership by nationality reveals that 45 percent of the firms were Chilean, 46 percent were foreign owned, and the remainder were of mixed or unknown ownership. Not surprisingly, food and drink processing was the principal industry at this time, and it accounted for more than 40 percent of the value of total industrial production. Some progress had been made in capital goods production, however, most notably in the machine tools, metal, and chemical industries.[18]

Unfortunately, no information is available on the sectoral origin of the Chilean GDP near the turn of the century. Census data on the distribution of the economically active population provide some idea of the country's changing economic structure, but these must be used with some caution. The proportion of the population engaged in mining, to take one of the most glaring examples, fails to reflect the sector's overall economic importance. Nitrates alone accounted for an estimated 24 percent of the GDP in this period,[19] but the mining industry employed only a small fraction of the labor force. The use of vague occupational categories, such as "manual and day labor," and the questionable accuracy of census counts create additional problems.[20] Nevertheless, census results do suggest that Chile's social structure had become quite diversified by 1895. Persons employed in nonagricultural pursuits accounted for nearly 60 percent of the working population: an exceptionally high figure for Latin America at this time and one, it should be noted, which a large number of countries on the continent had yet to reach as late as 1960.

The distribution of the economically active population did not shift dramatically between 1895 and 1907, but a comparison of the census results for these years points to important trends. First, employment in white-collar, professional, and managerial occupations grew very rapidly between 1895 and 1907, suggesting that the late nineteenth-century economic boom contributed to a sizeable expansion of Chilean middle-sector groups. Second, the relative size of the agricultural work force declined after 1895 in favor of the growth of employment in commerce, mining, transport, and industry. Census errors and classification problems, however, tend to mask this latter shift. The 1907 census seriously underestimated the number of mining workers in Chile[21] and subsumed manual labor employed both in the agricultural and

TABLE 2

CHILE: DISTRIBUTION OF ECONOMICALLY ACTIVE POPULATION
BY OCCUPATION, 1895 AND 1907

Occupation	1895[a]		1907	
	Number	%	Number	%
1. Professional, technical & related	11,259	1.1	23,744	1.9
2. Managers, proprietors & related	4,679	0.6	18,193	1.4
3. Sales, commerce & banking	65,241	6.3	82,383	6.6
4. Public admin. & office work	46,760	4.5	100,288	8.0
5. Agriculture & fishing	420,476	40.8	474,258	37.7
6. Mining	31,816	3.1	34,020[b]	2.7
7. Transport	19,281	1.9	41,100	3.3
8. Artisan & industrial	242,520	23.5	310,529	24.7
9. Manual & day labor	17,521	1.7	– – –[c]	– –
10. Services[d]	163,891	15.9	168,769	13.4
11. Other	4,363	0.4	3,490	0.3
Total	1,029,413	99.8	1,256,774	100.0

SOURCE: Chile, Oficina Central de Estadística, *Sétimo censo jeneral de la población de Chile levantado el 28 de noviembre de 1895*, 4 vols. (Santiago, 1900); Chile, Comisión Central del Censo, *Censo de la República de Chile levantado el 28 de noviembre de 1907* (Santiago, 1908).

[a]Figures do not include Tacna province which had approximately 12,000 workers.

[b]Unadjusted data; the actual figure was probably in the region of 55,000.

[c]Included in agriculture.

[d]Domestic servants accounted for 60 percent of the service category in 1895, 50 percent in 1907.

nonagricultural sectors of the economy under a single rubric. In addition, the occupational categories used both in 1895 and 1907 make it difficult to separate self-employed artisans or persons working in small, unmechanized workshops from industrial workers proper. Approximately 60,000 to 65,000 workers fell into the latter category in 1907; i.e., about 5 percent of the work force.[22] The size of the industrial work force at an earlier date remains unclear, but a comparison of provincial census data suggests that industrial development in the provinces of Santiago and Valparaíso accounted for most of the national increase in artisan and industrial employment between 1895 and 1907. In the majority of Chile's provinces the proportion of the working force engaged in artisan and industrial activities actually declined between 1895 and 1907.

The foregoing economic and occupational trends had significant political implications. From the middle of the nineteenth century, wealth in Chile had been shifting to urban areas, giving rise to an upper class that was a mixture of traditional landowning families and *nouveaux riches*. According to an article which appeared in *El Mercurio* in May 1882, entitled "Los millonarios de Chile viejo," there were fifty-nine personal fortunes in Chile of more than $1,000,000 pesos. Over half of these were based on mining, shipping, banking, railroads, commerce, and industry.[23] The nitrate boom and the growth of other industries accelerated this trend. Whereas agriculture accounted for approximately one-third of the total value of Chilean exports between 1870 and 1880, by 1895 the proportion was 13.1 percent. In 1900 it was only 6.5 percent.[24] Agriculture was not totally stagnant,[25] but its relative economic importance had definitely declined. Hence by the end of the nineteenth century the traditional predominance of landowning interests in national affairs could no longer be taken for granted.

At the same time it should be emphasized that the expansion of mining, industrial, and commercial activities did not give rise to a straightforward clash between urban and rural interests. The Chilean upper class remained relatively open. Indeed, although land ownership conveyed considerable social prestige and political power, no sharp distinction can be drawn between the traditional landed aristocracy and newer urban elites. Wealth enabled the latter to purchase land, sons of landowning families entered business and commerce, and the two groups intermarried. One indication of this process, as many observers have pointed out, is the large number of foreign names (MacIver, Edwards, Letelier, Walker, etc.) that can be identified in the elite circles of the time. Another is the relatively high proportion of persons of immigrant origin among the country's large landholders. In 1902 persons with surnames that clearly point to an immigrant background, such as Williams, Lynch, and Green, held title to approximately 15 percent of Chile's 527 most valuable privately owned estates. The largest single landowner in the country was Juana Ross de Edwards, the daughter of a merchant and widow of a second-generation immigrant who had made a fortune in banking and commerce.[26]

The growth of urban middle-sector and working-class groups also had important political implications. Teachers, professionals, public employees, and other middle-sector social elements were all well-qualified for political action, and their growing numbers created new opportunities for political leaders attempting to recruit a popular base of political support. The rapid growth in the number of mining, transport, and industrial workers had similar consequences, particularly since these workers tended to be highly concentrated and hence more easily organized than the traditional artisan. By the early twentieth century the Chilean working class was beginning to emerge as a political force in its own right.[27]

Demographic Shifts

Demographic movements reflected the shift in economic power from rural to urban areas. As Table 3 indicates, by the beginning of the parliamentary period approximately one-fourth of Chile's population lived in cities with over 5,000 inhabitants, and urban areas were growing far more rapidly than the population as a whole.[28]

The demographic shifts that occurred at the end of the nineteenth century, however, involved more than a simple rural to urban movement. After 1885 northern provinces lost population to the neighboring nitrate territories, particularly the mining centers of Iquique and Antofagasta, while the population of the

TABLE 3

CHILE: URBAN POPULATION, 1865-1920

	Cities over 5,000			Cities over 20,000		
Year	No.	Inhabitants	% Total Pop.	No.	Inhabitants	% Total Pop.
1865	20	348,462	19.1	2	185,815	10.2
1875	21	420,003	20.2	2	248,104	11.9
1885	33	587,172	23.2	5	362,651	14.3
1895	36	764,229	28.2	6	513,688	18.9
1907	49	1,092,231	33.6	8	716,587	22.1
1920	46	1,386,074	37.0	12	1,043,066	27.8

SOURCE: Chile, *Censo*, 1907, pp. 1266-1267; Chile, Dirección General de Estadística, *Censo de población de la República de Chile levantado el 15 diciembre de 1920* (Santiago, 1925), p. 104.

relatively stagnant central agricultural provinces migrated to the major commercial and industrial cities of Valparaíso, Santiago, and Concepción or joined a secondary migratory movement to the expanding southern frontier. Foreign immigration played no major role in this redistribution of population. Foreign nationals only accounted for 3.4 percent of the population in 1885 and 4.1 percent in 1907.[29]

These demographic shifts reflected and reinforced changes initiated by the rapid expansion of the Chilean economy after 1880. Together with increasing occupational diversification, they released a sizeable proportion of the population from the pervasive control of the traditional rural social structure and enlarged the social base from which political leaders might attempt to recruit popular support.

Growth in Literacy

The rising rate of literacy had similar implications. Between 1885 and 1907 literacy rates increased from 28.9 percent of the total population to 40.0 percent, rapidly expanding the size of the potential electorate. Simply between 1907 and 1920, when the average literacy rate rose from 40.0 percent to 50.3 percent, the number of Chileans who were adult, male literates and hence eligible to vote, more than doubled from approximately 429,000 to 981,000.[30] Because the growth in literacy was closely linked to the process of urbanization, the resulting increase in incentives and opportunities for organizing popular electoral support was particularly marked in urban areas. In 1907 literacy rates for towns and cities with over 1,000 and 10,000 inhabitants were, respectively, 54.3 and 62.0 percent. In contrast, only 29.0 percent of the rural population could read and write in 1907.[31]

These gaps between rural and urban literacy rates provide a further indication of the extremely uneven pattern of social and economic change in Chile and of the failure of large portions of the population to participate in the economic boom touched off by the growth in nitrate exports. Outside the large towns, the northern nitrate region, and the southern frontier, the social structure hardly changed between 1880 and 1920. Most rural areas experienced no real expansion in the number of potential political participants, no breakdown of the traditional and paternalistic pattern of class relations, and no erosion of the social and economic power of large landowners. Instead, as Arnold J. Bauer has emphasized in his study of Chilean rural society,[32] the opening of the country to market forces reinforced the archaic rural social system. The structure of the rural sector of the economy will be explored further below, but the significance of this uneven pattern of change for Chilean politics must be explicitly underlined. It severely circumscribed the ability of parties to recruit popular support outside the urban areas and enabled the rural elite, through the manipulation of a small and deferential rural electorate, to retain considerable political influence in the face of the declining importance of agriculture. Under these circumstances the Chilean rural elite, far from resisting political reforms favorable to party development, constituted a key source of pressure and support for competitive electoral arrangements. Hence, somewhat paradoxically, the extremely uneven pattern of socioeconomic change in Chile facilitated the emergence and consolidation of a competitive party system.

THE PATTERN OF SOCIOECONOMIC
DEVELOPMENT IN ARGENTINA

Turning now to the Argentine case, a similar but by no means
identical process of economic and social change was underway at
the turn of the century. As in Chile, an export boom in the 1880s
introduced an unprecedented period of national prosperity; but
in Argentina this boom was based on the expansion of rural production and was stimulated by a massive influx of foreign immigrants and capital. Partially as a result, the pace and magnitude
of change, particularly in the economic sphere, were much greater
than in Chile.

The indices presented in Table 4 provide a rough idea of the
relative rates of economic growth in the two countries. The point
of the comparison is not that the Chilean economy was expanding
slowly; emphasis must be placed instead on the extraordinary and
practically unequalled record of sustained growth achieved by the
Argentine economy between the late 1860s and the outbreak of
World War I. During this period the Argentine GDP increased at
an average rate of at least 5 percent per annum, allowing Argentina
to overtake Chile as the wealthiest country in Latin America.[33]
By 1914 Argentine per capita income had reached a figure of
approximately $1300 U.S. dollars at 1980 prices, while that of
Chile approached $1000.[34] Even by the standards of late twenti-
eth-century Latin America, these figures are impressive. In 1970
the per capita incomes of half of the countries in Latin America
still fell below the $1000 mark.[35] Hence in terms of per capita
wealth, Argentina and Chile more closely resembled the economically advanced North Atlantic nations than their Latin neighbors.
The resemblance was particularly striking in the case of Argentina,
which at the outbreak of World War I ranked alongside countries
such as Canada and the United States as one of the most dynamic
and important economies in the world.

External factors accounted for most of Argentina's growth.
During the latter part of the nineteenth century a plentiful supply
of foreign, particularly British, capital flowed into Argentina.[36]
Indeed, in 1889, which was the peak year for British investment,
Argentina accounted for between 40 and 50 percent of all British

TABLE 4

INDICES OF ECONOMIC GROWTH IN ARGENTINA AND CHILE
1865-1914

| | Argentina | | | Chile | | |
	1865	1895	1914	1865	1895	1914
Population	100	249	490	100	151	205
Exports	100	460	1,340	100	236	459
Imports	100	314	897	100	270	499

SOURCE: Chile, Oficina Central de Estadística, *Sinopsis estadística de la República de Chile* (Santiago, 1919), p. 11 (population); Chile, Oficina Central de Estadística, *Anuario estadístico de la República de Chile*, 1918, Vol. VI: *Hacienda*, p. 64 (exports and imports); Argentina, Comisión Nacional, *Tercer censo nacional levantado el 1 de junio de 1914*, 10 vols. (Buenos Aires, 1916-1919), VIII, 16.

funds invested outside the United Kingdom.[37] Much of this investment took an indirect form—loans to the government and *cédulas hipotecarias* or land mortgage bonds—but direct investments in social overhead capital were also important. It has been estimated that in the prewar years railroads, which were largely in British hands, accounted for a full one-third of total foreign investment.[38]

The extension of the railway network was of great significance, because it opened up vast areas of agricultural land to settlement and linked them with Buenos Aires and international markets. Foreign immigrants helped to develop this land for commercial purposes. Between 1871 and 1914 a total of 5,877,292 immigrants, mainly from Italy and Spain, entered Argentina.[39] Many of them returned to their country of origin, but the majority settled permanently. By 1914 approximately 30 percent of the country's population was foreign born, and in some areas, particularly the Federal District, and among adult males the proportion was considerably higher.[40]

The massive inflow of foreign labor and capital produced a tremendous expansion of agricultural production and exports.

Between 1872 and 1900 there was a twenty-five fold increase in the area of land under agricultural cultivation, while the value of agricultural exports grew almost 80,000 percent, rising as a proportion of total exports from 0.4 to 50.1 percent.[41] After 1890 the livestock industry also made considerable progress.[42] The improvement in stocks through selective breeding and developments in refrigerated transport led to the rapid growth of chilled and frozen meat exports to European markets. The value of these rose from an annual average of $3.6 million gold pesos in the years 1890-1894 to $62.9 million in the 1910-1914 period.[43]

Economic Diversification

The growth of the Argentine rural sector had a much more direct and positive impact on the rest of the economy than did the expansion of the Chilean nitrate industry. New processing industries, commercial establishments, and other services, such as transport, were required to handle the increased rural output, not to mention industries producing agricultural tools, equipment, and supplies. Forward linkages in nitrate production, in comparison, were quite negligible. Payments to domestic factors of production, mainly land and labor, were also much greater than in Chile. For one thing wage rates in Argentina were high, even relative to Europe, because of the relative scarcity of labor.[44] For another, the multiplier effects of the Argentine export boom were not vitiated as in Chile by the remission of profits abroad, because foreign capital was not directly invested in the rural sector. The situation is complicated since foreign capital did play an important role in processing, transport, commerce, and other services that added value to rural exports; however, factor payments abroad were probably still very low in comparison to other Latin American export economies.[45]

Evidence that the rural export boom spread out to other sectors of the economy is provided by Table 5, which shows that the rural sector actually grew more slowly than industry or commerce between 1900 and 1914. No information is available on sectoral growth rates before 1900, but the pattern was probably not very different.[46]

TABLE 5

ARGENTINA: GLOBAL AND SECTORAL GROWTH RATES
1900-04/1910-14

GDP, at factor cost	6.3
Agriculture, livestock and fisheries	3.4
Mining	11.5
Manufacturing	7.7
Construction	11.6
Services	6.8

SOURCE: Carlos F. Díaz Alejandro, *Essays on the Economic History of the Argentine Republic* (New Haven, 1970), p. 6.

In emphasizing the stimulating effects of the rural export boom on urban economic activity, the importance of immigration should not be overlooked. Not only did foreign immigrants provide the necessary manpower for the expansion of rural production, but they enlarged the domestic market and introduced new attitudes and skills that were highly conducive to further economic and industrial development. These trends became particularly important after 1890 when immigrants found opportunities to acquire land on favorable terms increasingly restricted.

Immigrants played a particularly important role in the growth of Argentine industry and commerce. In 1895 there were 44,100 commercial firms in Argentina; immigrants owned 74 percent of them. By 1914 the number of commercial firms had increased to 90,790, 71 percent of which were foreign owned. Over half were located in the capital or Province of Buenos Aires.[47]

Industrial development was similarly concentrated in the littoral region, where approximately 65 percent of the population lived. But, in contrast to Chile, there is little evidence that industrial growth combined with an increased capacity to import exacerbated existing regional imbalances. The number of industrial establishments increased in every province between 1895 and 1914, as did industrial employment and capital investment.[48] In the nation as a whole the number of firms more than doubled from 23,181 in 1895, 82.6 percent of which were foreign owned, to 48,779 in 1914, 64.5 percent of which were controlled by foreigners.[49] A great deal of this growth can be related directly to the expansion of rural exports. Flour mills, meat-packing plants, sugar refineries, and other food and drink processing industries accounted for 42.7 percent of the total capital invested in industry in 1914 and 53.2 percent of the total value of industrial production.[50]

By the turn of the century mining, construction, and manufacturing accounted for approximately 13 percent of the total GDP. While the economy as a whole clearly remained highly dependent on livestock and agriculture, the value added by the rural sector equalled only 38.1 percent. Services, including commerce, accounted for the remainder.[51]

Comparable figures are not available for Chile, but the contribution of mining, manufacturing, and construction to the GDP at the turn of the century was unquestionably much greater than in Argentina. The value added by manufacturing alone, on the other hand, was probably higher in Argentina. Whereas manufacturing employed an estimated 5 percent of the Chilean work force in 1907, census results for 1914 indicate that the percentage was more than twice as large in Argentina.[52] Because of the vague criteria used in defining industrial employment, too much reliance cannot be placed on these figures; however, the net output ratio between consumer and capital goods, which equalled 5.2 in Chile in 1912 as compared to 4.7 in Argentina in 1908, tends to confirm that Argentina was slightly more industrialized than Chile.[53]

A comparison of occupational data reveals only one other important structural difference between the two countries: the rural labor force was relatively larger in Chile.[54] Otherwise, as the reclassified census data presented in Table 6 indicate, the occupational distribution of the population in the two countries was quite similar and changing in the same directions. By the turn of the century the Argentine social structure, like the Chilean, had become quite diversified. Between the great property holders on the one hand and the domestic servants and rural workers on the other, there existed a wide variety of occupational groups accounting for at least 50 percent of the total economically active population.

TABLE 6

ARGENTINA AND CHILE: ECONOMICALLY ACTIVE POPULATION
BY MAJOR OCCUPATIONAL CATEGORIES (percent)

| Occupation | Argentina | | Chile | | |
	1895	1914	1895[a]	1907	1920
1. Professional, technical & related	1.8	2.9	1.1	1.9	2.4
2. Managers, proprietors & related	1.8	2.1	0.6	1.4	1.3
3. Sales, commerce & banking	6.0	9.1	6.3	6.6	8.2
4. Public admin. & office work	4.3	6.0	4.5	8.0	3.3
5. Agric. & fishing	35.6[b]	28.7[b]	40.8	37.7	36.2
6. Mining	0.1	– –	3.1	2.7	4.1
7. Transport	3.7	3.2	1.9	3.3	4.4
8. Artisan & industrial	21.9	22.4	23.5	24.7	20.5
9. Manual & day labor	9.4	9.9	1.7	– –[c]	3.0
10. Services	14.8	11.1	15.9	13.4	15.5
11. Other	0.7	4.5	0.4	0.3	1.1
Total	100.1	99.9	99.8	100.0	100.0

SOURCE: Chile, *Censo*, 1895, Vols. I-IV; 1907 and 1920. Argentina, *Segundo censo*, 1895, Vol. II; *Tercer censo*, 1914, Vol. IV.

NOTE: Percentages may not add up to 100 due to rounding.
[a]Excluding Tacna province.
[b]Estimates
[c]Included in category 5.

Despite these overriding similarities, occupational data do reveal important differences between Argentine and Chilean society. Partially because of the sheer magnitude of the immigrant flow, foreigners virtually monopolized enterpreneurial positions in Argentina and accounted for the majority of skilled workers. To note some of the most important disparities, in 1895 foreigners accounted for 38.7 percent of the total economically active population in Argentina, but they constituted 66.2, 54.7, and 41.8 percent respectively of the work force in commercial, transport, and artisan and industrial activities. Natives, on the other hand, were disproportionately represented in the service sector. In the case of more specialized occupational categories, even greater contrasts exist between the occupational distribution of the foreign-born and native population. Among professionals, for example, natives accounted for over 65 percent of the lawyers, teachers, and professors in 1895, while immigrants tended to monopolize the engineering and medical professions. In the artisan and industrial category, immigrants were disproportionately occupied as masons (67.9 percent), carpenters (63.5 percent), blacksmiths (65.7 percent), machinists and mechanics (79.5 percent), shoemakers (73.2 percent), and tailors (77.3 percent), while the highest concentrations of natives were found in occupational subcategories such as dressmaking (87.5 percent) and weaving (97.1 percent), where the majority of workers were women. Overall, almost three-fourths of the natives employed in artisan and industrial establishments in 1895 were female. Immigrants, in contrast, accounted for approximately 70 percent of all males employed in artisan and industrial activities but only 46.6 percent of the total male working force.[55]

By 1914 native Argentines had made up some ground, particularly in the professions, commerce, and white-collar work. Nevertheless, immigrants, who accounted for 45.8 percent of the work force, remained disproportionately represented in commerce (62.0 percent), artisan and industrial occupations (47.8 percent), and transport (52.2 percent).[56]

Immigrants also performed some distinctive social roles in Chile. In 1907, for example, half of the engineers in the country were foreigners.[57] Yet, in comparison to Argentina, immigration had a relatively minor social impact. Differences in national origin fragmented Argentine society at all levels. The rapid rate of foreign immigration to Argentina also worked against the expansion of political participation, because unnaturalized foreigners could not take part in Argentine elections.

The Rural Sector

The structure of the rural sector shaped the role played by immigrants in Argentina as well as the broad pattern of social change taking place in the period leading up to World War I. Argentina entered the second half of the nineteenth century with a massive supply of unsettled fertile land, a small population, and few structural remnants of the colonial period. *Latifundio*, labor intensive agriculture, and the exploitation of *inquilino* or service-tenant labor—all of which were typical of rural Chile—were virtually unknown. In Argentina labor was expensive and relatively mobile.[58] In these circumstances stock-raising, which required large tracts of land but relatively little labor, became the principle rural activity, and wool, hides, and salted and jerked beef the country's main export products. The cultivation of wheat and other cereals only began to become important during the 1880s, when the first large wave of immigrants reached Argentina. These immigrants found opportunities to acquire land in the nonpastoral zones of Santa Fe, Córdoba, Entre Rios, and Buenos Aires through both public and private colonization schemes.

After 1890 opportunities for small-holders to acquire agricultural land diminished steadily. Land values rose rapidly in response to the growth of world demand for rural produce and, more specifically, to the increased profitability of stock-raising. Exporting meat to the English market proved exceptionally lucrative, and largely as a result, land prices doubled and in some cases quadrupled between 1888 and 1911, moving well beyond the levels at which small-holders could hope to amortize a mortgage.[59] Rising prices also meant land speculation and a preference on the part of landowners for leasing rather than selling land.

Successive governments failed to take any positive steps to encourage further colonization or implement policies favorable to small-holders. At times national and provincial governments even seemed to discriminate against small farmers. For example, government authorities auctioned off public land in large lots, imposed burdensome taxes on cereal farmers, and, until 1910, favored landowning cattlemen in extending rural credit.[60] Other aggravating circumstances existed as well; e.g., the agricultural land most suitable for small-holdings was located in the pampean zone close to Buenos Aires and was already settled by 1890. The net result was that by 1914 only 40 percent of the agricultural holdings in the country were operated by their owner.[61] In the major cereal provinces of Santa Fe and Buenos Aires the proportion was even lower.

As Table 7 indicates, significant differences existed between the position of immigrants and natives in the rural sector. First, over three-fourths of the immigrants were farmers, whereas the majority of natives were ranchers. Second, immigrants settled mainly in the provinces of Buenos Aires and Santa Fe, where they were in charge of 62.3 and 74.5 percent, respectively, of all rural holdings and between 70 and 80 percent of the purely agricultural holdings.[62] The Argentines were much more widely dispersed. Third, in 1914 over 60 percent of the foreign immigrants directing rural holdings were tenants and employees, while over 60 percent of the Argentines who directed rural holdings were proprietors.[63] Finally, and most important, native Argentines accounted for the overwhelming majority of the large landholders. The census of 1895 showed that 86.3 percent of all *estancieros* and *hacendados* were natives, and the percentage had only dropped slightly to 79.5 by 1914.[64] Almost without exception, these large landholders were ranchers rather than farmers.[65]

TABLE 7

ARGENTINA: DIRECTORS OF AGRICULTURAL AND PASTORAL
HOLDINGS BY NATIONALITY, 1914

	Agricultural		Pastoral		Total	
	No.	%	No.	%	No.	%
Native	70,447	43.2	83,259	74.1	153,706	55.9
Foreign	92,441	56.8	29,056	25.9	121,497	44.1
Total	162,888	100.0	112,315	100.0	275,203	100.0

SOURCE: *Tercer censo*, 1914, V, 309.

Due to inequalities in the distribution of land, the native landowning elite in Argentina, as in Chile, wielded tremendous economic power vis-à-vis tenant farmers as well as urban interests. But in contrast to Chile, the orientation of the Argentine rural elite was thoroughly commercial. Land in Argentina was a commodity and the mobility of land ownership very high. Anyone with enough money to invest was likely to buy land, and it changed hands frequently. Thus as Rodolfo Puiggros has stressed, the great cattle barons who made up the Argentine rural elite were rarely members of a traditional aristocracy with roots in the colonial period or even the early 1800s. They appeared in connection with the opening up of the English market to beef exports.[66]

Capitalist forces shaped social relationships in the countryside as well. Landowners did not, as in Chile, inherit a labor supply with their land, but purchased it. As a result, rural labor was unquestionably better paid in Argentina where, relative to land, labor in 1914 was still scarce. Comparing the amount of agricultural land per head of population in Chile and Argentina gives some idea of the pressures on available land. In 1914 there were 20.6 hectares of agricultural and grazing land per person in Argentina; in Chile the figure was only just over four hectares.[67] Given the higher proportion of the population involved in agriculture in Chile, the relative scarcity of land there was even greater than this comparison suggests.

Because the structure of the rural economy conditioned the pattern of party development in both countries, it is worth elaborating this point further. According to the 1930 census of Chile, about 52 percent of the rural population lived on *fundos* or large rural properties.[68] Comparable figures are not available for Argentina, but 71 percent of the total agricultural and pastoral population in 1914 lived on a holding that was directed by a family member. Agricultural employees and their families accounted for the remainder.[69] The ratio between the number of persons employed in the rural sector and the number of rural holdings provides another rough indication of differences between the two countries. Official statistics suggest that in Chile only one out of every seventy-one persons employed in the rural sector controlled a holding, whereas in Argentina over one person in every three enjoyed this position.[70] Obviously few rural Chileans could have pretensions to middle-class status. The agricultural population was largely composed of service tenants and laborers, while in Argentina a very large proportion controlled their own holdings, either through ownership or rental contract. Finally, as might be anticipated on the basis of the previous evidence, the distribution of land was also more unequal in Chile than in Argentina. In 1917 449 estates held over half of Chile's agricultural land.[71]

The differences in rural social structure contributed to a higher degree of overall social inequality in Chile. No data on the distribution of wealth exists for the 1880-1930 period, but the relative equality of social conditions in the two countries clearly differed considerably. While wage rates in Argentina were high even relative to Europe, no shortage of cheap labor existed in Chile. The contrast in labor conditions is reflected in the failure of Chilean landowners to support efforts to attract foreign immigrants, except for a brief period between 1905 and 1908 when a variety of special circumstances encouraged workers to leave large estates in search of higher wages.[72] In addition, nitrate exports accounted for most of the increase in Chilean national income after 1880, and the ownership of the nitrate fields was clearly concentrated in the hands of a small number of investors. In contrast, a relatively sizeable proportion of the Argentine population participated in the agricultural export boom that formed the basis of that country's growing income.

The comments of an Argentine traveller in Chile in 1889, who was plainly struck by the poverty of the Chilean lower class, also support the view that greater inequalities existed in Chile. The traveller, Gabriel Carrasco, observed:

> Here, where the entire population is divided into two well-defined classes, without any others intervening—namely, the powerful and wealthy who form the aristocracy, and the common people, poor and completely subjected to the former—money has an importance unknown to us in Argentina. The poor, who are very numerous, find it very difficult to earn the necessary minimum . . . I point out as a fact . . . that a middle class almost does not exist in Chile, and that what we could call the aristocracy treats the mass of the population with evident severity . . . Daily wages are still very low, and cultivable territory of Chile is in the hands of a relatively small number of large landowners on whose domains

TABLE 8

CHILE AND ARGENTINA: DISTRIBUTION OF AGRICULTURAL LAND

	Chile		Argentina		
% Holdings		% Land	% Holdings		% Land
0.46	own	56.61	0.7	own	33.4
2.04	"	73.35	1.7	"	48.9
7.33	"	88.56	8.2	"	78.3
19.60	"	95.40	12.7	"	84.2
34.03	"	98.13	40.0	"	96.4
59.46	"	99.60	54.8	"	98.5
100.00	"	100.00	100.0	"	100.0

SOURCE: Chile, *Anuario estadístico*, 1917-1918, Vol. VII: *Agricultura*, pp. 20-21; Argentina, *Tercer censo*, 1914, V. 73.

live a hardy native population largely at the mercy of those we would call 'land lards' [*sic*] : a type of feudal gentleman who is cultivated, honorable, and very patriotic but who gives the poor man no hope of becoming himself the owner of a piece of land. . . .

The middle class, that which forms a large majority in the well-balanced nations . . . which exercises such a major influence in European countries, North America, and the Argentine Republic, this class I repeat can be considered nonexistent in Chile.[73]

The comments that James Bryce made about Argentina after a visit at the beginning of this century, are also apposite:

Society is something like that of North American cities, for the lines between classes are not sharply drawn, and the spirit of social equality has gone further than in France, and, of course, far further than in Germany or Spain. One cannot speak of an aristocracy, even in the qualified sense in which the word could be used in Peru or Chile, for though a few old colonial families have the Spanish pride of lineage, it is, as a rule, wealth and wealth only that gives station and social eminence.[74]

Urbanization

The difficulties the immigrants experienced in acquiring land in Argentina accelerated the growth of urban centers. Census data do not provide a clear picture of the distribution of immigrants by community size, because the census definition of "urban" was so generous as to be virtually meaningless. Nevertheless, the growth of the city of Buenos Aires provides an indication of the impact of immigration on urbanization. In both 1895 and 1914 over 60 percent of the population living in cities with over 20,000 inhabitants resided in Buenos Aires. As Table 9 shows, immigration was a major factor in the city's rapid growth. One-third of the total foreign population of Argentina lived in the Federal Capital and probably another third lived in other littoral cities.

TABLE 9

POPULATION OF FEDERAL CAPITAL BY NATIONALITY
1895 and 1914

	Native		Foreign		
	No.	%	No.	%	Total
1895	318,361	48.0	345,493	52.0	663,854
1914	797,969	50.7	777,845	49.3	1,575,814

SOURCE: Argentina, *Segundo censo*, 1895, Vol. II, p. CLIII; *Tercer censo*, 1914, I, 202.

Table 10 further underlines the impact of immigration in Argentina. In the 1860s Chile and Argentina had approximately the same number of inhabitants living in cities over 5,000. Between 1865 and 1914 that population tripled in Chile, but increased nearly eight times in Argentina. Large cities grew even more rapidly in the Argentine case, especially the Federal Capital, which, relative to Chile's largest urban center, Santiago, included an exceptionally high proportion of the total population. Despite these differences in the pattern and volume of urban growth, the proportion of the population living in cities in the two countries was quite comparable and relatively high by international standards. At the turn of the century Chile and Argentina were not only more urbanized than the majority of Latin American republics in 1950,[75] but the proportion of the population living in cities over 20,000 in the two countries was nearly the same as in the United States in 1910 (31 percent), or, to take two even

TABLE 10

ARGENTINA: POPULATION LIVING IN CITIES OVER
5,000 AND 20,000 INHABITANTS, 1869-1914

	Cities over 5,000		Cities over 20,000	
	Inhabitants	% Total Pop.	Inhabitants	% Total Pop.
1869	385,396	22.2	233,530	13.4
1895	1,270,399	32.2	957,491	24.2
1914	3,164,608	40.2	2,600,423	33.0

SOURCE: *Segundo censo*, 1895, Vol. II; *Tercer censo*, 1914, Vol. IV.

more striking examples, as in France or Sweden in 1950 (33 percent).[76]

Increased Literacy

As in Chile, literacy rates also expanded rapidly at the end of the nineteenth century in Argentina. Because Argentina had a large foreign population, 60.9 percent of which was literate in 1895 as compared to only 29.5 percent of the native population,[77] its overall level of literacy was higher than Chile's, both in 1895 and 1914; but the differences between the two countries were not very marked. According to census results, literacy rates in Argentina expanded from 17.9 percent in 1865 to 37.4 and 49.7 percent, respectively, in 1895 and 1914.[78] Starting from virtually the same base in 1865, the Chilean literacy rate reached a figure of 31.8 percent in 1895 and 50.3 percent in 1920.[79]

Perhaps the major contrast between the two countries in the expansion of literacy concerns the relationship of that process to urbanization. Unlike Chile, the literate population expanded much more rapidly than the urban population in Argentina, indicating that the discrepancy between rural and urban literacy rates was not as marked as in Chile. Nevertheless, important regional differences in literacy rates did exist in Argentina. In 1895 the average literacy rate in the littoral region equalled 44.9 percent. In other parts of the country literacy rates ranged between 20 and 29 percent.[80]

THE SOCIOECONOMIC CONTEXT:
SOME CONCLUDING REMARKS

In summary, after 1880 both Chile and Argentina experienced a period of very rapid socioeconomic change. External demand provided a dynamic impetus to economic growth that rapidly found expression in the expansion of urban economic activities. In the case of Argentina, new rural interests associated with agricultural, as distinct from pastoral, exports also emerged in the period. Concomitantly, urbanization and shifts in the occupational distribution of the population enlarged the number of urban middle-sector and working-class elements. Chilean and Argentine literacy rates also increased rapidly after 1880.

In both countries these changes created a set of conditions favorable to party development. Taken together they increased the variety of economic and social interests, fostered new rivalries and greater competition for political influence, and enlarged the number of potential political participants. Consequently, new incentives emerged for challenging the political status quo, as well as new opportunities for political leaders interested in enlisting popular support in their political struggles. The rapidly growing number of individuals with a capacity for independent political activity also exacerbated the problems involved in controlling a representative system through purely informal methods. No accurate information exists on the size of the electorate in either country before 1912, but the rise in literacy rates indicates that the number of eligible voters increased rapidly toward the end of the nineteenth century. It may also be inferred that the relative independence of the electorate increased, since rapid socioeconomic change, particularly urbanization, breaks down established social relationships.

The emergence of political parties in Chile and Argentina at the end of the nineteenth century reflected, more specifically, the growth in the number and relative importance of urban middle-sector groups. In both countries their search for greater political influence played an important role in the formation of parties modelled after European and North American examples and contributed to the collapse of systems of executive control over electoral outcomes that had previously limited opportunities for competitive party activity.

It should be emphasized strongly, however, that the process of party development did not involve clear-cut conflicts between urban and rural interests or upper and middle-class social elements in either country. The absorption of new elites into the upper class and the resulting overlap between urban and rural elites muted sectoral conflicts in Chile. Because of the rapid pace of development and the sheer number of new urban elites, who were mainly foreign in origin, rural and urban elites were not as thoroughly commingled in Argentina; but the interests of the two groups still overlapped considerably. Indeed, because the Argentine economy as a whole was geared to the export of rural products, far stronger economic linkages existed between urban and rural elites in Argentina. Thus while the growth of industry and commerce created new sets of economic interests, the pattern of socioeconomic change in both countries moderated sectoral conflicts.

The pattern of socioeconomic change also worked against the organization of a straightforward middle-sector challenge to established elites. The importance of foreign capital in the growth of urban activities, the nonantagonistic relationship between urban and rural sectors, and the nature of middle-sector groups in the two countries all checked such a development. In neither country did middle-sector groups constitute a class of self-employed and independent persons with a set of economic interests completely distinct from those of established elites. Employment opportunities for middle-sector elements remained very dependent on export-oriented development and the associated increase in foreign investment. The social gulf between middle-and working-class groups, which arose out of massive social inequalities in Chile and the division between natives and foreigners in Argentina, further impeded the development of a clear-cut middle-sector political challenge.

Despite these broad similarities, important differences existed between the two countries. The level of foreign immigration, the pace and magnitude of change, the concentration of the urban population, and the equality of social conditions were all greater in Argentina than in Chile. Even though standard socioeconomic indicators show that the two countries were quite comparable in 1900, Argentina was also slightly more modernized in terms of literacy rates, per capita income, urbanization, industrialization, and occupational differentiation. Even more significant, the pattern of socioeconomic change in the two countries differed considerably. The Chilean nitrate boom gave rise to an extremely uneven process of change, one which left the socioeconomic structure of rural areas relatively untouched. In Argentina, on the other hand, economic growth spread out from the rural sector to other portions of the economy. Imbalances existed between the littoral region and the rest of the country, but they were much less marked than regional differences in Chile. This contrast had important political consequences, because it meant that the Argentine rural social structure changed along with the urban one, enlarging the number of groups with a capacity for independent political activity and an interest in supporting challenges to the prevailing political order. Partially as a result, parties in Argentina were able to recruit a much broader base of popular support than in Chile, and rural elites experienced greater difficulty in retaining control over the political system.

CHAPTER III

THE FIRST CHILEAN PARTY SYSTEM

The first steps towards the formation of national political structures with a popular base took place in Argentina and Chile around 1890. The initial party-building effort in both countries is largely a matter of Radical party history and may be characterized as a struggle of middle-sector groups, acting in alliance with dissident elite elements, to achieve a greater measure of political power; however, parties representing urban working-class interests—the Democrats in Chile and the Socialists in Argentina—were also involved. The strategy that these groups adopted, which was basically that of using organized numbers as a political resource, first paid off in Chile.

Political conditions account for the relatively early appearance of party politics in Chile. In Argentina, where the principle of the legitimacy of political opposition had not won acceptance during the course of the nineteenth century, it proved extremely difficult for new groups to gain political representation. The Argentine Radicals found few legal channels of protest open to them. Confronted with growing dissent, popular aspirations for political participation, and the threat of repeated revolutionary movements on the lines of 1890, the leaders of PAN offered concessions that would enable them to control and co-opt the opposition; but they made a concerted effort to deny the Radicals access to power in their own right and blocked reforms that would have made genuine electoral competition possible. In response, the Radical leadership adopted a strategy of intransigence and abstained from electoral activity for twenty years. This lengthy exclusion from power, discouraging to all but the most dedicated, coupled with recurring threats of internal division arising out of attempts to neutralize the movement through some form of electoral *acuerdo*, meant that the Argentine Radicals faced a long uphill struggle in their effort to develop a national party structure.

The Chilean Radicals confronted far fewer obstacles. Because a tradition of peaceful competition among rival protoparties had been firmly established by 1891, the Radicals and other opposition elements obtained some political representation long before the end of the nineteenth century. Moreover, as the expansion of export tax revenues allowed the Chilean state to become increasingly autonomous during the 1880s, major conflicts developed between public and private sector elites. The Chilean Radicals thereby gained powerful allies in their struggle to open up the political system—notably, the Conservatives, whose influence had been restricted severely during most of the Liberal Republic and who therefore took up the theme of political reform and sided with the congressional forces against President Balmaceda.

THE INTRODUCTION OF THE PARLIAMENTARY REPUBLIC

The 1891 civil war significantly altered the relationship between the state and civil society in Chile by modifying institutional arrangements. The principle of cabinet responsibility was introduced and the power of the executive was severely circumscribed. Concomitantly, the national administration lost control over the electoral system, encouraging relatively free competition for political support and the organization of political forces outside the legislature. All these changes occurred without fundamental modification of the legal framework of government. Apart from the electoral law of 1890, which replaced the complete list or winner-take-all system with the cumulative vote in all elections, and the law of municipalities of December 1891, which enlarged the power of local government,[1] the constitution of 1833 survived until 1925, the year which formally marks the end of the "Parliamentary Republic."

Relatively little research has been done on this period. Devoid

of political crises, international adventures, and, at least until
1920, colorful presidential personalities, historians have usually
seen it as an interregnum: a fruitless, corrupt period which can be
summed up in a few critical phrases. The following quotations are
representative:

> Government in Chile reached its lowest ebb during the period of parliamentary rule.[2]
>
> The complexity of politics in the parliamentary period is exceeded only by its unimportance.[3]

Contemporaries could be even more scathing.[4]

From 1892 until 1920, when Arturo Alessandri assumed
office, the government was headed by a succession of bland, aging
presidents, whose passive attitude is beautifully summed up by
an aphorism attributed to President Ramón Barros Luco (1910-
1915): "There are two kinds of political problems—those that
have no solution and those that solve themselves."[5] Beneath them
were cabinet ministers, responsible to the legislature, who rarely
held their posts long enough to make any lasting mark on public
policy. Indeed, the rotation of cabinet officials is probably one of
the best-known and remarkable features of the period. Between
December 1891 and September 1924 the Ministry of the Interior
changed hands almost one hundred times, and the average cabinet
survived only four to five months.[6] Yet the system of parliamentary
rule proved remarkably stable. It survived for over thirty
years and for this reason alone warrants great attention.

THE DEVELOPMENT OF POLITICAL PARTIES

The factions and parties that competed for power in the 1891-1925
period in Chile included the Radicals, Nationals, Liberals, and
Conservatives plus two newer groups: the Liberal Democrats and
Democrats. Of these the Radicals were the first to organize on the
lines of a modern political party.

The Radical Party

In November 1888 the Radicals held their first national convention,
composed of delegates from all parts of the country, in the
rooms of the Club Radical in Santiago. Agreeing on a party con-

stitution and national party platform, they established the basis
for a political association with a national structure, explicit program, and formally recognized leadership. The constitution, which
was to become the model for most other parties, called for the
formation of a *junta central* or central committee, elected by the
local Radical *asambleas*, to coordinate the work of the party at
the national level.[7] Until this time the departmental *asambleas* had
been independent of one another, and such unity and cooperation
as had existed had been achieved informally in the legislature and
owed much to the personality and leadership of Manuel Matta.[8]
The *junta central*, from which legislators were explicitly excluded,
was elected during the following month.

The program adopted at the first Radical convention chiefly
addressed the issue of political reform. It called for the strict
responsibility of the cabinet to parliament, decentralization of
government, reform of the public administration to establish a
system of appointment and promotion according to professional
rather than political criteria, municipal autonomy, proportional
representation in congressional and municipal elections, the formation of provincial assemblies, and "the most absolute respect
for the right of suffrage."[9] Many of these demands were being
voiced by other political groups, and a few materialized in the
aftermath of the 1891 civil war. Other important planks incorporated in the program include free, secular, and compulsory primary
education; the expansion of secondary and technical education;
the improvement of the legal position of women; a progressive
system of taxation; the improvement of the condition of the
working class; protection of the national merchant marine; and
state action to stimulate and promote national industry.[10]

Radicals had emphasized anticlericalism and political reform
from the middle of the century onwards. The concern for socioeconomic problems was newer, and it reflected the changing
composition of the party as well as its effort to secure a more
widespread base of popular support.

The attitude of the Radicals towards the Chilean working class
at this stage can only be described as ambivalent. Two months
after the convention the party issued a circular underlining the
significance of the demand for state action on behalf of the
working class:

The convention has printed in its program a proposition relating to the improvement of the moral and material condition of the poor and working class.

Few problems are more serious than that described under this heading and of greater consequence for the general development of the republic. Its importance is beyond controversy.[11]

But the impoverished condition of the mass of the population, which led to this expression of concern, also tended to inhibit the spread of democratic sentiments within the party. The Radical leader Enrique Mac-Iver is quoted as having said at this first convention, "The workers have neither sufficient culture nor preparation to understand the problems of government, much less participate in it."[12]

During the course of the 1891-1925 period the orientation of the party gradually changed, and its commitment to state intervention in the social and economic sphere became more explicit. The third party convention of 1906, which was marked by a famous debate between Mac-Iver and Valentín Letelier over the issue of broadening the party's program, represents a key turning point. Letelier, who won the support of the majority, argued that the Radicals should take their bearings from Western Europe where Mac-Iver's laissez-faire conception of government had been exposed as a sterile and conservative doctrine. He observed that new parties emerge out of the failure of older ones to satisfy certain collective aspirations and that "all the cultured peoples of the world have at this moment something of socialism."[13] The resulting program did not openly endorse socialism, but it did assert the obligation of government to assist the helpless and destitute and called for state intervention in the areas of health and housing. The rest of the program dealt mainly with the need for further institutional reforms, reflecting the growing disillusionment of the Radicals with the system of parliamentary rule which they had helped bring into existence.[14]

By 1919 the party had completely abandoned its laissez-faire line. The convention held in that year approved a platform that recognized the duty of the state to provide the broadest form of economic and social assistance. It proposed free public education up to the university level, social security and minimum wage legislation, the regulation of female and child labor as well as hours and working conditions, the protection and promotion of national industry, limits on the export of food and basic necessities, the improvement of housing conditions, progressive taxation, and state involvement in labor disputes.[15] Despite this reorientation, tensions between those who thought the party should actively concern itself with the plight of the lower class and those who held a more traditional conception of the Radicals' mission persisted long after 1906 or even 1919. The problem was not only that the Radicals attempted to occupy the difficult middle ground in a society characterized by tremendous social inequalities, but the social composition of the party was far from homogeneous. A contemporary observed:

> Its leadership does not perhaps differ much from that of other parties: it includes men of social position such as Ascanio Bascuñan, Javier Gandarillas, Francisco Puelma, Jorge Huneeus, Enrique Mac-Iver, Juan Castellón, and many others . . .[16]

He went on to argue, however, that the bulk of the party's members were drawn from less prestigious social elements, such as shop assistants, and that this class character made the Radicals a disruptive social force.[17] But, precisely because the leadership of the party was in the hands of eminently respectable men, this tendency was muted. Northern mine owners and southern *hacendados* continued to play a powerful role, and without their wealth and influence the strength of the party would have been diminished considerably.

At the time of their first convention the Radicals held only seven seats in the Chamber of Deputies and one in the Senate.[18] In the years that followed their political importance increased rapidly, and by 1915 only the Conservatives held more legislative seats. Several factors account for the growth in the Radicals' strength. First, the civil war of 1891 made it possible for the Radicals to compete with other political groups on more equal terms. Whereas the intervention of police chiefs, judges, intendants, governors, and other public officials had previously deprived elections of almost all meaning, after 1891 their outcome was determined largely by the number of votes counted. Electoral abuses did not disappear entirely. Lengthy and heated debates over the disqualification of candidates on the grounds of fraud followed every election, and the impartiality of authorities, especially at the municipal level, was frequently called into question.[19] Nevertheless, most observers agree that after 1891 the fraud became less systematic and less centralized and was perpetrated not by the national administration, but by party agents whose chief instrument was bribery.[20] The difference is not merely academic. As Carlos Pellegrini pointed out in 1905 with reference to the spread of electoral bribery in the Argentine capital,

> Votes are not bought or sold where there is no electoral freedom, and if this is doubted, let someone try to buy votes in the Province of Buenos Aires.
> Bribery is a vice of liberty and it has existed among all free peoples.[21]

The socioeconomic changes outlined in the previous chapter also enhanced the Radical party's influence, because they released large numbers of men from the hegemony of the hacienda and enlarged the social base from which the party might draw support. While the Radicals elected representatives from rural districts, they drew a disproportionate amount of electoral support in communes with higher than average literacy rates.[22]

The gains made by the Radicals in the years after 1891 may, finally, be related to their organizational efforts. Between 1888 and 1899, when the party held its second convention, the number of *asambleas* quadrupled, reaching eighty-five.[23] By 1919 there were over one hundred plus a number of youth clubs.[24] As the Radicals were quick to point out, and with some pride, no other party in Chile had a comparable organization. Others, however, soon imitated the Radicals' initiative.

The Democratic Party

The Democrats (Demócratas), who emerged as a discrete political group during the administration of Balmaceda, were the first to follow the Radical lead. The party was formally founded on November 20, 1887 by a group of Radical dissidents, headed by Malaquías Concha and Avelino Contardo, who sought to create a party to defend the interests of the working class. The party's first program defined the Democrats' central objective as the political, social, and economic emancipation of the Chilean people, and to this end it called for free, secular, and obligatory education, state support for the aged and infirm, the abolition of taxes on food and industrial production, progressive taxation, and a protective customs policy. The program also endorsed several political reforms: the reduction in the size of the armed forces, municipal autonomy, and the incompatibility of legislative and administrative posts.[25]

This program was amplified at the party's first convention, which was held in July 1889. The need for a protective commercial policy, which the party claimed would benefit not only industry but workers and agricultural interests, was explicitly underlined, as was the need for the abolition of taxes on food and artisan or industrial activities. The platform of 1889, however, placed greater emphasis on political reform. Democrats saw the improvement of the socioeconomic condition of Chilean workers as inseparable from the problem of achieving a more democratic form of government and, in particular, effective and widespread participation in elections. Finally, to mention two planks relating specifically to the economic position of the working class, the 1889 platform advocated metallic conversion to stabilize the constantly depreciating peso and the prohibition of foreign immigration.[26]

Because Democrats supported Balmaceda, their organization was suppressed until 1892. In July of that year the party held a second national convention, and in the months that followed it established over thirty local party units.[27]

Importance is attributed to the Democratic party in the historical literature chiefly because it was the first party in Chile to identify with the urban working class. It should be noted, however, that the party also represented the interests of domestic industry. Among its most prominent leaders were men such as Artemio Gutierrez and Angel Guarello: men originally of low social rank who owned, or whose families owned, workshops, factories, and small firms.

The Democrats' influence remained quite restricted throughout the parliamentary period. The party elected its first deputy, Angel Guarello, in 1894 from Valparaíso, but it was not until 1912, when four Democrats were seated in the lower house, that the party succeeded in electing a senator. Significantly, in that year the party suffered a serious split as Luis Emilio Recabarren, one of its more prominent and militant leaders, broke away to form the Socialist Worker party. A central dilemma facing the Democrats after 1892 was that influence could only be secured through interparty electoral pacts, which tended to compromise its basic principles. Splits over electoral strategy had developed on previous occasions, most notably at the convention of 1906 when the party decided to cooperate with the Conservatives. Recabarren's dissatisfaction had similar origins.[28]

The nature of the trade union movement during the parliamentary period shaped the role played by the Democratic party. Prior to the civil war of 1891 few attempts had been made to establish anything more militant than mutual aid societies (*socorros mutuos*) in Chile. The 1890s witnessed several tentative organizational efforts, including the formation of the Central Social Obrero, the Agrupación Fraternal Obrera of Santiago, the Unión Socialista, and the Partido Obrero Socialista Francisco Bilbao—all of which collapsed within one or two years—and the publication of numerous socialist and anarchist periodicals, mainly in Santiago, Valparaíso, and the northern nitrate areas. The labor movement made greater progress during the succeeding decade, when a large number of trade unions were founded and the country experienced its first serious wave of strikes.[29] By 1910 unions or mutual-help type associations included 4 to 7 percent of the total work force.[30] During this initial period of organization the Democrats cooperated with unionized labor and helped organize a series of strikes and popular demonstrations against rising living costs. These protest activities culminated in the popular manifestations of October 1905, which attracted 30,000 to 50,000 participants in Santiago alone and degenerated into several days of violence known subsequently as "Red Week."[31]

During the second half of the parliamentary period the trade union movement continued to grow and became increasingly radicalized in response to the diffusion of socialist and anarchist ideologies, low wages, inflation, and repression. While the movement as a whole remained decentralized, union activities also became increasingly coordinated through the formation of union federations, such as the Federación Obrera de Chile (FOCH), and other working-class organizations. Union activity reached a peak in the 1917-1920 period, which witnessed a series of mass protest rallies organized by the Asamblea Obrero de Alimentación Nacional as well as a major strike wave.[32] Trade union membership in this period has been estimated as high as 270,000 workers or approximately 22 percent of the work force; however, the real size of the movement, which was certainly much smaller, remains unknown.[33]

The spread of radical ideologies created a growing gap between the labor movement and the Democratic party. By 1925 all major unions, except that of the railroad workers, had clearly defined Communist or anarcho-syndicalist affiliations.[34] The Democrats, on the other hand, retained a parliamentary orientation. As a result the growing strength of the trade union movement did not significantly enhance the Democrats' political position, and the demands of organized labor largely bypassed the parliamentary system. The anarcho-syndicalists eschewed parliamentary politics in favor of strikes and other direct means of exerting pressure on behalf of the working class, while other trade union elements extended support to Recabarren's Socialist Worker party, which affiliated with the Communist International during the early 1920s.

The Socialist Worker party, which held its first national congress in 1915,[35] remained a less than impressive organization. Its membership, generously estimated, was only 2,000 in 1922; and although it was well financed and directed, publishing a number of newspapers and periodicals,[36] its electoral importance was negligible. Socialists received less than 0.5 percent of the vote in 1915 and 1918, and only 1.4 percent in 1921.[37] Thus the party's formation scarcely affected the distribution of political power in Chile, although it did serve an educational function. The removal of the most militant socialists from the ranks of the Democratic party also allowed the latter organization to pursue a much more compromising strategy after 1912.

The organization of the Democrats and Radicals into national political structures with local units, a national leadership, concrete programs, and sizeable popular followings provoked other political groups to follow suit, albeit with varying degrees of enthusiasm and success. This development has often been overlooked; indeed, historians have portrayed the politics of the parliamentary period in terms of the dissolution rather than the organization of political parties. The confusion surrounding this issue arises out of the very large number of competing political groups as well as the persistence of factions alongside parties. Multipartyism, as Maurice Duverger pointed out in his classic study of political parties, can easily be confused with the absence of parties.[38] Edwards Vives, who had few flattering things to say about political parties after 1891, recognized this point in 1903 when he wrote that the chief problem in Chile was not the lack of organized parties but the absence of any powerful parties, for which the dissolution or fusion of some would have been necessary.[39] Given a mixture of multipartyism and factional politics, the possibilities of confusion increase. The term party system, although fully applicable, hardly begins to convey the real complexity and character of the situation.

The Conservatives

The Conservatives were unquestionably the most unified and powerful political group in Chile during the parliamentary era. They benefitted directly from the civil war of 1891, increasing their legislative representation from only a small fraction of seats in 1888 to the largest single block in the years that followed. This gain chiefly resulted from the loosening of the executive's control over electoral outcomes, which allowed large landowners to take advantage of socioeconomic conditions in the countryside and manipulate large numbers of voters.[40] In this connection it should be emphasized that the electoral system had a decidedly antidemocratic and upper-class bias. Not only were rural areas overrepresented in the legislature—a tendency persisting well beyond the parliamentary period—but the largest taxpayers in each electoral district continued to exercise authority over the registration of voters and supervision of elections after 1891.[41] This authority could be and was abused for partisan purposes, particularly since the administration of the electoral process was decentralized after 1891 and placed under the direct control of local government officials. Other parties used the system to their advantage. In the northern Province of Tarapacá, for example, where mining rather than agriculture was the principle source of wealth, the Liberal Democrats maintained a tight grip on the electoral machinery.[42] But in most rural districts the Conservatives were in the best position to profit from the decentralization of electoral administration.[43] The influence of the church also represented an important political asset. As Valentín Letelier noted with reference to the elections of 1891 and 1892, the clergy actively supported Conservative candidates.[44]

Although the support and leadership of large landowners remained important throughout the parliamentary period, after 1900 the Conservatives, influenced by the encyclical Rerum Novarum of Pope Leo XIII, as well as by practical considerations, deliberately attempted to strengthen their organization and base of popular support. Conservatives began describing themselves as "advanced reformers"[45] and took an increased interest in socio-economic issues. The program presented by a group of Valparaíso Conservatives to the party convention of 1901 illustrates this tendency. In harmony with recently espoused Catholic social doctrine, the program proposed the construction of entertainment centers and cheap housing for urban workers, the regulation of hours and working conditions in factories and workshops, the prohibition of child labor, workmen's compensation for industrial accidents, laws to ensure that workers were paid in cash rather than in coupons only redeemable in company stores, legislation to protect tenant farmers, the colonization of public lands, and the expansion of educational opportunities of all types.[46] The concern with developing a broader following and more popular image also led the Conservatives to establish a nominally democratic party structure, which was modelled after the Radical party's organization and based on a system of departmental assemblies. There is no indication that the Conservative organization actually functioned in a democratic manner; however, it did permit greater coordination of party activities, more widespread diffusion of Conservative propaganda, and a widening of the party's social base. In 1910 a leading Conservative claimed with regard to the party's social composition:

Its forces are distributed through all the social classes. Its popular base
is much greater than that of the liberal parties. It is true that a great
majority of old aristocratic families support it; but it is no less true that
they are far from constituting the bulk of such a large party. One can
say that the Chilean aristocracy is Conservative, but not that the Conservatives are aristocrats.[47]

The Liberal Democrats

The Liberal Democrats or Balmacedists,'as their political opponents
frequently called them, consisted largely of remnants of Balmaceda's government: former legislators, army officers, public officials, and friends. Scattered by persecution and exile after the
civil war, they reunited in June 1892 under the leadership of
Manuel Arístides Zañartu, a former Minister of Finance, and
prepared the foundations for a new party. With the death of the
party's provisional president in August 1892, the leadership fell
to Adolfo Valderrama who, with the assistance of a directorate
of thirty members, began organizing the party throughout the
country. In November 1893 the Liberal Democrats held their
first national convention in Talca. They elected national officers;
adopted a constitution, which provided for the popular election
of departmental leaders; and promulgated a platform, which
essentially endorsed Balmaceda's ideas on questions such as the
superiority of presidential over parliamentary forms of government.

The government allowed the party to contest the elections of
1894 and, despite a certain amount of official harassment, it did
surprisingly well. The Liberal Democrats emerged, with twenty-six
seats, as the second largest legislative bloc after the Conservatives,
who held twenty-nine.[48] Once in the legislature, the Liberal
Democrats worked to obtain a law of amnesty and pensions for
officials dismissed after the civil war. The party held no cabinet
posts in Jorge Montt's administration (1891-1896), but thereafter Liberal Democrats were constantly at the center of political
intrigue, shifting support from one coalition to another, making
and breaking ministries. Paradoxically, no one played the parliamentary game with more zest and to greater effect than the members of the party whose chief and distinguishing tenet was the

return of the pre-1891 presidential system.

Liberal Democrats played a highly confusing political role between 1896 and 1901, because during these years the party was divided into two personal factions: the *vicuñistas*, who followed Claudio Vicuña Guerrero, and the *sanfuenistas*, who were led by Enrique Sanfuentes, Balmaceda's handpicked successor. This split meant that at many points one faction of the party participated in the cabinet while the other cooperated with the opposition. The union of these two factions under the leadership of Juan Luis Sanfuentes, the brother of Enrique, during the administration of Germán Riesco (1901-1906) greatly increased the party's influence and involvement in ministerial shuffles.[49]

By all accounts Juan Luis Sanfuentes was the most devious, dexterous, and powerful figure in Chilean political life from 1900 until the end of his term as president in 1920.[50] With six different political groups competing for power during the parliamentary period, success depended not only on electoral resources but on the possibility of negotiating advantageous political alliances. Since complex electoral pacts and governing coalitions could only be worked out at the national level, a premium was placed on the centralization of authority. Even the Radicals, with their tradition of autonomous local assemblies, conceded this point and delegated greater authority to their national committee. Because the Liberal Democrats carried this tendency to an extreme, Sanfuentes had much more freedom to maneuver than the leaders of the other major parliamentary groups. In addition, the Liberal Democrats were relatively pragmatic, even opportunistic, and were prepared to form an alliance with any party. The Conservatives and the Radicals, on the other hand, had ideological commitments that prevented such flexibility, while the Liberals were simply too fragmented to make maximum use of their parliamentary strength.

Although the Liberal Democrats were not founded by Sanfuentes and survived his retirement from politics,[51] the tremendous authority he wielded raises questions about the structure of his party. If most electoral pacts and important decisions were made in the *casa azul* of Sanfuentes, as Edwards Vives implies,[52] did the formal constitution of the party have any reality or were the Liberal Democrats only a legislative faction with connections in the countryside? Several facts suggest that the Liberal Democrats did develop a national party structure. First, although local units of the party did not enjoy much autonomy, they were not just paper organizations. The national committee issued circulars to the provincial *directorios* to coordinate their activities,[53] and contemporary newspapers indicate that party meetings were held at the local level to nominate candidates.[54] Moreover, the national *junta ejecutiva* and larger *directorio* met frequently to decide on party strategy.[55] Sanfuentes was capable of acting in a rather cavalier fashion, bypassing both these bodies; but, interestingly, his influence owed less to the support of Liberal Democrats within the legislature than to his control over formal party institutions.[56]

The Liberals, Nationals, and Independents

In contrast to the parties described above, legislators played a key role in the leadership of the Liberals and Nationals. For much of the period neither of these groups was well organized. The Nationals, who owed their existence more to historical memories than to anything else, basically remained a small legislative group with no distinctive program. At times they did not even constitute a separate group. After the revolution of 1891 the Nationals and Liberals attempted to unify and form an influential Liberal party under the leadership of José Besa Infantes. The unity of this political combination was precarious, to say the least, but during the administration of Federico Errázuriz Echaurren (1896-1901) the Nationals virtually disappeared. Referring to this period in a speech before the Senate in 1911, Arturo Besa said: "We Nationals had no president, no directorate, no secretaryship; we all met at the house of Ismael Tocornal [a Liberal] ."[57]

The nomination of Pedro Montt, a National, to the presidency in 1901 revived the separate identity of the group, since the majority of the Liberals refused to support his candidacy. The style of Montt's nomination is revealing. Leaders of the Conservative party plus a group of Montt's friends simply announced his candidacy at a banquet given in his honor in Valparaíso. Montt's supporters even failed to organize a formal convention of delegates to ratify the decision.[58] With only the support of the Conserva-

tives and Nationals, Montt lost the election; but in 1906 the hopes
of the Nationals were finally realized. In this election Montt received support from the Radicals, Nationals, a Liberal faction,
and a small group of Conservatives called the Monttinos.[59] Since
the majority of the Liberals sided with the Conservatives, Liberal
Democrats, and Democrats supporting Fernando Lazcano Echaurren, the election widened the gap between the Liberals and Nationals even further. Thereafter the latter acted quite independently.
Nevertheless, there is little evidence that the Nationals developed
a national party structure, and for all practical purposes they
might be considered a Liberal faction. As late as 1914, by which
time other political groups had established active local units and
at least a nominally democratic party framework, the Nationals'
executive committee was still selecting legislative candidates.[60]

The Liberals were unquestionably the least disciplined parliamentary group, and they divided in almost every presidential election. The party consisted of two main factions. One, the *liberal
doctrinario*, which traced its origins back to the dissident Liberals
of Santa María's time, tended to align with the Radical party.
Whenever the Liberals joined the Coalition, the electoral alliance
whose nucleus was the Conservative party, the *liberales doctrinarios*
split off to operate independently. The other faction, the *liberal
coalicionista*, displayed more flexibility. Although it usually cooperated with the Conservatives in presidential elections, it readily
entered into alliances with the Radicals.

Until the middle of the parliamentary period the Liberals had
no party structure. Elections were essentially do-it-yourself opera-
tions, which is to say that virtually anyone with enough influence
and money could proclaim himself a Liberal candidate. After the
party's national convention of 1907 the situation began to change.
Under the leadership of Ismael Valdés Valdés, who presided over
the party from 1906 to 1912, the Liberals actively began to imitate the Radical party and set up a system of departmental assemblies.[61]

The 1907 convention also led to innovations in the Liberal
program. It was broadened to include not only traditional planks
relating to freedom of suffrage, the separation of church and state,
and other political reforms, but demands for socioeconomic re-

forms.[62] However, the Liberals went much less far in this direction than the Conservatives. As late as 1919 their platform still emphasized political reform, although it also called for the expansion and improvement of the state educational system.[63]

To complete this sketch of the forces competing in Chilean politics after 1891, it should be mentioned that a number of parliamentary seats were regularly filled by independent candidates: men such as Augusto Bruna, a Senator from Antofagasta from 1915 to 1921 with nitrate interests and links with the Liberal party, who had enough money and prestige to defeat regular party candidates.

THE STRUCTURE OF POLITICAL COMPETITION

Table 11 shows the relative strength of the parties described above in the legislative elections of 1912 and 1915. These are the first elections after 1891 for which official data are available and, significantly, the first Chilean elections for which the government published information on the distribution of the vote by political party.[64] It should be noted that a coalition of at least three parties was necessary to secure a majority in the Chamber of Deputies after both these elections. The need for coalitions was typical of the period as a whole.

During most of the parliamentary period Chile was governed by one of two basic alliances: the Coalition, built around the Conservative party and usually a portion of the Liberal party or the Liberal Democratic party, and the Liberal Alliance, which was the name applied to any alliance including the Radicals and *liberales doctrinarios*. Usually the Democrats participated in the Liberal Alliance as well. Beyond this one cannot generalize. Alliances were made and broken with tremendous rapidity, and the only stable points of reference in the whole system were the two parties with strong views on the issue of relations between church and state.

The Radicals, intensely anticlerical, attacked all forms of state support for religion, from religious ceremonies in the armed forces to subsidies to religious institutions. The most controversial issue of all, however, was state control of education. The Radicals were deeply entrenched in the state's educational establishment and

TABLE 11

CHILE: PERCENTAGE OF TOTAL VOTES CAST AND NUMBER OF
CANDIDATES ELECTED BY POLITICAL PARTY IN LEGISLATIVE
ELECTIONS, 1912 AND 1915

1912 Elections	Senate		Deputies	
	% Total Vote	Candidates Elected	% Total Vote	Candidates Elected
Conservative	18.1	4	21.5	25
Democrat	5.8	1	6.0	4
Liberal	24.5	8	18.3	22
Lib. Dem.	14.3	5	18.5	25
National	9.3	1	13.1	14
Radical	19.6	5	16.3	25
Socialist	— —	— —	— —	— —
Independent	7.6	1	6.6	3
Dispersed	0.4	— —	0.1	— —
Total	100.1	25	100.1	118

1915 Elections	Senate		Deputies	
	% Total Vote	Candidates Elected	% Total Vote	Candidates Elected
Conservative	24.5	2	21.5	26
Democrat	0.3	— —	9.2	5
Liberal	46.2	4	13.8	16
Lib. Dem.	6.4	2[a]	16.9	22
National	9.3	2	9.6	15
Radical	6.8	1	17.9	26
Socialist	0.6	— —	0.6	— —
Independent	3.2	1	10.4	8
Dispersed	2.8	— —	0.1	— —
Total	100.1	12	100.0	118

SOURCE: Chile, Oficina Central de Estadística, *Censo electoral: Elecciones ordinarias de Senadores, Diputados y Municipales, verificadas el 3 de marzo de 1912* (Santiago, 1912), pp. 46-53; idem, *Censo electoral: Elecciones ordinarias de Senadores, Diputados, Municipales y Electores de la República, 1915* (Santiago, 1915), pp. 28-31.

[a]Both these seats were later awarded to Liberals.

sought to extend public education at the expense of private schools, particularly religious ones. Almost all their programs included demands for free, secular, and compulsory education, and many attacked the church even more directly. The Radical program of 1912, for example, called for the abolition of the university's faculty of theology and the replacement of religious instruction in secondary schools with courses in "scientific morality."[65] The Conservatives, in contrast, fought the extension of the public school system and demanded "freedom of teaching," which basically meant that they wanted degrees obtained in ecclesiastical schools placed on the same footing as those granted by the state, a demand which aroused considerable passion because only the latter were recognized in the appointment of public officials.[66]

For other parties, however, the religious issue had lost much of its former significance.[67] It thus failed to produce a stable alignment of parties. Other questions of a social and economic nature were becoming important, but they cut across party lines and the preexisting religious cleavage. Monetary policy, for example, was a great source of political controversy, but it was usually not considered a party question.[68] The Radicals and Democrats favored monetary conversion and the stabilization of the peso on the grounds that the inflation associated with the constantly depreciating peso tended to reduce the living standards of the lower class, while the Liberal Democrats resolutely opposed such a policy.[69] The other parties were thoroughly divided. Many of their members, particularly the Nationals, favored monetary stability in principle, but often not in practice.[70]

Party lines were drawn even less firmly on commercial policy, although here the two extreme ends of the political spectrum were held by the Conservatives, who generally favored free trade, except where agricultural imports were concerned, and the Democrats, who enthusiastically supported protectionism, with the exception of tariffs raising the prices of imported food. The Radicals formally advocated protectionism too, as Jorge Huneeus reminded his colleagues during the debate on the 1897 customs law:

> . . . for many Radicals, one could say for all, support for the protection and development of national industry is a question of principle, even more than of program . . . the ills that weigh upon the country, the almost complete absence of industrial development, are due to the dreadful doctrine of free trade . . .[71]

Yet prominent figures within the party, notably Enrique Mac-Iver who announced "soi libre-cambista" during this same debate,[72] took a different line.

On the issue of social reform, which grew increasingly important during the course of the parliamentary period, the party alignment was different but again not very clear.[73] The Conservatives had much in common with the Democrats and Radicals, arguing that if efforts were not made to solve the "social question," workers would turn to socialism and undermine the entire social order.[74] The Conservatives' attitude was thoroughly patronizing and most of their concrete proposals related only to urban workers. Nevertheless, during the 1892-1920 period they probably sponsored as many reforms as the Radicals and Democrats, and they certainly outdistanced the Liberal Democrats and Nationals.[75] As with most issues, it is difficult to generalize about the Liberals, but certain individuals within the party, such as Eliodoro Yáñez, did take a serious interest in social problems.[76]

Not surprisingly, even contemporaries found it hard to define the differences among the parties in programatic terms. In 1913 Abraham König, a Radical, observed that nothing important separated the Radicals from the Liberal Democrats, Nationals, or Liberals. Their distinct identities were due to "historical memories, nothing more."[77] In a similar vein, Ramón Subercaseaux, a Conservative, argued that the Conservatives and Liberals were not divided by any significant issues. In fact, he proposed that the two parties should unite—a suggestion, he later admitted, which was made from want of political experience.[78]

As these comments indicate, partisan identities in this period crystallized around purely political questions and past conflicts rather than policy issues or contemporary socioeconomic realities. This tendency reflected the very gradual development of party competition in Chile, where, unlike Argentina, several parties could trace their origins back to the middle of the nineteenth century. The early solidification of partisan differences had important consequences for the structure of competition, because new issues crosscut the political rivalries that had persisted over time, creating the system of overlapping cleavages described above. Thus serious obstacles existed to the formation of a governing alliance on programatic grounds.

The clientelistic character of the Chilean party system reflected and intensified these difficulties. As Arturo Valenzuela's ecological analysis of the 1921 elections indicates, the various parties did not represent significantly different social groups, but drew support from a heterogeneous clientele.[79] Party leaders thus concentrated on providing tangible rewards for their followers, rather than fulfilling party programs.[80] Given the necessity for coalition government, some gap between program and practice was virtually inevitable, but political compromise in the ordinary sense does not explain the situation in Chile. Disagreements over the allocation of public posts almost superceded all others and more often than not led to the collapse of ministries. The appointment of governors, intendants, and diplomats and disputes over contested elections were a particular source of tension, but differences also arose over lesser posts. Because demands for patronage came from almost every quarter, ministries seldom survived for more than a few months.[81] This cabinet instability and the related preoccupation of party leaders with meeting demands for specific favors worked against the representation of subordinate group interests or the implementation of social reforms. Indeed, since clientelistic politics encouraged the formation of very heterogeneous coalitions and cabinets, positive action on any redistributive as opposed to purely distributive issue was almost inconceivable.

The electoral system must be held partially accountable. Not only did proportional representation discourage the consolidation of parties, but districts were small. On the average, deputies represented only 1,300 voters,[82] making legislators vulnerable to pressures from their constituents, particularly wealthy ones.[83] Even more to the point, elections were incredibly expensive. Estimates vary, but in his autobiography Ramón Subercaseaux claimed that he spent $30,000 pesos as a candidate in the 1906 election (roughly $9,000 U.S. dollars at the time) and suggested that this election was relatively cheap, since he did not really have to buy votes but only provide a small "gratification" to encourage voters to go to the polls.[84] This level of expenditure is quite possible: figures as high as $1,000,000 pesos have been quoted, although the usual price for a seat in the upper house was probably in the region of $100,000 pesos and for the Chamber of Deputies

$10,000.[85] Politicians used these large sums mainly to bribe voters, a practice that became deeply established in this period.[86] Moreover, as mentioned above, electoral regulations gave the economic elite significant control over the registration of voters and supervision of elections. Again, the implications for the political influence of groups at the middle or lower end of the socioeconomic spectrum were anything but positive.

Even if two or three parties did agree to give general policy objectives precedence over others of a more particularistic nature, it proved difficult to form a viable coalition. The distribution of seats in the two houses of the legislature, both of which could overturn a ministry, did not necessarily correspond. Since neither house could be dissolved, ad hoc ministries were frequently necessary. Party factionalism constituted another persistent source of difficulty, particularly among the Liberals. There was no guarantee that a coalition negotiated by the executive committee of the party would be accepted by its legislative members, nor even that Liberals in the Senate would support a ministry backed by Liberal deputies. Greater party discipline characterized the other parliamentary groups, leading to complaints that party leaders were vested with too much authority and influence;[87] however, because the number and relative strength of the parties made it difficult to form a majority, the defection of just a few individuals could be critical. In addition, the opportunities for congressional obstructionism were enormous. There was no limit on debate in either chamber, so virtual unanimity was required for laws to be passed.[88]

Low rates of electoral participation reflected and exacerbated these obstacles to the representation of popular interests. After 1874 all literate males over the age of twenty-five became eligible to vote,[89] but only a small proportion exercised this right. The growth of party competition did not significantly alter this situation. While the number of voters in Chile doubled between 1888 and 1918, even during the last decade of the parliamentary era, when the number of voters as a proportion of literate adult males rose from 19.4 to 39.2 percent,[90] the electorate remained quite restricted by the standards of most other liberal democracies. Whereas the percentage of the population voting in countries such as Britain, France, and the United States regularly reached figures in the 10 to 25 percent range during the 1900-1925 period, in Chile the rate of electoral participation was typically around 5 percent. In this respect, Chilean political history bears some resemblance to that of Sweden, where the expansion of the electorate was also unusually slow and where the percentage of the total population voting equalled only 5.6 percent in 1908 and 11.2 percent in 1920.[91] As indicated by Table 12, however, in the case of Chile the tendency towards limited electoral participation persisted well into the twentieth century. Until women began to vote in the 1950s, liberal democratic institutions in Chile were based on the electoral participation of less than 10 percent of the population.

The small size of the electorate can be related to several factors. First, restrictions on voting by women and illiterates excluded more than 70 percent of the adult population from the electoral system. Despite educational advances, 27 percent of the adult male population still was illiterate in 1920.[92] Second, regulations governing electoral registration and voting coupled with socioeconomic conditions allowed the upper class to manipulate the electoral system and contain pressures from below. Such manipulation prevailed particularly in the countryside, where the traditional social structure remained largely intact. In addition, the complicated and multipolar party system that emerged in the 1891-1925 period limited incentives for the expansion of the electorate. Competing groups could hope to increase their influence through the formation of new alliances rather than the mobilization of new support.

Political parties and electoral competition thus emerged in Chile under conditions unfavorable to policy innovations beneficial to a wide array of social groups. A new expression of concern for the needs of less privileged citizens did accompany party development, but the limited scope of political participation and the complicated structure of competition inhibited the translation of this concern into public policy. Cabinets represented very heterogeneous legislative majorities and were formed less on the basis of general issues than on questions of particular interests, material gain, or electoral advantage. Due to administrative continuity the

TABLE 12

EXPANSION OF THE CHILEAN ELECTORATE, 1873-1949[a]

| | Registered Voters | | Votes Cast | |
	Thousands	% Total Population	Thousands	% Total Population
1873	– – –	– – –	26	1.3
1876	– – –	– – –	80	3.9
1879	– – –	– – –	104	4.7
1882	– – –	– – –	97	4.2
1885	– – –	– – –	79	3.2
1888	– – –	– – –	90	3.5
1912	598	17.6	295	8.7
1915[b]	185	5.3	150	4.3
1918	342	9.4	183	5.0
1921	383	10.2	197	5.3
1925	302	7.7	256	6.6
1945	641	12.0	450	8.4
1949	592	10.4	470	8.3

SOURCE: Chile, *Censo electoral*, 1912, p. XVI; *Censo electoral*, 1915, p. 24; idem, *Sinópsis estadística*, 1919, p. 19; ibid., 1926/27; idem, *Anuario estadístico*, 1921, III, 41; ibid., 1925, I, 78 (for population figures); Gil, p. 213 (figures for the 1940s).

[a]Figures refer to legislative elections.

[b]New system of permanent registration, renewable every nine years, introduced to cut down on fraudulent registrations.

resulting ministerial instability did not completely disrupt government,[93] but it did limit the impact of any cabinet on public policy and discouraged authorities from pursuing policies involving more than the distribution of short-term benefits. Most important of all, the structure of competition prevented the electorate from making meaningful choices. Policy issues failed to differentiate the parties, and with constant shifts in party alliances and the related rotation of cabinet officials no distinction could even be drawn between "ins" and "outs." Consequently, the electorate had no effective means of making its preferences felt or of holding government authorities responsible for policy. These characteristics of the parliamentary system chiefly benefitted the already privileged: the commercial, agricultural, and mining elites who stood to profit most from the possibilities for congressional obstruction and government inaction and who could buy votes, make large contributions to political campaigns, and otherwise use their socioeconomic resources to control political outcomes.

THE ELECTION OF ALESSANDRI AND THE COLLAPSE OF THE PARLIAMENTARY SYSTEM

Even after 1915, when there was a marked upsurge in the strength of the Liberal Alliance, policy inertia and cabinet instability persisted. In that year an alliance of Radicals, Democrats, and a faction of the Liberal party made serious inroads into areas of Coalition strength and secured a majority in the Senate, although they lost the presidency and failed to gain a majority in the lower house. Most notable was the election of Arturo Alessandri to the Senate from the northern Province of Tarapacá, an area that had been firmly controlled by the Liberal Democrats until the electoral reform laws of 1914 and 1915 eliminated local government control over the electoral system and brought a new system of permanent registration into effect. Alessandri, who recognized the potential of socioeconomic electoral appeals, championed the cause of the oppressed northern mining workers and generated considerable popular enthusiasm.

Five years later Alessandri led another remarkable and successful campaign, this time for the presidency. Against a background of widespread unemployment, labor agitation, and economic depression—products of the disastrous postwar collapse of the nitrate market—he attempted to rally the middle and lower class to his side, promising fundamental political and social reforms.[94] For the first time in Chile organized labor took an active part in the campaign.[95] Whatever view one takes of Alessandri's objectives, and some cynicism is quite justified,[96] his triumph in the presidential campaign brought the mounting social problems of early twentieth-century Chile to the forefront of national politics. The electorate divided along new lines and the stakes of political competition suddenly increased. The 1921 legislative elections, in which the Democrats and Radicals polled 42.8 percent of the vote,[97] reflected these changes.

The parliamentary system was strained to the point of collapse. Forces seeking to defend the status quo concentrated on blocking Alessandri's program of reforms,[98] but with the country in a state of serious social unrest and economic depression, the almost complete paralysis of government proved too much for the military. In 1924, encouraged by politicians from all sides to intervene, military officers took matters into their own hands and ended the stalemate.[99] A series of reforms, including legislation on social security and state arbitration of labor disputes, was pushed through the legislature, and in 1925 the promulgation of a new constitution formally abolished the parliamentary system in the form in which it had been known since 1891.

CHAPTER IV

THE FIRST ARGENTINE PARTY SYSTEM

Whereas political parties in Chile evolved out of established parliamentary factions that gradually expanded their organizational networks, the process of party development in Argentina involved the mobilization of political opposition against the ruling oligarchy and a protracted struggle for political reform. This struggle, which the Argentine Radicals led between 1890 and 1912, created stronger incentives for the organization of popular support than in Chile and a greater degree of political polarization. Other factors reinforced these contrasts and produced important differences between the first Chilean and Argentine party systems. Before analyzing these differences and their implications for the distribution of political power in the two countries, this chapter provides a brief description of political events in Argentina between 1890 and 1912. The efforts of the Argentine Radicals to develop a national political structure, the nature of their struggle against the old regime, and the attitudes both sides developed in the course of it are all relevant to the analysis of the party system that emerged at a later date.

THE DEVELOPMENT OF THE ARGENTINE RADICAL PARTY

After the unsuccessful revolt of July 1890, the leaders of the Unión Cívica decided to organize their forces on a national scale and participate in the forthcoming presidential election. To this end they invited delegates from all the provinces to meet at a national electoral convention in January 1891. The convention, which set a precedent in Argentina for popular consultation in the nomination of candidates, chose two of the most prestigious figures in the Unión Cívica, Mitre and Bernardo de Irigoyen, as the opposition's standard bearers.

Support for the Unión Cívica had originally come from a variety of sources, and its members pursued a rather diverse set of objectives.[1] This lack of unity became apparent almost immediately. Mitre, who had left for Europe before the 1890 revolt, returned to Argentina in March and rapidly reached a private agreement with former President Roca, who had reassumed control over PAN. To avoid conflict at the polls, Mitre consented to head a combined ticket, with a *roquista* as vice-presidential candidate. The announcement of this *acuerdo* divided the Unión Cívica into two groups. One faction supported Mitre and split off to form the Unión Cívica Nacional (UCN). The other, which became known as the Unión Cívica Radical (UCR), denounced the *acuerdo* and organized another convention, which nominated Bernardo de Irigoyen as presidential candidate. This second group was led by former Republicans, Leandro Alem and Hipólito Irigoyen, who took the view that pacts and *acuerdos* served personal ambitions at the expense of intraparty democracy and the reformist objectives of the Unión Cívica.[2] Without the support of the UCR, Mitre's candidacy floundered, leading to new efforts to solve the problem of presidential succession. Roca and Mitre eventually reached another agreement in February 1892 when Roca, in one of his more famous political maneuvers, persuaded Luis Saenz Peña to run for president.[3]

In preparation for the presidential elections in April 1892 the UCR conducted a campaign around the country. Its agitation created considerable anxiety in government circles, and on April 2 President Pellegrini declared a state of siege, suspended civil liberties, and arrested and deported many UCR members. In protest the Radicals decided to abstain from the election.[4]

At the beginning of 1892 the UCR had yet to create a national party structure, but in the course of the year it made real progress in that direction. In November UCR provincial representatives met to approve a national constitution, which provided for a federal and representative party structure and owed a great deal to

North American models.[5] The convention also approved a general program, which incorporated principles endorsed at the organizing September 1889 meeting as well as a later manifesto of the national committee. The program criticized peso depreciation, the system of public land sales encouraging the concentration of rural property, the lack of provincial autonomy, and the predominance of the executive over other branches of government. But above all, the program insisted on the need for electoral freedom and political reform.[6]

The structure formally established at the 1892 convention proved weak and impermanent, mainly because the leaders of the UCR rejected electoral activity in favor of armed insurrection. In 1893 the UCR led a series of provincial revolts in Buenos Aires, Corrientes, Tucumán, Santa Fe, and San Luis; and later in the same year Alem headed a second national insurrection. Leaders of the UCR were again imprisoned and sent into exile.[7]

By 1897 the only regularly functioning unit of the movement was that led by Hipólito Irigoyen in Buenos Aires.[8] In that year, as well as in 1903 and 1909, UCR supporters placed considerable pressure on the national committee to participate in electoral campaigns; but Irigoyen, who assumed leadership of the UCR after Alem's suicide in July 1896, tenaciously insisted on a policy of "austere intransigence."[9] The argument in favor of this strategy, however, was becoming less and less compelling over time. Sympathy for the Radicals' objectives had grown within government circles, and PAN itself approached collapse. In 1901 a rift developed between Pellegrini and Roca, and the former, turning against the regime in which he had played such a prominent role, joined the Radicals in urging political reform. The UCN also fell into a state of disarray. Mitre retired from politics in 1901, and his followers divided into two groups. Manuel Quintana led one, while the other, which began calling itself the "Partido Republicano," looked to Emilio Mitre for leadership. To add to the confusion, Governor Marcelino Ugarte of Buenos Aires led another independent group. Serious barriers existed to the unification of these disparate elements behind a single candidate, and a convention of notables, which was held in October 1903 to decide who would succeed Roca at the end of his second term, left the UCR, Republi-

cans, and *pellegrinistas* all dissatisfied. Nonetheless, when the
UCR's national committee met in 1904 for the first time in many
years, it declared in its usual moralistic and turgid style that the
Radicals would abstain from the forthcoming elections.[10] The
party leadership decided instead to organize another revolt. It
broke out in February 1905, and because it had considerable
military support, the UCR was confident of success. But the plans
had been betrayed to the government, and the Radicals were again
forced to capitulate.[11]

After 1905 the Radicals abandoned their efforts to seize power
through force. With President Quintana's death the weakness of
PAN became obvious. In a speech before the Chamber of Deputies
in May 1906 Pellegrini pointed to the disunity:

> We have seen in the Capital a party calling itself the Electoral Union, in
> the Province of Buenos Aires United Parties, in Corrientes a Liberal party,
> in Santa Fe a provincial or independent party: various names for small
> oligarchies or factions; but nowhere do I see that great Partido Autono-
> mista Nacional to which I have had the honor of belonging.[12]

Under José Figueroa Alcorta, who succeeded Quintana as
president, the legislature passed an amnesty law for the participants
in the 1905 revolt. The Radical exiles celebrated their return to
the country with a large parade in the Federal Capital and in a
more serious vein began an extensive reorganization of the UCR.
Between 1906 and 1908 Radical party units were set up in every
provincial capital plus at least 200 other towns.[13] Soon afterwards
a national convention met to select a new national committee.
This organizational effort proved quite durable.

THE COLLAPSE OF THE OLD REGIME

President Figueroa Alcorta initiated a process that gradually opened
up the Argentine political system. He ruled with the support of
the *pellegrinistas* and Republicans, two factions of PAN that
favored political reform and accommodation with the Radicals on
practical grounds. The exclusion of the Radicals from power
through electoral fraud posed the constant threat of rebellion,
which disrupted economic life and did nothing to enhance the
image of Argentina as a field for foreign investment.[14] Moreover,
political reform offered a means of destroying Roca's influence,

which was based on the provincial oligarchies of the interior.

Opposition elements, led chiefly by Roca and Ugarte, dominated the national legislature when Figueroa Alcorta assumed office. Reflecting the deep division of the ruling elite, both major factions of PAN sought to win the support of the Radicals. Figueroa Alcorta, seeking to undercut the opposition, offered Irigoyen electoral control over Buenos Aires and Córdoba, while from Roca, who was hoping to depose Figueroa Alcorta, came an offer of the presidency.[15] By 1908 the situation had reached crisis proportions. To defend himself against the *roquistas*, who blocked all essential legislation, Figueroa Alcorta closed the congress and prepared to destroy the opposition in the national legislative elections of March 1908. In response opposition leaders gathered in Ugarte's house to discuss plans for an uprising.[16] The president, however, won the battle. Using the traditional weapons at his disposal, especially the threat of federal intervention, Figueroa Alcorta ensured that the electoral returns were favorable to his administration.[17] The last bastion of *roquismo*, Córdoba, was eliminated in April 1909 by direct intervention. The deaths of Pellegrini (1906), General Mitre (1906), and Emilio Mitre (1909) further helped clear the way for the president to impose a successor, Roque Saenz Peña, whose presidency was to mark the end of the old system of semi-competitive oligarchical politics.

Presidents Luis Saenz Peña, Uriburu, Roca, Quintana, and Figueroa Alcorta had all promised electoral reforms.[18] Unlike his predecessors, Roque Saenz Peña, who was particularly concerned about the low level of electoral participation in Argentina, fulfilled that pledge.[19] The president invited the Radicals to participate in his administration, and although they refused to collaborate officially, Irigoyen did meet with Saenz Peña to prepare new electoral legislation.[20] The resulting reform law, which was first put into effect in 1912, contained the following provisions: (1) a permanent register of voters based on the *padrón militar*, (2) the secret ballot, (3) universal male suffrage without literacy requirements, (4) compulsory voting, (5) prohibitions against fraudulent electoral practices, (6) the supervision of the electoral process by the federal judiciary, and (7) the incomplete list system under which the majority and minority parties in a province were to be represented in the Chamber of Deputies in the ratio of two-thirds to one-third.[21] Prior to this legislation all provincial seats were legally allocated to the party receiving the majority of votes, although in practice the complete list system had been modified by electoral pacts under which parties or factions might be represented according to their respective strengths.[22] Senators, as before, were to be elected by provincial legislatures.

Few Argentines accurately predicted the impact of the new law. Saenz Peña himself did not think that the Radicals could win free elections, nor did the representatives of the provincial oligarchies who voted for the law, apparently expecting that the incomplete list system would work to their advantage.[23] In any case, legislation was one thing, Argentine electoral practice another. La Nación argued on February 7, 1912 that in many provinces "the incomplete list will continue to be as complete as it has been up to now."[24] Everything depended on how the legislation was implemented.

The elections of 1912 and 1914 alarmed many. Shortly before the 1912 elections the UCR national committee authorized Radicals to present candidates in two districts, the Federal Capital and Santa Fe. Santa Fe was under federal intervention, so in both districts there was direct federal responsibility for supervision of elections. The majority slate in both went to the UCR. Two years later the party did even better, winning the majority delegations in Santa Fe and Entre Ríos and the minority in the Federal Capital, Buenos Aires, Córdoba, Corrientes, and Mendoza. In the capital the Socialists won the majority delegation. Ideas of deposing the president or of altering the reform law circulated as the oligarchy began to recognize the real implications of the new legislation.[25]

In 1916 Hipólito Irigoyen won the presidential election with 45.6 percent of the national vote.[26] A contemporary observed: "The old system has been destroyed like an anthill struck by a shell."[27] To some extent this comment exaggerated the degree of change. Many essential characteristics of the pre-1916 political situation persisted over time, including the concentration of political power in the hands of the president, one-sided competition for political office, and profound antagonism between government and opposition elements. In addition conservative forces in 1916 still retained control over most provincial governments as well as the upper house of the national legislature. Yet the Saenz Peña law did undermine dramatically the political base of conservative groups. With the exception of the Senate, which remained under the control of the conservatives, the Radical party dominated Argentine political institutions from 1916 until 1930.

THE STRUCTURE OF PARTY COMPETITION, 1912-1930

The structure of political competition in Argentina after 1912 differed markedly from Chile. In contrast to the multipolar Chilean party system, a clear distinction between "ins" and "outs" characterized Argentine politics.[28] The previous pattern of political development, the dominant position of the UCR, and the formal rules governing the system of political representation all contributed to this contrast.

Whereas in Chile a relatively well-institutionalized system of inter-elite rivalries dating back to the middle of the nineteenth century fostered multiple and overlapping political party cleavages, in Argentina the previous pattern of political development sharply divided government and opposition elements. The process of transition to a competitive system exacerbated this tendency. The introduction of a competitive regime in Chile was supported by a wide variety of political groups, including conservative ones, and did not give rise to any overriding political cleavage. In contrast, a single party, the UCR, led the battle to reform the Argentine system, creating a profound political division.

The role played by the UCR in bringing down the "viejo regimen" contributed to its political predominance after 1912. During their twenty years of opposition to PAN governments, the Radicals developed organizational skills, a tremendous partisan élan, and a strong base of popular support. Moreover, because of their leadership of the reform movement, they became closely identified with the electoral system introduced by the Saenz Peña law. In the long run this identification weakened competitive institutions in Argentina. When the world depression hit the country and the military turned the aging and increasingly incompetent Radical leader

Irigoyen out of office, the competitive system went with him. But in the short run, the UCR's role in promoting political reform enabled it to swamp all electoral opposition.

The powerful political position of the UCR after 1912 added to the tendency towards political polarization. In Chile the distribution of party strength necessitated political alliances and provided all parties with an opportunity to participate in the administration, blurring the distinction between "ins" and "outs." Partisan lines were much more firmly fixed in Argentina, because no party other than the UCR stood any real chance of controlling the national government.

Formal rules governing the system of representation reinforced contrasts between the structure of competition in the two countries. The Argentine incomplete list system gave majority and minority parties two-thirds and one-third, respectively, of the seats in the lower house, whereas in Chile congressmen were elected under a system of proportional representation. Institutional differences were also important. In Chile the locus of political power was the legislature, where all political parties were represented, while in Argentina the presidency, a nondivisible office, dominated other representative institutions, intensifying the distinction between government and opposition elements.

The Distribution of Party Strength

Tables 13 and 14 provide a basis for understanding the structure of party competition in Argentina after 1912. Technically the system was a multiparty one, like the Chilean; but as a practical matter only the Radicals stood any chance of securing control over the national government through elections. The opposition was so disorganized that other parties received only a fraction of the Radical vote. Indeed, most opposition groups were so small or ephemeral that they cannot even be classified as parties. Only three of them—the Socialista, Conservador, and Demócrata Progresista—normally received over 5 percent of the total national vote, and their strength was limited to just one or two provinces.

TABLE 13

ARGENTINE NATIONAL ELECTIONS OF DEPUTIES:
PERCENTAGE VOTE BY POLITICAL PARTY, 1912-1930

Party label	1912	1914	1918	1920	1924	1926	1930
Unión Cívica	8.9	3.6	– –	– –	– –	– –	– –
UCR	16.8	33.3	47.1	44.4	25.9	38.2	41.6
UCR-Unificada	– –	– –	– –	– –	10.8	8.4	3.6
UCR (Tacuarí)	– –	– –	– –	– –	– –	10.9	– –
UCR-other	– –	– –	8.5	4.6	12.8	6.8	9.2
Demócrata	– –	3.1	7.4	– –	1.0	– –	– –
Democ. Progres.[a]	2.6	2.9	– –	10.1	9.4	5.2	9.2
Socialista	5.4	9.3	8.3	11.2	14.6	11.1	8.3
Socialista-other[b]	– –	– –	4.5	0.5	0.6	0.8	8.2
Oficial	5.0	– –	– –	– –	– –	– –	– –
Conservador	16.9	10.8	9.9	13.7	5.1	4.4	10.3
Unión Nacional	8.7	– –	– –	– –	– –	– –	– –
Liberal	6.4	– –	1.3	3.8	2.2	2.6	2.7
Other conservative[c]	14.8	31.8	10.4	3.8	10.7	8.2	3.9
Blank votes	– –	– –	– –	2.5	2.0	2.3	2.7
Unknown	14.5	5.3	2.1	5.4	4.9	1.3	0.5
Total	100.0	100.1	100.0	100.0	100.0	100.2	100.2

SOURCE: Darío Cantón, *Materiales para el estudio de la sociologia política en la Argentina*, 2 vols. (Buenos Aires, 1968), I, 81-106.

[a]Including votes for Liga del Sur.

[b]Including votes for Communist candidates.

[c]All parties included in this category regularly received less than 5 percent of the vote.

The Major Opposition Parties

The Socialist party, organized by Juan B. Justo during the mid-1890s, obtained support mainly in the Federal Capital where the industrial and immigrant population of the country was concentrated.[29] It was probably the best-organized party in the country,

TABLE 14

ARGENTINE PRESIDENTIAL ELECTIONS
PERCENTAGE VOTE BY POLITICAL PARTY, 1916-1930

Party label	1916	1922	1928
UCR	45.59	47.75	57.41
UCR-Antipersonalista	– –	– –	10.63
UCR-other	– –	6.68	6.15
Socialista	8.88	8.96	4.49
Democ. Progresista	13.23	8.31	– –
Conservador	12.86	7.07	5.00
Concentración	2.40	8.02	– –
Frente Unico	– –	– –	6.11
Other conservative[a]	12.92	7.75	3.61
Unknown	4.15	3.83	2.14
Blank votes	– –	1.63	4.46
Total	100	100	100

SOURCE: Cantón, *Materiales*, I, 86, 92, 102.

[a]Parties consistently receiving less than 5 percent of the vote, including for 1916 and 1928 votes of Communists and dissident Socialists (0.05 percent in 1916, 0.42 in 1928).

having a durable structure and definite criteria of membership, and it was also the only party with anything approaching a full-blown ideology or an extensive and specific program of political action.

Juan B. Justo had participated in the formation of the Unión Cívica, and during the 1890s his party joined the Radicals in pressuring for political reforms; however, the objectives and strategy of the Radicals and Socialists differed considerably. The Socialists were committed formally to the promotion of the trade union movement and working-class solidarity, and from 1896 on they took an active part in elections in the Federal Capital, mainly for educational purposes. Also unlike the UCR, they put forward a concrete program that called for the strict separation of church and state, the regulation of labor conditions, the creation of a Department of Labor, an eight-hour day, the removal of import duties and other indirect taxes, the extension of citizenship rights to foreigners after one year's residence, and monetary stability.[30] In 1901 the party issued a further program relating to the agrarian sector of the economy, which called for land reform through progressive taxation of property, the improvement of rural housing conditions, and legislation to protect tenant farmers and rural workers.[31]

The Socialist program did not change much over time, so by the early 1920s, if not earlier, it sounded less than radical. The party itself mellowed, rejecting international socialism and driving more militant members, who formed the International Socialist party in 1918, from its ranks. But signs that radical socioeconomic reform, not to mention revolution, ranked low on the party's list of priorities were evident long before the emergence of the *contubernio* of the mid-1920s, which involved a tacit agreement between certain Socialists and conservative opposition parties, or even the party split of 1918. In 1902 Justo wrote an article for *La Vanguardia*, the Socialists' official mouthpiece, in which he explained that the party had abandoned its demand for a progressive income tax, partially because such a tax would tend to discourage foreign or "advanced" capital investment.[32] As Justo's argument suggests, the Socialists attached so much importance to the capitalist transformation of the economy, they lost sight of many of their other professed goals.[33]

After 1916 the Socialists succeeded in extending their influence into the Provinces of Buenos Aires, Mendoza, and Tucumán, but basically the party depended on the support of workers in the Federal Capital. Thus even in the elections of 1924, when the party received an unprecedented 14.6 percent of the national vote, approximately three-fourths of its support came from the port city.[34]

The Progressive Democrat Party (PDP) also appealed to the immigrants for support, but in the agricultural areas of the littoral region, particularly southern Santa Fe and Córdoba. The party was organized by Lisandro de la Torre: an ex-Radical like Justo who had come into personal conflict with Irigoyen over the issue of electoral abstention in 1897.[35] De la Torre broke away to found the Liga del Sur, a provincial party based in Rosario that represented the political interests of southern Santa Fe vis-à-vis the North. In 1914 the Liga del Sur entered into an alliance with other provincial groups to form the Partido Demócrata Progresista. Originally its leaders hoped that the powerful provincial party of Buenos Aires would join this alliance, allowing disuinited conservative forces to defeat the UCR in the 1916 presidential election; but inflexibility on both sides and fear of de la Torre's "advanced ideas" destroyed this plan.[36] After 1916 the PDP received electoral support in only three districts: Santa Fe, where it occasionally won the minority slate; Córdoba, which it usually carried; and the Federal Capital, where it drew support from middle- and upper-class groups but rarely received more than a small fraction of the vote.[37]

The PDP, like the Radical party, emphasized political reform, clean elections, and intraparty democracy; however, its program also addressed other issues, most notably agrarian reform.[38] De la Torre thought the elimination of *latifundios* was essential to both political democracy and the growth of rural production, and in 1914 he submitted a bill to the national legislature to encourage land subdivision.[39] In 1919, in a famous speech on agrarian problems, he proposed "to convert all professional farmers, tenants and rural workers into property owners."[40] The party's concern with agrarian reform issues reflected its strength in the cereal provinces, as well as its failure to secure the support of the cattle-raising elite of Buenos Aires.

The Conservatives created even less of a national organization than the PDP. Their party was led originally by Marcelino Ugarte, Governor of Buenos Aires, who sought to unify former members of PAN around a program of institutional reaction. To protect provincial elites from the threat of a UCR national government, the Conservatives proposed modifying the constitution "so that the political autonomy of the provinces is not dependent on the good or ill will of the central powers."[41] As a corollary to this, the Conservative program called for greater provincial control of public funds.[42]

Elites in the smaller provinces generally followed the lead of the Conservatives in Buenos Aires who, after 1916, formed the nucleus of a series of anti-UCR coalitions contending for the presidency: the Concentración Nacional, which supported Dr. Norberto Piñero in competition with Radical, Socialist, and PDP candidates in 1922, and the Frente Unico in the 1928 election. But the Conservative party's organization never transcended the provincial level. In the legislative elections of 1914, 1924, and 1926, 100 percent of the Conservative vote was cast in the Province of Buenos Aires. In 1918 and 1920, when the party received electoral support in two districts, this proportion was, respectively, 88.7 and 68.5 percent.[43]

The Conservatives only differed from the other parties and factions competing for power in the 1912-1930 period in that they were organized in the most populous province and therefore received a higher proportion of the national vote. Of the twenty-seven other groups contesting the 1924 legislative elections, for example, only four—the UCR, Socialist, Progressive Democrat, and UCR Anti-Personalist—received votes in more than two provinces.[44] In short, the UCR's opposition was organized at the provincial rather than the national level. In the Federal Capital competition came chiefly from the Socialists, in Buenos Aires from the Conservatives, in Córdoba and Santa Fe from the Progressive Democrats, in Corrientes and Tucumán from the Liberals, and in Salta from the Unión Provincial. In other provinces the opposition was more ad hoc, and during the 1920s it came principally from dissident factions of the UCR.

Political Cleavages and the Disunity of the Opposition

The failure of conservative groups to create a successor to PAN to defend their interests at the national level is striking. The federal form of government, as in the United States, encouraged party disunity and the organization of forces at the provincial level; yet one might have expected to see the emergence of a more unified anti-Radical coalition, particularly since opposition bastions in the provinces were anything but secure while the UCR controlled the national government. Irigoyen made full use of the power of federal intervention to oust provincial governments he considered to be undemocratic or the products of fraud. Between 1916 and 1921 the federal government assumed control over provincial affairs on a record number of occasions—twenty in all—and the interventions lasted an average of eleven months. In the case of one province, San Luis, intervention lasted almost four years.[45] Thus the failure of conservatives to develop a national party cannot be explained in purely institutional terms. The bitter divisions that developed within PAN between 1901 and 1912 are relevant, but the failure of political cleavages in Argentina to develop along socioeconomic lines provides the best explanation for the Radicals' dominance.

The UCR did not, at least initially, represent a serious enough threat to established socioeconomic elites for the latter to set aside their differences and create a national structure to defend their interests. The UCR was a populist party, a heterogeneous collection of social interests with a vague anti-status quo ideology, and none of its *national* pronouncements indicated an interest in fundamental socioeconomic reform.[46] Indeed, the party deliberately eschewed concrete policy proposals in favor of general pledges to strengthen and support the wealth, culture, morality, and democratic institutions of the nation; and it positively prided itself on the breadth of its following.

A long and bitter dispute developed between Irigoyen and Pedro C. Molina in 1909 over this very point. Molina resigned from the UCR in July of that year, arguing that the party did not offer any real program but only "good intentions and honest objectives."[47]

> We are individualists and socialists, federalists and unitarians, liberals and conservatives, believers and sceptics, church-goers and atheists. What unites us then? At the present we have only this: hatred for the ruling clique . . .
> What will we do tomorrow if we should take power? We will divide, for one thing, and reveal only too clearly the poverty and divergences in our beliefs; for another, we will perpetuate the existing regime with new men, because what characterizes the present government is its complete lack of principles . . .[48]

But Irigoyen preferred vague principles, such as *reparación institucional*, to a detailed program of government, since such principles enabled the party to appeal to the broadest possible range of social interests. In 1915 the party declared to the voting public:

> The Unión Cívica Radical is not opposed to any legitimate interest; on the contrary there is room in its ranks for all those who sincerely wish to serve the true well-being of the country. If it does not exhibit seductive, detailed platforms, it is because the great party is only preoccupied with the strict fulfillment of the sacred right to vote . . .[49]

This deliberate disavowal of any concrete policy aims or even links with broad socioenomic groups, which at times was taken to absurd lengths,[50] created, as Molina had predicted, difficulties for the UCR once it assumed power. The party represented a wide variety of different social class, regional, and economic interests. The battles among them were carried on largely within the UCR's own ranks.

The division of the UCR after 1922, when an Anti-Personalist sector appeared in opposition to Irigoyen, provides an indication of the breadth of the party's original base of political support. Both social and regional differences played an important role in this division, although the resulting alignment of political forces varied from province to province. In some, notably San Juan, where the traditional elite controlled the UCR, the Anti-Personalists represented a distinctly populist political force.[51] In general, however, the national leadership of the Anti-Personalists was both more aristrocratic and more oriented towards the interests of the interior provinces than the leadership of the Personalist sector.[52]

The Anti-Personalists had a long list of grievances against Irigoyen: personalism, administrative corruption, unconstitutional interventions in the provinces, and the involvement of the police, military, and public administration in electoral politics, to mention only a few.[53] They accused him of creating a "gobierno de círculo" in imitation of General Roca and a *círculo*, moreover, formed not around intellectuals or capable leaders but "lower orders." "He demands neither long-standing in the party nor intelligence, character, and experience; he only wishes for blind obedience . . ."[54] Revealingly, Anti-Personalist leaders also claimed that Irigoyen flattered the proletariat and attempted to stir up class warfare.[55]

Most of these charges contained some substance. Once in office the Radicals' first priority was politics in the narrowest sense of the word. As mentioned above, Irigoyen stretched the

power of federal intervention to new limits in his effort to consolidate control over the provinces. As in Chile party patronage
also consumed much time and energy. Not only were civil administrative posts "radicalized," but Irigoyen used the military as a
source of political patronage.[56]

The charges of personalism were also justified, even though
Irigoyen had repeatedly scorned personal recognition and even
public office. However, it appears that the Anti-Personalists ob-
jected not to personalism per se, but to Irigoyen's immense
popularity. At best only one Argentine political leader has ever
rallied more popular enthusiasm and that leader, of course, was
Perón. Irigoyen's popularity remains something of a puzzle, because his language was abstruse and bombastic at the best of
times, and he was no public speaker; nor did he possess other
personal qualities normally associated with a charismatic political
leader.[57] Yet if he promised nothing but national reparation, that
slogan was translated to mean all things to all men.

The nomination of the wealthy and aristocratic Marcelo T. de
Alvear as Radical presidential candidate in 1922 comforted conservatives both in and outside of the party.[58] Irigoyen favored his
nomination, but obviously miscalculated, because his successor
quickly demonstrated that he intended to pursue an independent
political course. By 1924 a leadership struggle between the two
men had split the UCR in two, and the outlines of a coalition between Conservatives and Anti-Personalist Radicals began to emerge.

In 1928 at the age of seventy-six Irigoyen ran for a second
term of office and scored a tremendous electoral victory. This
election made the split in the Radical party irrevocable. The Anti-
Personalists combined with conservatives to oppose Irigoyen's
election and, subsequently, to block almost all legislative activity.
The composition of Irigoyen's cabinet reflects the new division of
political forces. Whereas in 1916 and 1922 five of the eight initial
cabinet ministers could, by virtue of their membership in the Argentine Rural Society, be described as upper class, in 1928 only
the Minister of Agriculture could be classified in this way.[59]

The conservative influences in the first two Radical administrations reflect the broad range of social interests accommodated
within the UCR's ranks and suggest that the rural elite became

reconciled to Radical rule after 1916 largely because it appeared in no way to threaten their interests. During the 1920s the situation changed, and the opposition began to unify. By 1930 the Anti-Personalists had no compunction about joining other conservative groups in supporting a military coup to overthrow their former leader whom they now affected to regard as a dangerous demagogue.[60]

The UCR's Electoral Appeal

The failure of the conservatives to organize a national party after 1912 also reflects the Radicals' sudden electoral success, which both surprised and demoralized the opposition. After 1914 many men who had held office under PAN administrations switched political allegiances and entered the UCR's electoral lists.[61] Others just withdrew from politics. The Saenz Peña law altered the Argentine electoral system so rapidly the conservatives were literally overwhelmed.

After over twenty years of propaganda, agitation, and experience in organizing popular support, the UCR, in contrast, was well-equipped to take advantage of the new electoral system. It was a party to which all those who had been dissatisfied with the previous regime could look for a solution to their grievances: a party that avoided close identification with any single set of social or regional interests but nonetheless claimed to represent the interests of the people vis-à-vis an oligarchical elite. Compared to most other political groups, the UCR had also developed a strong sense of partisan identity that was reinforced by a panoply of symbols and myths, such as the revolution of 1890—"a great civic sacrifice"—and the tomb of Alem, before which Radicals could congregate "in periodic renovation, to render homage and gather inspiration."[62] The party had also educated the populace:

> The citizen has learned . . . that his vote is not the property of his *patrón* and that his will ought to be taken into account in elections. The feelings of dignity, aroused or quickened by these new political concepts; the energetic defense of his personality and rights against the abuses of power, the temptations of money or the wiles of electoral fraud; and the conferring of full participation in the life of the party, with a vote in the election of its authorities, with a local center permanently open for its

meetings, with speakers and a daily newspaper as means of propaganda: all these things have linked the populace with the Radical party.[63]

Perhaps even more important, the Radicals had created a national organization with a committee structure reaching down to the precinct level in major cities. As David Rock has emphasized,[64] the expansion of this structure after 1912 established the basis for the creation of a party patronage system that was important both in recruiting electoral support and in surmounting objective conflicts of interest among various electoral groups. The conservative provincial parties, closely identified with a discredited regime, without any sense of common purpose or experience in organizing popular forces, competed with the Radicals at a real disadvantage.

THE SCOPE OF POLITICAL PARTICIPATION

The scope of political participation clearly differentiates the early Chilean and Argentine party systems and goes a long way towards explaining the varying consequences of competitive party politics in the two countries. Political activities involved a much higher proportion of the population in Argentina than in Chile. As a result Argentine political leaders were recruited from a broader social base and faced greater pressures to take the opinions and needs of middle- and lower-class groups into account in formulating public policy.

The Expansion of the Electorate

The pace at which the electorate expanded affected the ability of traditional elites to adjust to competitive party politics in the two countries. Only 9 percent of adult males or approximately 2 percent of the total Argentine population voted in presidential elections before 1916. As Table 15 indicates, after the introduction of the Saenz Peña law these proportions rose immediately to 30 and 9 percent, respectively.[65] The expansion of the Chilean electorate was very slow in comparison. Leaving to one side the fraudulent Chilean elections of 1912, electoral participation during the parliamentary period peaked at a figure of 6.6 percent of the total

TABLE 15

EXPANSION OF THE ARGENTINE ELECTORATE, 1912-1930

| | Registered Voters | | | Voters | |
| | | % Total | | % Total | % Reg. |
Year	Thousands	Pop.	Thousands	Pop.	Voters
1912	935	13.1	641	9.0	68.5
1914	1010	12.7	563	7.1	55.7
1916	1189	14.6	746	9.2	62.7
1918	1303	15.5	751	9.0	56.4
1920	1436	16.5	762	8.8	53.0
1922	1586	17.3	876	9.5	55.3
1924	1580	16.1	699	7.1	40.7
1926	1799	17.4	875	8.5	48.6
1928	1808	16.6	1462	13.4	80.9
1930	1981	17.3	1482	12.9	74.8

SOURCE: Cantón, *Materiales*, I, 81-104; Juan José Guaresti, *Economia y finanzas de la Nación Argentina* (Buenos Aires, 1933), p. 223.

population in 1925. Perhaps even more striking, electoral participation in Chile failed to reach the 1916 Argentine rate until the 1950s, when women were finally enfranchised.

Variations in the development of party competition, electoral regulations, and socioeconomic conditions account for this important contrast. The character of the struggle for political reform in Argentina and the related polarization of the party system created far greater incentives for enlarging the scope of political conflict. Electoral regulations, which, unlike Chile, did not limit the suffrage to literates, facilitated this process, as did socioeconomic conditions. Not only did Chile lag behind Argentina in terms of literacy, urbanization, and industrial development, but large parts of the country did not participate in the late nineteenth-century economic boom. In contrast, economic growth transformed both rural and urban social structures in Argentina, allowing parties challenging the political hegemony of the rural-commercial elite to recruit electoral support in the countryside and small towns as well as the large cities.

Contrasts in the size of the electorate appear even more marked when one considers differences in the qualitative aspects of suffrage expansion. In Chile bribery and the manipulation of the rural electorate diluted the significance of the vote. There is no evidence that abuses were perpetuated on a comparable scale in Argentina. In national elections legal remedies existed to reduce fraud, and the record of complaints made in the Chamber of Deputies indicates that the falsification of electoral registers and voting results, the use of public funds, and the active intervention of public employees in campaigns constituted the chief electoral irregularities.[66] More subtle methods probably influenced voters in rural areas without attracting outside attention, particularly since electoral data indicate that provincial elections continued to be marked by irregularities. Anomalies appear, for example, in the results of the gubernatorial elections of Mendoza in 1922 and 1926, where the total number of votes cast exceeded that of the national elections of those years. The same is true of the gubernatorial elections of Córdoba of 1912, 1915, and 1918 and of those held in Santa Fe in 1924, where the number of registered voters in two northern districts, Vera and San Javier, was even greater than in the 1928 presidential elections.[67] In general, however, the electoral influence of rural landlords in Argentina, who had to deal with relatively independent farmers rather than a mass of ignorant, deferential, and very dependent peasants, was very restricted in comparison with Chile.

The Argentine Immigrant Community

Because the immigrant took no active part in elections, the level of voter participation in Argentina was much lower than it might otherwise have been. It was relatively easy for immigrants to become naturalized citizens. After two years of residence they theoretically had only to make a formal application; but for a variety of reasons, including the absence of concrete incentives, the overwhelming majority preferred to retain the citizenship of their country of origin.[68] In 1915 only 2.25 percent of foreign men had become naturalized citizens.[69] The electorate therefore consisted almost exclusively of adult males who had been born in

Argentina. Gino Germani has presented figures that show that 64 percent of this population category voted in 1916 and 77 percent in 1928, while the proportions for all adult males in these years reached only 30 and 41 percent, respectively.[70]

Political attitudes partially accounted for the immigrants' isolation from electoral politics. At the national level only the Socialists, the Liga del Sur, and a few isolated individuals such as Roque Saenz Peña—who in 1912 expressed the hope that political reforms would make Argentine citizenship more attractive—[71] took an active interest in the problem of integrating foreigners. Xenophobia prevailed in the upper class as well as in the ranks of the Radical party.[72] This tendency should not be exaggerated, however. In some parts of the country important links did develop between the party and the immigrant community. In Santa Fe, for example, immigrant farmers supported Radical uprisings in 1890 and 1893, and the UCR incorporated many key tenant-farmer demands in its provincial platform.[73] In addition, over time the sons of immigrants, who were eligible to participate in electoral politics, emerged as an important group of Radical party supporters and activists. According to David Rock, 46 percent of the individuals elected to posts within the Radical party of the Federal Capital in 1918 had non-Hispanic surnames indicating immigrant origins.[74] Since Spaniards accounted for a sizeable proportion of Argentine immigrants, the leadership role played by immigrants within the UCR was certainly even greater than this figure suggests. Nevertheless, attitudes towards the foreign community and the related failure of immigrants to participate in elections did bias the electoral system against the representation of important social interests, notably those of the urban working class and cereal farmers.

Yet the vote was not the only channel of political influence, and the failure of the immigrants to exercise it does not necessarily indicate political ignorance or apathy. Long before the Saenz Peña law, immigrant workers in the capital were making their voices heard in public life. Indeed, their militancy, as much as anything else, aroused feelings of hostility and suspicion towards the foreigner.

Due to the influx of Spanish and Italian workers, the trade union movement in 1900 was more organized and aggressive than in Chile. By 1895, a year in which there were nineteen strikes involving some 22,000 workers, twenty-five unions had been formed.[75] As in Chile the organization and militancy of workers increased steadily in the subsequent decade and reached an unprecedented high in the years 1902-1910, when the anarchists, the dominant influence in the labor movement up to World War I, led a series of terrorist attacks and strikes that created a strong reaction in government circles.[76] The record year 1907 witnessed general strikes in both Rosario and Bahia Blanca, and after the military intervened to repress the workers, the strike action spread further, threatening serious economic disruption. In the Federal Capital alone, 169,017 workers participated in 231 strikes in 1907.[77] Strike action declined sharply after 1907, but terrorist activity continued. The assassination of the chief of police in 1909 led to a two-month state of siege and a government crackdown on all labor organizations. In 1902 a law had been passed that allowed the president to evict foreigners "whose conduct compromises national security or public order."[78] In June 1910, after a bomb incident, a frightened government sought even more sweeping powers. The Law of Social Defense, passed in that month, denied foreigners advocating anarchism or similar doctrines the right of immigration, outlawed anarchist associations, and required previous permission to be granted for all public meetings.[79] This legislation effectively banned the anarchist movement and paved the way for the rise of syndicalism as the dominant trade union force.

Despite military intervention, states of siege, and other repressive measures, the workers' campaign achieved some success. In 1905 new legislation restricted the length of the working week in the Federal Capital. In 1907, 1912, and 1915 the government responded to other union demands: the regulation of female and child labor, the formation of a department of labor, public provision of cheap housing, and the establishment of employers' liability in cases of industrial accidents.[80] Notwithstanding its low level of electoral participation, the immigrant working class maintained its pressure on the government after 1916. The trade union movement was particularly well organized in the 1915-1922

period of the syndicalist federation FORA IX,[81] and as in Chile
trade union membership and strike activity burgeoned in the postwar period, reaching a peak in the years 1917-1921.

Other sectors of the immigrant community also pursued political goals through nonelectoral channels. The cereal belt, where
nearly 80 percent of the tenant farmers were immigrants, experienced frequent outbreaks of agrarian unrest. Rent strikes in 1912,
1913, 1917, and 1919 were coupled with crop-burning, the de-
struction of agricultural machinery, and violence. In 1912 tenant
farmers organized the Federación Agraria Argentina (FAA) that
published a weekly newspaper, made representations to the government, and organized strikes and demonstrations. Rural labor was
slower to organize, but made some progress during World War I.
In December 1919 *bracero* or migrant labor strikes spread throughout the cereal belt.[82]

If the immigrant bourgeoisie was less obstreperous, it still
ensured that its voice was heard by the government through the
Unión Industrial Argentina, formed in 1877, and local pressure
groups, such as the Cámara Sindical de la Bolsa de Comercio de
Rosario. Hence while the immigrants' failure to vote checked the
rate of electoral mobilization and distorted the representative
system, the much-belabored image of the totally apolitical immigrant is misleading. The foreign community constituted an important source of pressure on policy makers, both before and after
1912. In addition, the shift to a competitive system offered new
opportunities for the immigrant community to make its weight
felt through electoral channels. Important regional parties, notably
the Socialists and the Liga del Sur, represented immigrant interests,
and the second generation of immigrants played an active role in
partisan affairs.

MAJOR CONTRASTS BETWEEN THE FIRST CHILEAN AND ARGENTINE PARTY SYSTEMS

The critical differences between the first Argentine and Chilean
party systems may be summarized by two general concepts: the
scope of participation and the structure of political competition.
Because of these differences, the shift to a competitive party

system created greater opportunities for less privileged social groups to exercise political influence in Argentina than in Chile.

The size and independence of the electorate, the strength and militancy of working-class associations, and the related level of political education were all much greater in Argentina than in Chile. These differences reflected underlying socioeconomic conditions, particularly the rural social structure, but a variety of other factors also affected the scope of participation. These included legal regulations governing the exercise of the vote, most notably those relating to the eligibility and registration of voters. The net result was that popular involvement in politics was much greater in Argentina than in Chile, the electoral influence of conservative groups much less significant, and the political system in general more democratic, at least in one sense of that word.

The incentives and opportunities for changes in policies and recruitment practices favorable to groups at the middle or lower end of the socioeconomic spectrum varied accordingly. In Chile, where wealth and social prestige remained key electoral assets due to attitudes of deference, the prevalence of bribery, and the system of voter registration, policy makers could not ignore the pressures of socioeconomic elites, nor could men of modest social origin ordinarily aspire to high political office. Inequalities in the distribution of political resources certainly existed in Argentina as well; but, because of the scope of participation, political leaders confronted demands for action on behalf of a wider range of social interests than in Chile and sought means of generating more widespread popular support. Similarly, the social base from which political leaders might be drawn was much broader in Argentina than in Chile, diluting the tendency for political leaders to be recruited from upper socioeconomic echelons.

The structure of competition reinforced the contrast in the scope of political participation. The multipolar structure of conflict in Chile encouraged party leaders to negotiate advantageous political alliances rather than enlarge their base of popular support. In Argentina, on the other hand, the polarization of political conflict between "ins" and "outs" provided strong incentives to expand the scope of participation.

The variations in the structure of competition primarily reflected political rather than socioeconomic conditions. The line between the "haves" and "have-nots" was much more firmly drawn in Chilean society, but it was not translated into partisan conflict. Multiple and overlapping cleavages, the heterogeneity and instability of cabinets, and the institutional and electoral arrangements that reflected and supported the foregoing all inhibited the emergence of clearly defined electoral alternatives. In Argentina, on the other hand, the relative equality of social conditions and the close integration of the rural and urban economies discouraged the polarization of political forces along socioeconomic lines; but the preexisting political situation combined with electoral and institutional arrangements did produce a relatively sharp distinction between government and opposition elements. As a result of these differences, Argentine voters confronted more clear-cut electoral choices than Chilean voters. The significance of this contrast was partially undercut by the vague programs that most Argentine parties presented to the electorate. Specific proposals for reform, particularly with respect to the lower class, played a more important role in electoral campaigns in Chile than in Argentina. Indeed, the national programs of the Chilean Democrats, Radicals, *and* Conservatives all displayed more concern for socioeconomic reform than those of the Argentine Radical party. The tendency of Chilean parties to employ the rhetoric of the left is evidently not just a recent phenomenon; nor, for that matter, is the inflexibility of conservatives in Argentina. During the 1916-1930 period the latter left most initiative in the field of social reform to other parties and supported few progressive measures. Yet while conservative resistance to reform and vague electoral programs blunted the tendency towards action on behalf of less privileged social groups in Argentina, the structure of political conflict still created far stronger incentives and opportunities for policy reform than in Chile.

CHAPTER V

THE CHANGING SOCIAL BACKGROUND OF ARGENTINE AND CHILEAN POLITICAL ELITES

The development of political party competition in Chile and Argentina led to important changes in the process of political recruitment. During most of the nineteenth century government officials had played a key role in the selection of political representatives. With the shift to competitive electoral systems, parties gained control over the nomination of candidates to public office, and voters began to exercise real influence over the choice of political authorities. Since the process of political recruitment theoretically affects the kinds of individuals who enter public life as well as their policy orientations, the composition of political elites in Chile and Argentina provides a useful starting point for assessing the impact of party competition in the two countries.

The subsequent analysis focuses primarily on the social backgrounds of national legislators during the 1880 to 1930 period. While the inferences that may be drawn from such an analysis are necessarily limited,[1] information about the occupations, landholdings, family backgrounds, and association memberships of national legislators in the two countries is highly revealing. In both Argentina and Chile legislators played significant political roles, and no alternative group of political influentials of comparable size can be identified very readily. Analysis of the social backgrounds of legislators consequently facilitates comparisons of the nature of the political elite in the two countries, both over time and between cases. Such comparisons provide important insights into the impact of party competition on the distribution of political power and the relative equality of political opportunities in Chile and Argentina.

EDUCATIONAL AND OCCUPATIONAL BACKGROUNDS OF NATIONAL LEGISLATORS

The occupational status and educational qualifications of public officials typically exceed those of the average citizen. The literature on political recruitment suggests that party competition mitigates this tendency by drawing larger numbers of people into politics and by expanding political opportunities.[2] Nevertheless a recruitment bias in favor of upper- and middle-class social groups characterizes most competitive systems.[3]

Educational data indicate that the social gap between citizens and their political representatives was particularly pronounced in turn-of-the-century Chile and Argentina. In 1912, for example, less than half of the population was literate in Chile, but 74 percent of the members of the Chamber of Deputies had university education.[4] Similarly, at least 79 percent of the deputies and 92 percent of the senators holding office in Argentina in 1916 had attended a university.[5] Unfortunately, however, information about the educational training of legislators is too limited to assess changes in the composition of the national legislatures over time. Darío Cantón's study of the Argentine legislature, for example, provides no information on the educational backgrounds of 39 percent of the deputies and 14 percent of the senators holding office before 1916.[6] Similarly, in studying the Chilean political elite between 1834 and 1891, Gabriel Marcella found no educational data for 43 percent of the senators and 67 percent of the deputies.[7]

Occupational data are less fragmentary and hence somewhat more revealing. As Tables 16 and 17 indicate, the Argentine and Chilean legislatures not only included a highly disproportionate number of persons with privileged occupational backgrounds, but no major change in the composition of the legislatures followed the introduction of competitive party politics. Both before and after the emergence of competitive systems, landowners and professionals dominated both houses of the Chilean and Argentine legislatures. Nevertheless, certain changes did occur over time. In both countries the military steadily lost its importance as a channel for political recruitment. In the case of Chile, occupational data also point to the increased representation of industrialists over time and to the growing separation of legislative and judicial careers. But the most notable trend in both countries is the growth in the percentage of lawyers or lawyers/professionals in the legislature. Due to the ambiguity of occupational data, however, the meaning of this change is rather unclear. Aristocrats as well as men of modest social origins became lawyers in Chile and Argentina. Consequently, the growth in the number of lawyers in the two legislatures does not necessarily mean that members of the middle class were displacing aristocrats from the political elite. Expanding opportunities for higher education probably provide a better explanation.

This interpretation is strengthened by the absence of any trend away from the representation of landholders. In Argentina the proportion of landholders or landholders/professionals increased in the lower house after the passage of the Saenz Peña law and remained fairly constant in the Senate. In Chile the percentage of legislators holding land increased over time in the upper chamber. Trends in the Chilean Chamber of Deputies are less clear, but no marked decline in the percentage of landholders can be discerned from occupational data. Compared to the years before 1891, landholders held a very high percentage of seats in the Chilean lower house in 1909.

With respect to comparisons between the two countries, the data suggest that landholders played a more significant political role in Chile than in Argentina, both before and after the shift to a competitive system. Industrialists, who in the Chilean case frequently held agricultural land, also apparently enjoyed greater access to positions of political influence in Chile than in Argentina. Despite these differences, longitudinal trends in the two countries appear very similar. In neither case do occupational data provide a basis for arguing that political party competition enhanced the representation of middle-or lower-class groups in the legislature. If anything, occupational data indicate that the correlation between socioeconomic status and political power increased over time.

TABLE 16

OCCUPATIONAL BACKGROUNDS OF CHILEAN NATIONAL
LEGISLATORS IN SELECTED YEARS[a]
(in percentages)

Occupation	Chamber of Deputies				Senate			
	1834-91	1882	1909[b]	1912	1834-91	1882	1909[b]	1912
Landowners[c]	41.1	33.3	46.3	39.8	45.3	43.2	53.1	56.8
Rentiers	n.a.	n.a.	12.6	n.a.	n.a.	n.a.	53.1	n.a.
Lawyers	7.7	47.2	53.7	57.6	29.6	43.2	46.9	59.5
Other professionals	3.7	10.2	11.6	11.9	5.0	13.5	12.5	10.8
Merchants	3.0	5.6	2.1	5.9	11.3	8.1	3.1	5.4
Industrialists	2.7	4.6	13.7	11.0	1.3	– –	18.8	18.9
Mining entrepreneurs	3.5	8.3	3.2	5.9	8.2	8.1	9.4	13.5
Bankers	1.8	4.6	2.1	1.7	11.3	10.8	3.1	8.1
Judges	6.2	3.7	4.2	5.9	24.5	10.8	– –	2.7
Public officials	8.2	23.2	9.5	25.4	18.9	35.1	12.5	24.3
Military	7.2	1.9	– –	– –	11.9	5.4	– –	2.7
Journalists	10.1	8.3	1.1	6.8	15.1	8.1	– –	8.1
Educators	12.7	13.0	13.7	16.1	24.5	10.8	25.0	24.3
Writers	7.5	1.9	– –	1.7	3.7	8.1	– –	8.1
Other	2.2	0.9	2.1	0.8	2.5	5.4	– –	5.4
No information	33.5	18.5	1.1	3.4	0.6	2.7	– –	– –
Number	(623)	(108)	(95)	(118)	(159)	(37)	(32)	(37)

SOURCE: Gabriel Marcella, "The Structure of Politics in Nineteenth Century Spanish America: The Chilean Oligarchy, 1833-1891" (Ph.D. dissertation, University of Notre Dame, 1973), p. 90; Joaquín Rodríguez Bravo, *El Congreso de 1882: Retratos políticos de sus miembros* (Santiago, 1882); Virgilio Figueroa, *Diccionario histórico biográfico y bibliográfico de Chile*, 5 vols. (Santiago, 1925-1931); Alfredo Valderrama Pérez, *Album político: El gobierno, el Parlamento y el Consejo de Estado en la República de Chile (1912-1915)* (Santiago, 1914); Chile, Oficina de Estadística e Informaciones Agrícolas, *Indice de propietarios rurales i valor de la propiedad rural según los roles de avalúos comunales* (Santiago, 1908); Enrique Espinoza, *Jeografía descriptiva de la República de Chile*, 4th ed. (Santiago, 1897); ibid., 5th ed. (1903); *El Congreso Nacional de Chile de 1909 a 1912* (Santiago, 1909); Luis Valencia Avaria, ed., *Anales de la República*, II (Santiago, 1951).

Table 16 (*Continued*)

[a]All occupations of legislators have been included in the calculations. Since a significant percentage of legislators held more than one occupation, percentages total more than 100.

[b]Data reflect mainly legislators' occupations at the time of election.

[c]Includes legislators controlling large estates according to the 1894-97, 1902, and 1908 tax rolls as well as those whose biographical records indicate major involvement in agriculture.

TABLE 17

OCCUPATIONAL BACKGROUNDS OF ARGENTINE NATIONAL
LEGISLATORS IN SELECTED YEARS
(in percentages)

Occupation	Chamber of Deputies			Senate		
	1889	1908	1916	1889	1908	1916
Landowners	6	14	14	3	23	– –
Landowners/ professionals	10	n.a.	26	21	n.a.	24
Professionals	40	61	41	48	53	62
Military officers	6	4	5	7	3	– –
Industrialists	– –	8	– –	– –	10	– –
Journalists	– –	2	– –	– –	3	– –
Teachers	2	3	1	3	– –	– –
Other	1	– –	2	– –	3	– –
No information	35	8	11	17	3	14
Number	(84)	(120)	(117)	(29)	(30)	(26)

SOURCE: Darío Cantón, *El Parlamento Argentino en épocas de cambio: 1890, 1916 y 1946* (Buenos Aires, 1966), p. 40; José Nicolás Matienzo, *El gobierno representativo federal en la República Argentina*, 2nd ed. (Madrid, 1917), pp. 176-177.

NOTE: Percentages may not total 100 due to rounding.

The analysis of legislators' occupations by political party points to a similar conclusion about the impact of political party competition. In the case of the Argentine legislature of 1916, differences exist between the occupational backgrounds of Socialists and Democratic Progressives, on the one hand, and Conservatives and Radicals, on the other. Cantón's data indicate that nearly all of the Socialist and Democratic Progressive legislators in 1916 fall into the "solely professional" category and that none of them held land.[8] Virtually no distinction can be drawn between the occupational backgrounds of the two largest blocs of legislators in 1916, the Conservative and Radical.[9] Occupational data consequently provide no indication that the rise of the Radical party enhanced the representativeness of the Argentine legislature. The significance of this finding is limited, however, due to the fragmentary character of Argentine occupational data as well as the complete absence of information for the years after 1916. Other evidence, presented below, suggests that contrasts in the social backgrounds of UCR and Conservative legislators became more marked over time and that the composition of the legislature in 1916 was not typical of the 1916-1930 period as a whole.

As indicated by Tables 18 and 19, occupational data reveal greater differences among the representatives of the various parties in Chile. Whereas the percentage of all legislators who can be classified as landowners and/or rentistas equalled 50.4 percent in 1909-1912 and 41.9 percent in 1912-1915, the proportion in the case of Conservative party legislators reached 68.8 percent in 1909-1912 and 55.6 percent in 1912-1915. The parliamentary delegations of the National, Liberal, and Liberal Democratic parties included a somewhat lower percentage of landholders or landholders/ rentiers; but these parties' legislators differed from those of the Conservative party chiefly by virtue of their greater involvement in banking, commerce, mining, and industry. Although Tables 18 and 19 provide only limited information about economic involvements outside the rural sector, the relatively low proportion of Conservatives classified in the fourth and fifth occupational categories reflects this contrast. At least twenty-four of the men in the 1909 legislature can be classified as merchants, industrialists, bankers and/or mining entrepreneurs. Seven of these men belonged

TABLE 18

OCCUPATIONAL BACKGROUNDS OF CHILEAN
LEGISLATORS BY POLITICAL PARTY, 1909-1912

Occupation	Con.	Nat.	Lib.	Lib. Dem.	Rad.	Dem.	Ind't & Lib. Doc.	Total
1. Solely landowners and/or rentiers	9	3	4	8	1	— —	— —	25
2. Landowners &/or rentiers with profession	13	10	6	4	3	— —	3	39
3. Solely professionals or professionals/ educators[a]	7	2	4	9	14	1	1	38
4. Solely merchants, industrialists and/or mining entrepreneurs	— —	1	1	2	— —	— —	1	5
5. Other	3	4	3	2	2	3	2	19
6. No information	— —	— —	— —	— —	— —	1	— —	1
Total	32	20	18	25	20	5	7	127

SOURCE: Figueroa; Valderrama Pérez; Valencia Avaria, II; *El Congreso Nacional de Chile de 1909 a 1912*; Chile, *Indice de propietarios.*

[a]Includes professionals employed as civil servants.

to the National party, but the parliamentary delegations of the Liberal, Liberal Democratic, and Radical parties all included a higher proportion of men with occupational involvements outside the agricultural sector than the Conservative party. Similarly, available information indicates that in 1912 only 13.9 percent of Conservative legislators were involved in mining, commerce, industry, or banking. The proportions for the Nationals, Liberals, Liberal Democrats, Radicals, and Doctrinaire Liberals/Independents, respectively, equalled 38.5, 19.4, 19.4, 20.0 and 50.0 percent.

Radical and Democratic party legislators differed even more markedly from Conservative ones. Comparatively few of the legislators from these two parties can be classified into either of

TABLE 19

OCCUPATIONAL BACKGROUNDS OF CHILEAN LEGISLATORS
BY POLITICAL PARTY, 1912-1915

Occupation	Con.	Nat.	Lib.	Lib. Dem.	Rad.	Dem.	Ind't & Lib. Dem.	No Info.	Total
1. Solely landowners and/or rentiers	4	– –	5	7	4	– –	– –	– –	20
2. Landowners &/or rentiers with profession	16	3	9	10	4	– –	2	1	45
3. Solely professionals or professionals/educators[a]	11	5	9	11	13	2	1	1	53
4. Solely merchants, industrialists and/or mining entrepreneurs	2	4	3	1	2	– –	1	– –	13
5. Other	3	1	5	7	2	4	– –	– –	22
6. No information	– –	– –	– –	– –	– –	– –	– –	2	2
Total	36	13	31	36	25	6	4	4	155

SOURCE: As for Table 18.

NOTE: The list of names used is identical to that presented in Valencia Avaria with the exception of three legislators who died in the early stages of the 1912-1915 legislative session: Carlos Maira, Ricardo Matte Pérez, and Manuel Gallardo González. The table reports the occupations of the men who replaced them: Juan Castellón, Luis Aníbal Barrios Ugalde, and Francisco Valdés Vergara.

[a]Includes professionals employed as civil servants.

the first two occupational categories presented in Tables 18 and 19. Professionals, mainly lawyers, accounted for 70 percent of the Radical party's delegation in 1909-12 and 52 percent in 1912-15. The occupational backgrounds of the Democrats were even more modest. None of the Democrats in the 1909 or 1912 legislature was a landowner, industrialist, merchant, banker, or mining entrepreneur, and only three Democrats can even be classified as professionals. The party's other representatives included a journalist, a typesetter, a business firm employee, and an accountant. One of them, Nolasco Cárdenas, had only three years of schooling.[10]

This evidence indicates that the growth of the Radical and Democratic parties in the years after the 1891 civil war did alter the kinds of individuals entering public life in Chile. But because the two parties' parliamentary delegations remained relatively small until the end of the parliamentary period, the overall composition of the legislature did not change significantly as measured in terms of legislators' occupational backgrounds. Indeed, the analysis of legislators' occupational backgrounds by political party suggests that the Chilean congress became a more elitist body between 1891 and 1915, since the party most closely linked with traditional upper-class landed interests—the Conservative party—secured the greatest gains in representation through the shift to a competitive electoral system.

THE CHANGING SOCIAL STATUS OF ARGENTINE LEGISLATORS

Because data on the occupational backgrounds of legislators are fragmentary and susceptible to major problems of classification and interpretation,[11] it is necessary to turn to other sources of information to obtain a more complete picture of how regime changes affected who governed Argentina and Chile during the 1890-1930 period. In the Argentine case further analysis of the social backgrounds of legislators demonstrates that occupational data are misleading and that important changes in the composition of the Argentine political elite did follow the emergence of a competitive system. By the early 1920s the Argentine legislature was a significantly less aristocratic body than in the early 1900s.

The data collected by Peter H. Smith on the social backgrounds of deputies during the 1904 to 1930 period, which are summarized in Table 20, provide evidence of this change. Smith's data show that the percentage of aristocrats in the Chamber of Deputies dropped both rapidly and steadily after the passage of the Saenz Peña law, reaching a figure in the early 1920s that was approximately half that of 1910. Overall, the percentage of aristocrats in

TABLE 20

TRENDS IN THE REPRESENTATION OF ARISTOCRATS IN THE
ARGENTINE CHAMBER OF DEPUTIES, 1904-1930

Party Affiliation	1904-15 No. of Dep.	1904-15 % Aristo-crats	1916-18 No. of Dep.	1916-18 % Aristo-crats	1922-24 No. of Dep.	1922-24 % Aristo-crats	1928-30 No. of Dep.	1928-30 % Aristo-crats
Conservative	192	63.0	39	77.0	33	57.6	28	57.2
Radical	36	63.9	75	48.0	100	27.0	111	19.8
(Personalist)	– –	– –	– –	– –	(49)	(14.3)	(100)	(19.0)
(UCRAP)	– –	– –	– –	– –	(29)	(41.4)	– –	– –
(Unclassified)	– –	– –	– –	– –	(22)	(40.9)	(11)	(27.3)
Other or unknown	105	59.0	20	45.0	33	18.2	21	19.0
Total	333	61.9	134	55.9	166	31.3	160	26.2

SOURCE: Peter H. Smith, "The Breakdown of Democracy in Argentina, 1916-30," in *The Breakdown of Democratic Regimes: Latin America*, ed. Juan J. Linz and Alfred Stepan (Baltimore, 1978), p. 14; idem, *Argentina and the Failure of Democracy: Conflict among Political Elites, 1904-1955* (Madison, 1974), pp. 30-31.

[a]Includes deputies from PAN, Unión Nacional, Unido, Autonomista, Oficial, Unión Popular, Popular, Conservative and local conservative parties.

the Chamber of Deputies averaged less than 40 percent in the 1916-1930 period as compared to 61.9 percent for the years 1904-1915.[12]

After 1916 important variations also emerged among the social status of deputies from different parties. During the 1904-1915 period the social status of Radical legislators did not differ significantly from that of deputies belonging to PAN or other conservative groups. Aristocrats dominated all of the major parliamentary blocs. In contrast, less than one-third of UCR deputies came from aristocratic backgrounds between 1916 and 1930.[13] As indicated by Table 20, differences in the social backgrounds of Radical and Conservative deputies became particularly pronounced during the 1920s, when partisan conflict in Argentina began to crystallize along socioeconomic, rather than purely political, lines. Significantly, this trend coincided with the split between the "Personalist" and "Antipersonalist" Radicals. The contrast between the social backgrounds of deputies from these two blocs is particularly interesting, because it provides a relatively concrete indication that social as well as regional differences contributed to the division of the Radical party's initially heterogeneous base of political support.

A variety of questions can be raised about the reliability and validity of Smith's data. Smith classified legislators as "aristocrats" on the basis of social prestige as indicated by club memberships and the opinions of three persons interested in Argentine genealogy. A legislator qualified as an "aristocrat" if (a) he belonged to the Sociedad Rural or Jockey Club, or (b) at least two of the three genealogists placed him in the aristocracy.[14] On the basis of these indicators it cannot be assumed that all of the individuals Smith identified as "aristocrats" possessed both social *and* economic power, particularly since his operational definition of "aristocracy" fails to take into account the importance of politics as a channel for social mobility. Political prominence may well have opened the door to membership in exclusive social clubs or enhanced a family's social reputation. Consequently, Smith's data probably exaggerate the extent to which the country's socioeconomic elite dominated the lower house of the legislature, both before and after 1916. At the very least the label "aristocracy" appears to provide a somewhat misleading description of the social group to which the individuals identified by Smith's operational definition belonged. In the Argentine context the terms "aristocracy" and "rural elite" tend to be used as synonyms. Yet occupational data indicate that a relatively high proportion of the men Smith identified as "aristocrats" possessed no land. The percentage of landholders in the lower house in 1916, including those owning only modest properties, equalled only 34.2 percent. Yet over 55 percent of the deputies in 1916 qualified as "aristocrats" on the basis of Smith's operational definition.

The relatively low correlations among Smith's various indicators of aristocratic status raise additional questions about the data presented in Table 20. For the 1904 to 1955 period as a whole, the correlation coefficient for SRA membership and aristocratic status as identified by the three genealogists only equals .22. The three genealogists also disagreed quite frequently on the classification of deputies. While one judge identified 581 deputies as aristocrats, another identified only 206. The highest correlation coefficient reported by Smith, that measuring the overlap between membership in the SRA and the Jockey Club, only equals .42.[15]

As a result of these difficulties, the precise number of aristocrats in the legislature at any given point in time remains open to question. Nevertheless, *all of Smith's indicators point to similar trends in the representation of aristocrats in the Chamber of Deputies over time*.[16] If anything, Smith's data may underestimate the decline in the representation of aristocrats, because the importance of politics as a channel for social mobility probably increased, rather than decreased, after 1916.

The observations of contemporaries certainly support the view that the social origins of political leaders became less aristocratic over time. A foreign observer commented that Argentine Radicalism, concerned with jobs rather than programs or reforms, represented "above all the advent of a new layer of society."[17] A Conservative, evidently reacting against this change, observed that the legislature had become "filled with rabble" and "the usual parliamentary language had been replaced by the coarse utterances of the suburbs and of the Radical committees."[18]

Although their data covers only the legislature of 1916, Ezequiel Gallo and Silvia Sigal's analysis of contrasts between the social backgrounds of Radical and Conservative legislators provides further confirmation that new social elements gained access to positions of political leadership during the Radical era. Gallo and Sigal found no significant difference between the economic positions of Radical and Conservative legislators, but the Radicals came from families that had arrived comparatively recently in Argentina and had played less important roles in politics. Combining their findings on the date of family arrival in Argentina and past family activity in politics, Gallo and Sigal constructed an "index of antiquity." As Table 21 shows, this index suggests that even at the beginning of the Radical period marked differences existed between Conservatives and Radicals and that new social

TABLE 21

FAMILY ANTIQUITY AND PARTY OF CONGRESSMEN IN 1916

Index of Antiquity	Radicals		Conservatives	
Old	35%	(15)	62%	(34)
New	61%	(27)	34%	(19)
No data	4%	(2)	4%	(2)
Total	100	(44)	100	(55)

SOURCE: Ezequiel Gallo and Silvia Sigal, "La formación de los partidos políticos contemporáneos: La U.C.R. (1890-1916)," in *Argentina, sociedad de masas*, Torcuato S. Di Tella et al. (Buenos Aires, 1965), p. 167.

elements were displacing the traditional social elite from positions of political power.

THE CHANGING SOCIAL STATUS OF CHILEAN LEGISLATORS

In the Chilean case, previous research provides comparatively few insights into the impact of party competition on the social status of legislators.[19] The comments of both contemporaries and historians suggest that aristocrats remained an important force in the legislature after 1891; but the lack of systematic research makes it difficult to assess how the relationship between social status and political power changed, if at all, over time. According to one contemporary, the social status of legislators increased after 1891 due to the rising importance of wealth and estate ownership as political resources.[20] In contrast, Arturo Valenzuela argues that standard interpretations of the parliamentary period exaggerate the degree of aristocratic control and overlook the "democratization trend" of the years 1891-1912. In his view, party development allowed political bosses and electoral brokers from popular-sector groups to gain a significant measure of control over the electoral system at the expense of the upper class.[21] Although Valenzuela notes that national politicians were a distinct group with university education and legal training,[22] this line of analysis raises the possibility that the social status of legislators declined after 1891.

A third interpretation, which stresses the unchanging relationship between socioeconomic status and political power, suggests that the rise of party competition led to no real change in the composition of the Chilean political elite.[23]

To evaluate these competing views, data has been collected on the percentage of large agricultural estate owners in the Chilean congress between 1888 and 1925. These data are not only more complete than those on occupation; they also offer more precise information about the socioeconomic status of legislators. Moreover, unlike club memberships or retrospective judgments by genealogists, large estate ownership provides an empirical means of identifying members of the socioeconomic elite that does not raise basic questions of causality. Political prominence may have opened the door to Santiago's exclusive Club de la Unión or, as in the case of the Alessandri family, established the basis for upperclass social status; but the argument that large estate ownership depended on politics in the short run is highly implausible. Obviously, every aristocrat in Chile did not personally own a large estate, nor did every large estate owner enjoy aristocratic status. Land changed hands surprisingly frequently in Chile and was often purchased by *nouveaux riches* who had accumulated capital in nonagricultural activities. Nevertheless, land ownership conveyed considerable social prestige, and by virtually any standard large estate owners constituted a highly privileged elite.

For the years 1888-1912 large estates have been defined as those appraised at more than $200,000 pesos in the tax roles of 1894-97, 1902, and 1908. Despite inflation and a few unexplained and rather erratic shifts in large estate appraisals,[24] tax roll values remained highly constant over time, as did the number of large estates in each of the Chilean provinces. The tax rolls of 1894-97 appraised 558 privately owned estates at more than $200,000. In 1902 and 1908, respectively 527 and 565 privately owned estates fell into the $200,000 plus category.[25] Allowing for church, government, and corporate landownership, which was not significant,[26] it can be estimated that these large estates accounted for only 0.5 percent of the total number of agricultural properties in Chile.[27]

Due to the unavailability of other information, large estates for the years after 1912 have been identified primarily on the basis of size, as reported in Juvenal Valenzuela's 1923 *Album de informaciones agrícolas*, which provides information on the 1800 "most important" estates in Chile's central valley. Following the same procedure used by Arnold J. Bauer in analysis of landowner- ship,[28] 619 privately owned larger estates have been drawn from Valenzuela's list on the basis of a formula that weights irrigated land at ten times the value of unirrigated land. Together the 543 owners of the 619 estates chosen through this formula controlled approximately 3,373,000 hectares of land, a figure equivalent to 47.9 percent of the total agricultural land of central Chile in the early 1920s.[29]

Table 22 traces the percentage of these large estate owners in the Chilean legislature over time. In contrast to information on the social status of Argentine legislators, these data tend to con- firm the trends suggested by the analysis of legislators' occupa- tions. They indicate that party competition produced no immedi- ate or very drastic reduction in the representation of socioeconomic elites within the Chilean legislature. Despite the changing structure of the economy, the representation of large estate owners in the legislature actually increased in the wake of the 1891 civil war. In the case of the Chilean Senate, where the percentage of large estate owners rose 16 percent between 1888 and 1894, the increase was particularly marked. The significance of this trend might be dismissed on the grounds that Chilean parties were only beginning to become organized on a national basis between 1891 and 1900; however, the percentage of large estate owners in the upper house also remained high over time and only fell below the 1888 level in 1924.

In the case of the Chamber of Deputies the data indicate a slightly different trend. After rising to a peak of 27.7 percent in 1897, the percentage of large estate owners declined relatively steadily over time and reached a level of only 11 percent in the 1921-1924 period. Trends in the representation of large estate owners within the Chamber of Deputies consequently do support the view that Chile's socioeconomic elite lost a measure of direct control over the political system during the parliamentary period.

TABLE 22

TRENDS IN THE REPRESENTATION OF LARGE ESTATE OWNERS
IN THE CHILEAN NATIONAL LEGISLATURE, 1888-1924

	Chamber of Deputies			Senate	
No. of Deputies	No. of Large Estate Owners	% Large Estate Owners	No. of Senators	No. of Large Estate Owners	% Large Estate Owners
1888-91	126	29	23.0	42	17	40.5
1891-94	94	22	23.4	32	15	46.9
1894-97	94	21	22.3	32	18	56.3
1897-00	94	26	27.7	32	17	53.1
1900-03	94	23	24.5	32	18	56.3
1903-06	94	20	21.3	32	16	50.0
1906-09	94	16	17.0	32	15	46.9
1909-12	95	15	15.8	32	13	40.6
1912-15	118	22	18.6	37	18	48.6
1915-18	118	19	16.1	37	15	40.5
1918-21	118	18	15.3	37	16	43.2
1921-24	117	13	11.1	37	15	40.5
1924	118	13	11.0	37	11	29.7

SOURCE: Valencia Avaria, II; Espinoza, 4th ed.; ibid., 5th ed.; Chile, *Indice de propietarios*; Juvenal Valenzuela O., *Album de informaciones agrícolas: Zona central de Chile* (Santiago, 1923).

NOTE: Congressmen elected before 1912 qualified as large estate owners if near the time of their election they personally owned a rural property assessed at $200,000 or more pesos. For the years after 1912 congressmen have been identified as large estate owners if they personally owned a rural property (1) which was assessed at more than $200,000 pesos in the 1908 tax roll, or (2) which included at least 500 irrigated hectares or 5,000 unirrigated hectares of central valley land according to the 1923 *Album de informaciones agrícolas*.

Nevertheless, the decline in the percentage of large estate owners in the lower house, which only began in the second decade of the period, appears less than impressive given the length of the parliamentary era, the declining economic importance of agriculture, and the extremely small number of individuals who owned large estates.

By Argentine standards the composition of the Chilean lower house certainly did not change very significantly or very rapidly. Smith's data show that the average percentage of aristocrats in the Argentine lower house dropped 22.8 percent between the 1904-15 and 1916-30 periods. In the six years between 1916 and 1922 alone the percentage of aristocrats in the lower house fell from 55.9 to 31.3 percent. No six-year period between 1888 and 1925 witnessed as dramatic a shift in the social composition of the Chilean lower house. The percentage of large estate owners in the Chilean Chamber of Deputies was only 4.4 percent less in 1912 than in 1888. If the rising trend in the representation of large estate owners in the Chilean Chamber of Deputies between 1888 and 1900 is considered a consequence of party competition, the contrasts between the two countries obviously appear even more marked.

These findings on the importance of large estate owners in Chilean politics do not conform fully to those reported by Arnold J. Bauer in his analysis of the Chilean congress in the years 1854, 1874, 1902, and 1918.[30] According to Bauer's data, in 1918 large estate owners controlled more congressional seats than in 1854 or 1874 and virtually the same number as in 1902. The broad trends suggested by Bauer's data and Table 22, however, are very similar. Both underline the continuing importance of landownership in Chilean society, and both indicate that large estate ownership remained a valuable resource in the political recruitment process after 1891. In view of the nature of the parliamentary system and the powers exercised by the Senate under it, an extremely narrow socioeconomic elite clearly wielded an exceptionally disproportionate amount of political power throughout the 1891-1924 period.

How large estate owners utilized this power is a separate question. Large landowners frequently had investments in other sectors of the economy, and their access to positions of political influence did not necessarily work against the representation of other interests in the legislative process. At the same time, as indicated by the higher percentages of landowners reported both by Bauer and by the previous occupational tables, Table 22 unquestionably understates the weight of landholding interests in the legislature. Other congressmen held one or more smaller estates or managed properties for their families. Still others were related to large estate owners or acquired large estates in later years. To take only one example, Guillermo Subercaseaux Pérez, a Conservative who represented the Department of San Carlos in the Chamber of Deputies between 1909 and 1918 and the Province of Nuble in the Senate after 1924, did not own a large estate. However, his father-in-law, Juan Francisco Rivas, owned two exceptionally valuable haciendas in the Department of San Carlos of Nuble province. Only legislators directly owning at least one of Chile's larger estates near the time of their election have been included in the calculations presented in Table 22.

The major question about the trends portrayed in Table 22 concerns the comparability of information for the last decade of the parliamentary period with that for earlier years. In Chile estate size provides a limited guide to estate value. The Chilean land reform law of 1967, for example, rated the productive capacity of irrigated central valley land in Santiago at seventy-seven times that of mountain property in the same province.[31] The formula used to draw up a list of large estates for the latter years of the parliamentary era attempts to control for the discrepancy between estate size and value by taking the importance of irrigation into account; but it fails to allow for the highly variable productive value of land in different regions of the central valley or the importance of factors such as transportation links and capital investments.[32] Comparisons between Valenzuela's *Album* and earlier tax rolls suggest that these problems create important differences between the 1923 list of large estate owners and those for earlier years.[33]

The relative availability of information on large estate ownership over time also represents a difficulty. Large estate ownership in the latter half of the parliamentary period has been assessed primarily on the basis of a single list, as compared to three separate lists for the first half. The fifteen years gap between the 1908 tax roll and the appearance of Valenzuela's *Album*, in particular, raises the possibility that large estate owners controlled just as many seats at the end of the parliamentary period as in earlier years and that the decline reported in Table 22 is entirely spurious.[34]

To check on this possibility, the family backgrounds of deputies elected in 1897 and 1921 have been compared. The data on large estate ownership indicate that deputies holding office in the earlier session constituted a much wealthier and socially prestigious group. Information on the fathers of the deputies holding office in 1897 and 1921 only partially confirms this finding. Forty-five percent of the deputies elected in 1897 had fathers with enough prominence to merit a separate entry in Virgilio Figueroa's authoritative five-volume dictionary of Chilean biography.[35] Two-thirds of these socially prominent fathers had held public office. In comparison, the proportion of deputies elected in 1921 with socially prominent fathers equalled only 35 percent. The proportion of these socially prominent fathers who had held public office was approximately the same as in 1897. These data confirm that some shift toward the recruitment of deputies from more modest social backgrounds did occur at the end of the parliamentary period. The contrasts between the deputies elected in 1897 and 1921, however, are far less marked than the information on large estate ownership tends to suggest.

The number of Sociedad Nacional de Agricultura (SNA) members in congress at various points in time also indicates that the data on large estate ownership exaggerate the change in political recruitment patterns. The SNA, which represented large landholders, had more members in both the Senate and Chamber of Deputies in 1924 than in 1885 or 1895. In percentage terms SNA representation in the lower house rose from 19.3 percent in 1885 to 27.7 percent in 1901 and then declined slowly to 19.5 percent in 1924. In the Senate SNA members held 37.8 percent of the seats in 1924 as compared to 27.5 and 34.4 in 1885 and 1895, respectively.[36]

In summary, the percentage of legislators owning large estates indicates that the representation of a relatively narrow socioeconomic elite within the Chilean legislature increased in the aftermath of the 1891 civil war and only declined in the last years of the parliamentary period. If anything, the landholding data for the years 1915-1924 exaggerate the magnitude of this decline. Other evidence points towards an even more modest and gradual shift away from the recruitment of legislators from socioconomic elite backgrounds during the latter part of the parliamentary era.

The importance of large estate ownership as a political resource during the parliamentary period is further emphasized by the high proportion of the very largest estate owners who managed to secure a legislative seat. According to the 1894-97 tax rolls, 129 men owned an estate appraised at more than $400,000 pesos or more than one $200,000 peso estate.[37] At some point during their lives, 49.6 percent of these men held a seat in the legislature.[38] The access to public office created by great wealth, social prestige, and/or political control over a dependent rural population did not wane over time. According to the 1908 tax roll 126 men held at least one estate appraised at more than $400,000 or more than one $200,000 estate.[39] Sixty-nine of these men, or 54.8 of them, were elected to the legislature during the course of their life-times.[40] Thus the odds of a very large estate owner reaching congress were not only astronomically high by the standards of the average Chilean, but they apparently increased slightly over time. Consequently, the evidence again suggests that in the Chilean case party competition failed to equalize political opportunities and may even have enhanced the importance of wealth and social status in the political recruitment process. Whereas before 1891 the executive was free to place men of talent in legislative positions, during the parliamentary period this channel for the recruitment of men of modest social origins was closed.

Table 23 provides an additional indication of the impact of party competition on the kinds of individuals recruited into Chilean public life. The table presents information on the percentage of legislators whose paternal surnames indicate a family relationship to one of the fifty-nine millionaires in Chile in 1882. Possibly because of the hazards involved in identifying family relationships solely on the basis of paternal surnames, the trends portrayed in the table do not fully correspond to those indicated by large estate ownership. For example, in 1912 the percentage of large estate owners in the congress increased from 22.0 to 25.8, whereas the percentage of legislators with surnames indicating economic

TABLE 23

CHILEAN NATIONAL LEGISLATORS SHARING A PATERNAL
SURNAME WITH ONE OF CHILE'S "OLD MILLIONAIRES"

	Chamber of Deputies		Senate		Total	
	Number	%	Number	%	Number	%
1870-73	19	19.8	7	35.0	26	22.4
1873-76	26	27.4	7	35.0	33	28.7
1876-79	20	18.7	12	32.4	32	22.2
1879-82	29	27.6	12	32.4	41	28.9
1882-85	31	28.7	11	29.7	42	30.0
1885-88	29	25.4	11	27.5	40	26.0
1888-91	28	22.2	11	26.2	39	23.2
1891-94	28	29.8	9	28.1	37	29.4
1894-97	21	22.3	9	28.1	30	23.8
1897-00	20	21.3	11	34.4	31	24.6
1900-03	16	17.0	14	43.8	30	23.8
1903-06	19	20.2	9	28.1	28	22.2
1906-09	19	20.2	10	31.3	29	23.0
1909-12	18	18.9	8	25.0	26	20.5
1912-15	13	11.0	6	16.2	19	12.3
1915-18	20	16.9	6	16.2	26	16.8
1918-21	17	14.4	9	24.3	26	16.8
1921-24	21	17.9	10	27.0	31	20.1
1924	16	13.6	5	13.5	21	13.5

SOURCE: Names of legislators drawn from Valencia Avaria, II. Names of millionaires drawn from "Los millonarios de Chile viejo," *El Mercurio* (Valparaíso), LV, 26 April 1882, p. 2 as reprinted in Bauer, pp. 246-247.

NOTE: Including only the married names of widows, the 1882 list of fifty-nine millionaires yields a total of fifty-four different paternal surnames. Legislators between 1870 and 1924 held thirty-nine of these names as patronymics: Balmaceda, Barazarte, Bravo, Collao, Correa, Cortés, Cousiño, Covarrubias, Dávila, Díaz, Eastman, Echeverría, Edwards, Errázuriz, Escobar, Gallo, González, Gormaz, Herquíñigo, Huidobro, Irarrázaval, Lazcano, Lyon, Matte, Muñoz, Naranjo, Ossa, Ovalle, Pereira, Puelma, Subercaseaux, Toto, Urmeneta, Urrejola, Valdés, Valenzuela, Varela, Vergara, and Vicuña.

elite membership reached an unprecedented low point. Nevertheless, important similarities exist between Tables 22 and 23. Both show that the representation of socioeconomic elites within the legislature increased after 1888 and remained at a relatively high level until the last decade of the parliamentary period, despite a gradual and somewhat unsteady decline after 1900.

Taken together the legislators included in the calcuations in Table 23 held a total of only thirty-nine different family names. The table consequently emphasizes not only the importance of wealth in the political recruitment process, but the relatively closed and socially exclusive nature of Chilean public life.

By tracing the number of legislators who shared both paternal and maternal surnames during the parliamentary period, the high degree of inequality in the political opportunity structure becomes even more obvious. One hundred seventy-six legislators holding office between 1891 and 1924 shared both a patronymic and matronymic with another individual elected in the same period.[41] While identical maternal and paternal surnames do not invariably indicate a fraternal relationship, for the sake of brevity these legislators may be described as belonging to fraternal sets, seventy-six of which can be identified in the 1891-1924 period. Taking into consideration the many other possible types of family relationships among legislators as well as the number of legislators whose matronymics cannot be traced, the number of sets of relatives in the legislature was unquestionably much higher.

Since over one hundred fraternal sets can be identified in the 1870-1891 period, the level of kinship relationship among Chilean politicians declined over time, as might be anticipated simply on the basis of population growth. As measured by the number of fraternal sets in the legislature, family linkages among legislators also diminished over the course of the parliamentary period. Nevertheless, the number of family relationships among congressmen remained surprisingly high even in the latter half of the 1891-1924 period. For example, the 1912-1915 legislature included six fraternal sets with a total of fourteen members. Obviously, the odds against one set of three brothers, let alone two sets, sitting in the same session of congress would be extremely high unless marked inequalities characterized the political recruitment process.

By Argentine standards the number of relatives holding office in Chile between 1891 and 1924 was extraordinary. In 1916, for example, only nineteen Argentine legislators even shared a *paternal* surname.[42] In contrast, forty-six legislators in the Chilean congress of 1912-1915 shared a paternal surname. Factors such as Argentina's federal political structure, its larger population size, and the traditionally fragmented character of its socioeconomic elite may account partially for this contrast; but basic differences in the process by which political leaders were selected in the two countries are also important. The exceptionally high level of consanguineous relations among Chilean parliamentarians clearly points to the existence of a much more highly oligarchical selection process favoring the recruitment of national leaders from a relatively exclusive and narrow base of the population.

In the Chilean case analysis of trends in the social composition of the national legislature consequently provides no support for the hypothesis that party competition reduces the odds favoring the recruitment of political leaders from the upper end of the socioeconomic continuum. Whether one looks at the occupational backgrounds of legislators, the relationship between large estate ownership and election to national office, the social prestige of legislators' fathers, SNA members in congress, surnames indicating economic elite membership, or consanguineous relationships among Chilean legislators, the evidence indicates that socioeconomic elites retained a high degree of control over representative institutions in Chile throughout most of the parliamentary period. As in Argentina a break with past patterns of upper-class domination occurred during the early 1920s, but in Chile this break took place long after the introduction of a competitive system and can be as plausibly attributed to the electoral intervention of the Alessandri administration as to party competition.[43] Moreover, in the Chilean case no consistent pattern of change in the social composition of the national legislature can be associated with the emergence of a competitive system. The ability of large estate owners to convert their economic and social resources into political office actually increased in the wake of the civil war and only declined slowly over time. The evidence thus provides a basis for arguing that party competition in Chile raised, rather than reduced, the odds favoring the recruitment of political leaders from elite backgrounds.

Information on the social status of Argentine legislators, on the other hand, indicates that a comparatively steady and rapid shift away from the recruitment of leaders from elite backgrounds followed the emergence of a competitive party system. Taken together with Gallo and Sigal's analysis and the comments of contemporaries, this evidence supports the view that party competition equalized political opportunities in Argentina and allowed a new segment of society to participate in the formulation of public policy.

CHAPTER VI

THE IMPACT OF PARTY COMPETITION:
FISCAL, MONETARY, AND EXCHANGE POLICIES

The analysis of patterns of political recruitment leaves open a set of fundamental questions about the consequences of party competition in Argentina and Chile. How did the regime changes associated with party development affect public policy? It is widely assumed that regime changes do alter the distribution of policy costs and benefits. Equally prevalent is the assumption that competitive political processes encourage policy makers to respond to the preferences of the many rather than the privileged few. To what extent do the political experiences of Argentina and Chile in the 1890-1930 period bear out these assumptions? Is there any evidence that shifts in public policy favorable to ordinary citizens followed the emergence of competitive regimes? Did party competition enable a broader spectrum of social groups to exercise political influence or did decision makers respond primarily to the demands and interests of those at the upper end of the socioeconomic spectrum? How similar was the pattern of policy change in Argentina and Chile? Were differences in the relative equality of political opportunity reflected in policy outcomes? In an attempt to answer these questions this chapter examines the fiscal, monetary, and exchange policies adopted by the governments of Argentina and Chile during the initial period of party competition.

TABLE 24

CHILE AND ARGENTINA:
NATIONAL GOVERNMENT EXPENDITURES, 1870-1930
(thousands of pesos)

	Argentina		Chile	
	Expenditures $ gold	Per Capita	Expenditures $ of 18d	Per Capita
1870	19,440	10.3	32,249	16.8
1872	26,463	13.3	35,826	18.2
1874	29,784	14.2	49,899	24.7
1876	22,153	9.9	41,894	20.2
1878	20,841	8.9	32,223	14.9
1880	26,919	10.8	43,950	19.5
1882	58,007	21.9	76,055	32.5
1884	56,440	20.1	72,890	30.0
1886	39,179	13.2	67,282	26.6
1888	51,597	16.3	59,575	23.2
1890	38,146	11.3	91,049	35.0
1892	38,685	10.7	67,554	25.7
1894	40,114	10.4	48,745	18.3
1896	78,213	19.2	102,756	37.9
1898	121,290	27.8	88,302	31.6
1900	68,580	14.9	92,374	32.1
1902	85,335	17.5	103,120	34.7
1904	85,781	16.8	110,251	36.0
1906	118,911	21.6	119,128	37.8
1908	111,049	18.4	107,476	33.1
1910	180,948	27.5	163,247	49.0
1912	177,828	24.9	186,004	54.7
1914	184,642	23.3	153,559	44.2
1916	164,844	20.3	150,749	42.4
1918	185,263	22.1	221,616	61.1
1920	214,634	24.7	264,171	71.2
1922	270,688	29.5	198,673	52.5
1924	295,684	30.1	215,691	55.9
1926	328,553	31.8	– –	– –
1928	388,777	35.7	– –	– –
1930	480,997	42.2	– –	– –

SOURCE: Argentina, *Tercer censo*, 1914, X, 389; Guaresti, p. 223; Chile, *Sinopsis estadística*, 1919, p. 69; ibid., 1920, p. 64; Chile, *Anuario estadístico*, 1925, I, 78; ibid., VI, 18.

NOTE: Figures for Argentina exclude spending of autonomous institutions, such as the national universities, state banks, Consejo Nacional de Educación, and Ferrocarriles del Estado. The Chilean figures exclude spending of the state-owned railways.

GOVERNMENT EXPENDITURES AND SOCIOECONOMIC RESOURCES

The financial and social resources available to Argentine and Chilean government authorities expanded rapidly after 1890, creating a situation relatively favorable to policy innovation.[1] As indicated by Table 24, government expenditures in the two countries also grew considerably over time, more than doubling on a per capita basis between 1890 and 1920. A key question raised by these trends is the relationship between resources and expenditures. Is there any evidence that the emergence of party competition provoked rising expenditures and an expansion of government activity, or did expenditures simply grow in line with resources on an incremental basis?

Although the serial data are limited, Tables 25 and 26 provide a rough idea of the relationship between the growth of expenditures and resources in the two countries. In the Chilean case the data suggest that the emergence of a competitive system did not lead to any major expansion of government activity. Government expenditures grew at approximately the same rate as resources, both before and after 1890. The similarity between the indices of literacy and spending presented in Table 25 is particularly striking. Up until 1907 a very close correspondence also existed between the growth of exports and government spending. Thereafter government spending lagged behind the expansion of exports, suggesting that expenditures actually grew more slowly than resources. The export index is somewhat misleading, however, and has been included soley because better indicators of long-term economic development are not available. Other evidence suggests that the domestic economy was not expanding at anything like the rate of exports after 1907 and that government expenditures continued to expand in line with the nation's resource base. According to Mamalakis' growth estimates, for example, the GDP expanded at an annual rate of 4.0 percent between 1915 and 1924, or only slightly faster than the average annual increase in government spending, which equalled 3.8 percent.[2]

The relationship between the growth of public expenditures and socioeconomic resources differed in Argentina. As Table 26 indicates, national government spending increased more slowly

TABLE 25

CHILE: INDICES OF GROWTH IN NATIONAL GOVERNMENT
SPENDING, LITERATE POPULATION, URBAN POPULATION,
AND EXPORTS, 1875-1920

	Government Expenditures	Literate Population[a]	Urban Population[b]	Exports[c]
1875-79	100	100	100	100
1880-84	159	— —	— —	155
1885-89	158	153	140	163
1890-94	170	— —	— —	185
1895-99	201	179	183	200
1900-04	240	— —	— —	241
1905-09	277	292	260	372
1910-14	394	— —	— —	448
1915-19	418	396	330	662
1920-24	530	— —	— —	688

SOURCE: Chile, *Censo*, 1907 and 1920 (urban and literate population);
idem, *Anuario estadístico*, 1918, VI, 64 and ibid., 1925, VI, 66 (exports);
expenditures as for Table 24.

[a]For census years 1875, 1885, 1895, 1907, and 1920.

[b]Census years as above; cities over 5,000.

[c]Total value calculated in pesos of 18d.

than resources until 1895. Between 1895 and 1914 spending increased at approximately the same rate as the literate population,
slightly faster than the urban population, but slower than the expansion of exports. Again, however, export statistics appear to
provide a flawed indicator of economic expansion. According to
ECLA data, the GDP grew at an annual rate of 6.3 percent between
1900-04 and 1910-14, or somewhat more slowly than government
spending, which increased at an average annual rate of 6.9 percent.[3] No census data on urbanization or literacy are available
for the 1914 to 1929 period, but economic growth estimates
point to an accelerating gap between socioeconomic resources and
government spending in the wake of the introduction of competitive politics. Whereas the Argentine GDP grew an estimated 3.5

TABLE 26

ARGENTINA: INDICES OF GROWTH IN NATIONAL
GOVERNMENT SPENDING, LITERATE POPULATION, URBAN
POPULATION, AND EXPORTS, 1870-1914

	Government Expenditures	Literate Population[a]	Urban Population[b]	Exports[c]
1870-74	100	100	100	100
1875-79	89	– –	– –	118
1880-84	168	– –	– –	154
1885-89	184	– –	– –	218
1890-94	147	– –	– –	261
1895-99	301	476	330	334
1900-04	303	– –	– –	503
1905-09	496	– –	– –	855
1910-14	740	1123	823	1022

SOURCE: Argentina, *Tercer censo*, 1914, X, 389 (expenditures); ibid.,
I, 170 (literacy); ibid., Vol. IV and idem, *Segundo censo*, 1895, Vol. II (urban
population); idem, *Tercer censo*, VIII, 16 (exports).

[a]For census years 1869, 1895, and 1914.

[b]Census years as above; cities over 5,000.

[c]Total value calculated in gold pesos.

percent per annum between 1910-14 and 1925-29, public expenditures increased at an average annual rate of 5.2 percent.[4]

Thus in the Chilean case there is no evidence that political party activity led to greater government spending. The growth of expenditures closely paralleled the expansion of resources from 1875 to 1924. In Argentina, on the other hand, government expenditures increased rapidly after 1910 relative to economic indicators, suggesting that political party competition in that country significantly affected public policy.

PUBLIC POLICY IN CHILE

A second and more important issue is whether patterns of public spending and taxation changed over time in response to party competition. Did major shifts take place in government fiscal, monetary, or exchange policies that might reflect a redistribution of power in favor of subordinate groups, such as an increased emphasis on educational expenditures or greater dependence on direct taxation? Or was the distribution of policy costs and benefits much the same after the introduction of party competition as before?

Government Expenditures

Table 27 presents information on the allocation of Chilean government funds by ministry during the 1875-1920 period. The first point to be noted is that allocations to ministries did not grow incrementally, but fluctuated considerably over time, both in absolute and relative terms. In the case of four ministries—finance, war, navy, and public works—the year to year variations were enormous. For example, total government expenditures were approximately equal in 1901 and 1902, but the Ministry of Finance spent $37.2 million pesos in the former year, around 36 percent of total spending, and only $17.7 million in 1902, which was just over 17 percent of the total. Similarly, the Ministry of Industry and Public Works spent over $34 million pesos in 1912, the equivalent of 18.4 percent of total national government spending, and only $15.6 million in 1913, or 9.5 percent of the total.[5]

Despite such oscillations, certain long-term trends may be observed. First, the absolute level of expenditures increased for all ministries between 1875 and 1920 and, with one exception, reached a peak between 1910 and 1920. The exception is the Ministry of War, whose spending reached a high of $45 million pesos in 1883 during the War of the Pacific. Second, relative to 1875 the Ministry of Education increased its spending the most. Total government spending increased 455 percent between 1875 and 1920, while educational outlays increased 1000 percent. The next fastest growing departments were the war and naval ministries, whose expenditures each increased 900 percent in the period. These departments did not, however, receive a greater percentage of government funds during the latter part of the parliamentary period than they had previously.

TABLE 27

CHILE: NATIONAL GOVERNMENT EXPENDITURES BY MINISTRY
1875-1920
(millions of pesos of 18d)

Ministry	1875	1880	1885	1890	1895	1900	1905	1910	1915	1920
Interior	12.9	3.8	6.7	9.2	7.4	12.9	15.8	25.3	20.4	45.8
%	27.2	8.6	13.2	10.1	9.9	14.0	15.2	15.5	15.5	17.4
For. Rel.	1.4	0.5	1.3	3.9	2.5	3.3	5.3	8.0	3.0	4.7
%	3.0	1.1	2.7	4.3	3.4	3.5	5.1	4.9	2.3	1.8
Justice	1.4	1.1	2.2	4.8	3.4	4.9	4.8	5.5	4.4	8.0
%	3.0	2.5	4.3	5.3	4.6	5.3	4.6	3.4	3.3	3.0
Education	2.7	1.5	3.2	9.7	5.5	7.4	11.9	17.6	15.5	30.3
%	5.7	3.5	6.3	10.7	7.4	8.0	11.5	10.8	11.8	11.5
Finance	20.2	12.8	25.3	18.2	14.0	32.1	27.4	38.6	45.5	66.5
%	42.5	29.1	50.1	19.9	18.9	34.8	26.4	23.6	34.5	25.2
War	4.7	16.1	7.5	9.4	21.8	11.2	10.1	20.5	19.7	47.9
%	9.9	36.6	14.9	10.3	29.5	12.1	9.7	12.6	14.9	18.1
Navy	4.1	8.2	4.3	9.2	7.6	8.4	11.9	17.6	13.4	42.0
%	8.7	18.6	8.6	10.1	10.2	9.1	11.4	10.8	10.1	15.9
Pub. Wks.	– –	– –	– –	26.7	12.0	12.1	16.7	30.1	10.1	18.9
%	– –	– –	– –	29.3	16.1	13.1	16.1	18.5	7.6	7.2
Total	47.6	44.0	50.4	91.0	74.1	92.4	104.0	163.2	131.8	264.2
%	100.0	100.0	100.1	100.0	100.0	99.9	100.0	100.1	100.0	100.1

SOURCE: Chile, *Sinopsis estadística*, 1919, p. 69; *Anuario estadístico*, 1925, VI, 18-19.

NOTE: Expenditures of the railways are not included.

Only two ministries steadily increased their share of spending during the parliamentary period: the Ministry of the Interior and the Ministry of Education. Between 1890 and 1894 educational expenditures averaged 7.5 percent of total expenditures. They grew fairly steadily over time and averaged 8.4 percent of the total between 1900 and 1904 and 10.3, 12.3, 12.9, and 12.8, respectively, in the years 1905-1909, 1910-1914, 1915-1919, and 1920-1924.[6] The steady increase in spending by the Ministry of the Interior is less obvious from Table 27, because this ministry absorbed a high proportion of the budget in 1875. During the 1875-1890 period, however, its expenditures declined. This trend was sharply reversed in the wake of the civil war. From an average of only 8.9 percent of total expenditures in the 1890-1894 period, the Ministry of the Interior's expenditures rose to 11.5 percent of total national spending between 1895 and 1899, 11.9 percent from 1900-1904, and over 15 percent from 1905 to 1924.[7]

Lower- and middle-class groups in Chile derived some benefit from both of these major shifts in the pattern of government spending. As indicated by Table 28, the number of students in state primary schools more than tripled during the course of the parliamentary period. In view of the importance of public education for social mobility, particularly in a society characterized by rather modest rates of literacy, this development represented a clear policy gain for groups at the lower end of the socioeconomic continuum. At the same time there is no evidence that policy makers became any less responsive to the preferences of more privileged groups. Opportunities for state secondary and higher education, which chiefly benefitted individuals who could afford to pursue extended schooling, expanded even more rapidly than those at the primary level.

A similar shift in the distribution of policy costs and benefits was associated with the expansion of the Ministry of the Interior's national expenditures. The ministry's public health and welfare activities, which consisted mainly of subsidies to charities, vaccinations, and the provision of potable water and sewage, grew during the parliamentary period. After 1906 the ministry also assumed some responsibility for providing workers with low-cost housing. A comparison of the budgets of 1886 and 1916 provides evidence of the expansion in the ministry's activities in these areas. In the former year the budget earmarked only 7.7 percent of the ministry's funds for health and welfare; thirty years later the figure was 16.3 percent.[8] Hence the expansion of the Ministry of the

TABLE 28

CHILE: STUDENTS IN STATE SCHOOLS, 1896-1920

	Primary	Secondary	Higher	Total
1896	111,361	12,535	1,317	125,213
1910	258,875	30,731	1,824	291,430
1920	346,386	49,123	4,502	400,011

SOURCE: Chile, *Censo*, 1920, p. 402.

Interior's share of the national budget can be linked with changes in the pattern of public spending favorable to groups at the lower end of the socioeconomic continuum. Yet increased spending on health and welfare does not explain fully why the Ministry of the Interior's share of total national spending increased from 8.5 percent in 1891 to 17.4 percent in 1920. In the latter year expenditures on health, welfare, charity, and low-cost housing accounted for less than 3 percent of total national expenditures.[9] Growth of the ministry's other responsibilities, which included general government administration, police protection, and statistical, postal, telegraph, and telephone services, also fail to account for its rising share of national expenditures. The explanation rests instead with the very high proportion of the ministry's budget spent on salaries and wages.

Salaries and wages accounted for roughly 22 percent of the total national budget in 1896.[10] Table 29 presents comparable figures for the latter part of the parliamentary period, which show that an inflated bureaucracy developed in Chile long before the postdepression period.[11] Since the Ministry of the Interior was the largest government employer, its expenditures grew particularly rapidly. Between 1915 and 1920 wages and salaries accounted for over half of the ministry's budget. The second largest government employer was the Ministry of Education, which spent over 60 percent of its funds on wages and salaries. By 1920 these two ministries alone accounted for nearly one-half of the total budgeted wage and salary bill.[12]

TABLE 29

CHILE: BUDGETARY ALLOCATIONS FOR WAGES,
SALARIES, AND PENSIONS, 1913-1924
(percent of total budget)

	Salaries	Wages	Pensions	Total
1913	33.1	8.5	2.5	44.1
1914	25.7	7.0	1.9	34.6
1915	31.0	0.6	2.6	34.2
1916	32.4	1.2	2.9	36.5
1917	38.7	0.5	3.7	42.9
1918	42.5	0.7	3.9	47.1
1919	34.9	0.8	3.3	39.0
1920	35.5	1.0	3.6	40.1
1921	35.2	1.0	3.0	39.2
1922	35.5	0.8	2.8	39.1
1923	33.5	0.7	2.4	36.6
1924	34.3	0.9	2.6	37.8

SOURCE: Chile, *Anuario estadístico*, 1916, VI, 17 (1913-17); ibid., 1918, VI, 24-25 (1918-19); ibid., 1925, VI, 24-25 (1920-24).

Party competition directly affected this employment growth. Securing government positions for friends and partisans was a central preoccupation of politicians during the 1891-1924 era, and the expansion of the bureaucracy was a logical if costly means of satisfying demands for jobs. The chief beneficiaries of this expansion probably belonged to Chile's middle class, although members of elite families frequently held bureaucratic posts as well.

The Ministry of Industry and Public Works, which was established in 1888, provided another more traditional channel for political patronage. One cannot speak of a steady increase in public works spending, because the funds allocated to the ministry fluctuated considerably from year to year, reaching particularly high levels in the early 1890s as well as in the years 1907, 1910, and 1912. Nevertheless, the ministry's share of public revenues remained quite high until the outbreak of World War I, when the government became seriously pressed for funds. Between 1890 and 1914 public works accounted for 14 percent of total government spending, as compared to an average of only 6.5 percent in the years 1915-1924.[13]

Chilean Government Revenues

The rapid growth of the bureaucracy not only diverted funds from more productive forms of expenditure; it imposed a strain on the national treasury. The budget allocated $92.4 million pesos of 18d for wages in salaries in 1920: a sum equivalent to *total* expenditures in 1900. Government revenues also increased rapidly during the parliamentary period due to the nitrate boom, but they failed to keep pace with the growth in expenditures. As a result, the national debt increased tremendously.

The longitudinal data presented in Table 30 show that a trend towards spiralling indebtedness only developed in the aftermath of the 1891 civil war. Before the parliamentary period, the national public debt grew slowly and, despite the War of the Pacific, only registered an overall increase of approximately 60 percent between 1870 and 1896. In contrast, the debt more than tripled during the parliamentary period. Considering that ordinary revenues increased 400 percent between 1891 and 1918 but only 172 percent between 1870 and 1890,[14] the contrast between the periods before and after the introduction of party competition is truly striking.

The dramatic expansion of the national debt in the years following the civil war is explained largely by the failure of the government to expand adequately its revenue base. Whereas public expenditures grew at roughly the same rate as the economy as a whole, revenues did not. Data on the relative importance of various types of government revenue are presented in Table 31. These figures show that after the War of the Pacific customs duties normally provided the Chilean government with 70 to 80 percent of its income, the largest part of which was derived from a tax on nitrate exports.[15] The government remained highly dependent on customs duties throughout the 1891-1924 period, and no attempt was made to force large property owners or persons with high incomes to bear a heavier tax burden. Indeed, national direct tax revenues were *absolutely* lower between 1891 and 1912 than they had been as far back as 1860, and in most years between 1891 and 1924 they accounted for a smaller proportion of national revenues

TABLE 30

CHILE: GROWTH OF THE PUBLIC DEBT, 1870-1924
(Pesos of 18d)

	Thousands of Pesos	Index	Debt per Capita
1870	115,716	100	59.5
1875	152,268	131	73.4
1880	182,034	157	79.5
1885	152,362	131	60.3
1891	187,115	161	71.0
1892	202,458	100	76.5
1895	218,796	108	81.6
1900	303,897	150	105.5
1905	344,789	170	111.0
1910	510,325	252	153.4
1915	607,449	300	172.5
1920	597,536	295	161.0
1924	675,537	334	174.6

SOURCE: Chile, *Anuario estadístico*, 1918, VI, 32; ibid., 1925, VI, 66.

than during the 1870s and 1880s.[16] Moreover, national property
and inheritance taxes were virtually eliminated after 1891 and not
reintroduced until 1915, when the restriction of credit and disruption of foreign trade associated with the outbreak of war forced
the government to consider alternative sources of income.[17]

Indirect internal taxation also remained very low during the
1891-1924 period, although not in comparison with the 1880s.
The national government eliminated indirect taxes at the end of
the War of the Pacific, when the nitrate export tax began to yield
large revenues. After 1903, when a tax on alcohol was imposed,
indirect taxes increased in importance, but even between 1914 and
1924 they accounted for a lower proportion of revenues than in
the 1860s and 1870s.[18] Municipal taxes on property, licenses,
and patents failed to offset the decline in internal taxes collected
by the national government. Available data also indicate that
municipal taxes as a percentage of all internal tax revenues declined

TABLE 31

CHILE: RELATIVE IMPORTANCE OF VARIOUS TYPES OF
GOVERNMENT REVENUES, 1880-1922

| | Ordinary Revenues | | | | | | | |
| | Customs | | Internal Taxes | | Public | | Extra-Ordin- | |
Year	Imports %	Exports %	Direct %	Indirect %	Services %	Other %	ary %	Total %
1880	22.8	4.7	7.9	6.9	0.7	20.4	36.7	100.1
1882	48.1	27.8	11.9	– –	1.5	8.4	2.3	100.0
1884	45.1	35.9	11.2	– –	1.6	6.2	– –	100.0
1886	46.5	29.0	11.6	– –	1.8	11.1	– –	100.0
1888	42.2	38.8	5.9	– –	1.4	5.8	5.9	100.0
1890	31.1	46.6	3.8	– –	1.2	6.8	10.4	99.9
1892	33.3	40.4	2.6	– –	1.1	6.1	16.5	100.0
1894	21.5	59.6	0.7	– –	1.2	4.9	12.1	100.0
1896	24.6	39.0	0.5	– –	1.2	2.9	31.9	100.1
1898	17.1	35.5	0.4	– –	1.0	6.2	39.9	100.1
1900	26.0	45.7	0.5	– –	1.3	7.8	18.9	100.2
1902	30.3	52.6	1.3	– –	1.7	3.1	10.9	99.9
1904	27.0	43.7	0.8	1.0	1.7	3.3	22.6	100.1
1906	29.4	41.0	0.8	1.5	1.6	5.1	20.7	100.1
1908	28.0	50.0	0.5	1.4	1.5	5.9	12.6	99.9
1910	31.5	51.9	1.5	2.5	1.7	5.0	5.9	100.0
1912	26.7	40.3	1.4	2.5	1.7	4.9	22.5	100.0
1914	29.7	47.7	1.8	4.0	2.2	11.4	3.2	100.0
1916	20.0	55.5	4.8	3.7	3.0	4.6	8.5	100.1
1918	24.1	49.6	10.6	2.8	4.1	7.3	1.5	100.0
1920	19.7	48.0	5.8	9.1	6.1	7.8	3.4	99.9
1922	19.3	19.7	3.6	6.2	4.6	9.2	37.5	100.1

SOURCE: Chile, *Anuario estadístico*, 1918, VI, p. 15; ibid., 1925, VI, p. 15.

NOTE: Excluding revenues from state-owned railways.

in importance during the course of the parliamentary period as did property taxes as a proportion of municipal tax revenues.[19]

In short, the Chilean tax system became even more inequitable after 1891 than before. The national government used the nitrate revenues to reduce direct taxes and generally alleviate the internal tax burden. Because nitrate exports fluctuated from year to year, this shift created a tendency towards financial disequilibrium, one result of which was the growth of the national debt.

The Chilean Tariff

The growing dependence of the Chilean government on export taxes also involved a decline in the proportion of revenues derived from tariffs. Whereas import duties had accounted for over 40 percent of total state revenues during the 1880s, by the last decade of the parliamentary period import duties averaged only 21.9 percent of total revenues.[20] Despite growing political pressures from domestic industry, import duties as a percentage of total imports also declined over time. During the 1870s and 1880s duties had averaged 19.7 and 22.2 percent, respectively, of total imports. During the 1890s the average percentage fell to only 15.2 percent, and it remained low in comparison with earlier years, despite a partial recovery in the 1900s. Import duties as a percentage of total imports averaged 18.9, 15.2, and 13.8 percent, respectively, in the years 1900-1909, 1910-1919, and 1920-1924.[21]

Further information on the revenues collected from different categories of imports would be useful in comparing the tariff levels of the 1891-1924 period with those of earlier years, because changes in import duties collected as a percentage of total imports can reflect shifts in the composition of imports as well as changes in the incidence and structure of tariffs. Such shifts clearly played a major role in Chile, because raw materials accounted for a steadily increasing proportion of imports over time. Hence even though the ratio of duties to imports declined after 1891, domestic industry probably received greater protection during the 1891-1924 period than in previous years. The legislation passed during the parliamentary period points in the direction of such a trend, suggesting that industrialists made real gains through the introduction of a competitive system.

In 1897 congress passed a law that revised customs duties and imposed a general tariff of 25 percent on all imported goods.[22] To dispel any idea that the sole purpose of this legislation was revenue raising or that it failed to provide domestic producers with positive protection, it should be pointed out that a wide variety of manufactured goods were subjected to an even higher duty of 60 percent, while tariff exemptions were granted primarily for raw materials, tools, and machinery. A growing discrepancy between fixed tariff values and real import prices led to a decline in the ratio between duties and imports over time, and in 1909 the legislature began preparing a new law fixing specific rather than ad valorem rates of duty. The law eventually emerged in 1916,[23] and it offered domestic producers even more protection than the 1897 law.[24] A 1916 U.S. Department of Commerce study of Latin American customs legislation described the purpose of Chilean tariffs as "avowedly protective" and suggested that they were the highest on the continent.[25] When the real incidence of tariffs continued to fall in response to postwar inflation, congress passed another law (No. 3734) on 23 February 1921 raising customs duties 50 percent. The ratio between customs duties and total imports thereby increased to its highest level since the years 1899-1907.

The success of Chilean commercial policy is difficult to gauge, because no direct relationship exists between high tariff levels and effective protection; but domestic industry clearly received greater government support in the 1891-1924 period than most literature suggests. The widespread assumption that Chilean policy makers pursued a policy of free trade is well illustrated by Claudio Véliz' argument that Chile failed to make significant industrial progress before 1930 because the government was dominated by three pressure groups—southern agricultural exporters, mining exporters of the North, and large importing firms established in Valparaíso and Santiago—which opposed, both for reasons of economic interest and ideology, protective tariffs.[26] The evidence simply does not support such an argument. Compared to other countries, including even the United States, where the ratio of import duties to the total value of imports averaged 18.5 between 1910 and 1914 and only 8.1 in the years 1915-1919,[27] tariffs were reasonably high—certainly too high for Chilean commercial policy to be described as "free trade." Import duties as a percentage of Chilean imports averaged 16.1 during the 1891-1924 period as a whole, ranging from a high of 22.2 in 1900 to a low of 9.5 in 1920-1921.[28]

Chilean legislative debates and customs laws also indicate that the oft-cited Véliz argument seriously distorts the structure of political conflict in Chile during the pre-1930 period. The interests of the three powerful pressure groups Véliz identifies did not coincide on commercial policy. Moreover, while some prominent rural spokesmen argued that industrial development could only be promoted at the expense of agriculture,[29] commercial policy was shaped by cooperation between agricultural and industrial producers rather than conflict. In return for stiff tariffs on manufactured products, rural producers received strong protection from agricultural imports and the exemption of agricultural machinery and tools from duties. Given the strong representation of rural interests within the legislature as well as the opposition of mining and importing interests to protectionism, these trade-offs were critical to the passage of both the 1897 and 1916 customs laws.

Because tariff legislation responded to the demands of both industry and agriculture, no major redistribution of political power can be inferred from the shift in commercial policy that occurred after 1891. The 1897, 1916, and 1921 tariff laws reflected the growth of domestic industry and represented a victory for Chilean industrialists and their major pressure group, the Sociedad de Fomento Fabril (SFF);[30] but commercial policy also remained favorable to agricultural groups, whose economic interests and political demands had shifted over time in response to changing market opportunities. Declining international prices and markets for agricultural produce, urbanization and the related expansion of the internal market for agricultural goods, economic difficulties associated with Chile's return to the gold standard in 1895, and international trends toward increased protectionism all created rural support for a protectionist policy and thereby contributed to the 1897 policy change.[31]

The shift in commercial policy also contradicts the proposition that party competition encouraged political leaders to respond to popular demands. Because of the political weight of rural interests, tariff policy shifted in directions favored by a very narrow sector of Chilean society. Throughout the parliamentary period, groups representing popular-sector interests—including the Democratic and Socialist Worker parties that supported the protection of domestic industry—[32] expressed strong opposition to tariffs on imported agricultural products. A duty on imported cattle, which was introduced by the 1897 tariff law, served as a particularly important rallying point for urban lower-class and lower middle-class protest activity. Over time the duty became a symbol of inflationary pressures faced by urban consumers, and it provoked the organization of a long series of popular demonstrations, including that of October 1905, which degenerated into several days of violence. Congress responded to these pressures by suspending the cattle tax for two years in 1907. During the war congress also authorized the suspension of tariffs on food and created a special duty exemption for cattle that was exported and reimported across the Andes. Further concessions to consumer interests emerged during the volatile postwar period, which was characterized by massive street demonstrations against rising food costs. In 1918 congress temporarily suspended the cattle duty for the second time and authorized the purchase of food and medicine to be sold at retail prices to the public. Three years later the legislature exempted selected basic foodstuffs from the 50 percent across-the-board increase in tariff rates. Almost all of these concessions to popular pressures, however, were merely temporary measures designed to cope with short-term economic dislocations. Taking the parliamentary period as a whole, commercial policy responded to the demands of industrial and agricultural producers rather than consumers. Significantly, the cattle duty remained in effect until the collapse of the parliamentary period, when it was suspended almost immediately and then replaced by a sliding duty pegged to wholesale cattle prices.[33]

Chilean Monetary and Exchange Policies

Chilean exchange policy provided domestic producers with additional protection against foreign imports. Through devaluation the Chilean peso lost 75 percent of its value between 1890 and 1925,[34] benefitting both primary exporters and import-competing industries at the expense of wage earners, importers, and those remitting profits abroad.[35] While most literature on this period emphasizes the gains accruing to agricultural interests,[36] the economics of the situation were not lost on contemporaries, who explicitly recognized the benefits of the inconvertible peso for domestic industry.[37]

Great Britain was Chile's principal trading partner during the parliamentary period, and Table 32, which traces the rapid decline in the value of the peso relative to the British pound, provides an indication of the stimulus devaluation provided to exports and import substitution. The time period has been extended back to 1870 mainly to show that while the policy of exchange depreciation was not invented during the parliamentary period, the value of the peso did decline faster after 1891 than before.

Because rapid devaluation both reflected and intensified the inflationary pressures created by budget deficits, exchange policy had important implications for the distribution of income among social classes in Chile. Between 1891 and 1924 the cost of living

TABLE 32

CHILE: EXCHANGE RATES, 1870-1925

Year	Pence Per Peso	Index	Year	Pence Per Peso	Index
1870	45.6	100	1900	16.8	37
1875	43.8	96	1905	15.6	34
1880	30.9	68	1910	10.8	24
1885	25.4	56	1915	8.3	18
1890	24.1	53	1920	12.1	27
1895	16.8	37	1925	5.9	13

SOURCE: Chile, *Anuario estadístico*, 1918, VI, 8; ibid., 1925, VI, 13-14.

rose at an annual rate of 5 to 9 percent.[38] While not particularly crippling by modern standards, the rate of inflation inflamed contemporaries, who accurately perceived its differential social impact.[39] On the one hand, powerful socioeconomic interests stood well-placed to benefit from inflation, particularly exporters and large estate owners. While the real cost of mortgages, property taxes, and rural labor fell, rising property values outstripped the rate of inflation.[40] The lower class, on the other hand, bore the brunt of constantly rising price levels, a point that has been emphasized by Marxist historians.[41] Inflation also placed the middle class at a disadvantage, but it was better equipped to defend itself, especially that sector of it that was employed by the state, as the numerous laws raising salaries of government employees that were passed after 1891 suggest.[42]

Chilean policy makers may not have been solely responsible for the depreciation of the peso,[43] but they certainly did little to arrest it. After a disastrous attempt to return to the gold standard in 1895, the Chilean congress repeatedly rejected proposals to stabilize the currency and regularly approved large issues of inconvertible paper pesos, thereby exacerbating inflationary pressures. A return to the gold standard was only achieved in 1925, after the parliamentary system had collapsed.[44]

Exchange and monetary policies consequently emphasize the elitist thrust of Chilean government policy during the parliamentary period. Instead of responding to the demands of groups at the middle or lower end of the socioeconomic continuum, tax, commercial, exchange, and monetary policies all shifted in directions advantageous to Chile's socioeconomic elite. Changes in the pattern of government spending failed to offset these gains, particularly since direct taxes made only a minimal and decreasingly important contribution to the government's revenue base after 1891. The central characteristic of fiscal policy during the 1891-1924 period was irresponsibility: increased spending associated with increased indebtedness for no particularly productive end. The immediate political situation, especially the need to respond to demands for government jobs, concerned policy makers, rather than longer range goals. The one significant benefit the country derived from the pattern of spending was the growth in the public education system.

Increased public spending on education and the expansion of the bureaucracy both had positive implications for middle-sector groups. The lower class may also have derived some benefit from shifting patterns of expenditure, especially the expansion of spending for public education and health and welfare activities. Allocations for worker housing, although minute, did set a precedent for action on behalf of the working class. Yet these gains for popular-sector interests had no negative implications for groups at the upper end of the socioeconomic continuum. They were purchased instead at the expense of the rising living costs associated with revenue deficits, peso devaluation, and protective tariffs. Moreover, the two most marked shifts in the pattern of public spending—the growth in allocations for education and public-sector employment—did not exclusively benefit middle- or lower-class groups. Higher education, for example, expanded even more rapidly than primary education.

Overall, this evidence suggests that the shift to a competitive system failed to reduce inequalities in the distribution of political power. Chile's socioeconomic elite not only retained privileged access to decision-making positions; it derived major policy benefits from the introduction of the parliamentary system. Significantly, a reversal of controversial policies having a differential social impact, such as the cattle duty and peso devaluation, immediately followed the collapse of that system.

GOVERNMENT POLICY IN ARGENTINA

In the Argentine case the analysis of fiscal, commercial, monetary, and exchange policies yields a more mixed and tentative set of conclusions. Various aspects of Argentine government policy worked in opposition to one another, making it difficult to identify "winners" and "losers." The problems involved in drawing inferences about political influence from public policy are further complicated by the lack of reliable data on public expenditures and revenues. The national government, particularly during the 1920s, published little information about its finances, and serious discrepancies appear between various sets of statistics.[45] A related difficulty is that few published data series cover the whole of the 1900-1930 period. Given the disparities that exist among various sources, identifying trends becomes extremely difficult. In constructing the tables that appear in this chapter, every effort has been made to overcome this problem. When it has not been possible to locate a single data series or two overlapping and comparable ones, the time period has been reduced to minimize the chances of distortion. If contradictions among sources have raised serious questions about the rate and direction of change, this problem has been frankly indicated.

Argentine Government Expenditures

As indicated above in Table 24, Argentine national government expenditures grew rapidly after the introduction of competitive party politics.[46] The distribution of national government expenditures also shifted over time. As Table 33 shows, the proportion of funds allocated to public works dropped dramatically, while expenditures on pensions, salaries, and administration increased steadily, averaging 50.0 percent of total expenditures between 1905 and 1916 as compared to 59.5 percent between 1916 and 1922. The share of expenditures allocated to the public debt also rose from an average of 19.3 percent to 24.3 percent in these two time periods. The only category of spending that did not register significant change over time was defense, which on average received a 14 percent share of total expenditures both before and after 1916.

The increase in the proportion of government resources devoted to pensions, salaries, and administration after 1916 may be related directly to party competition, which, as in Chile, created new pressures and incentives for the expansion of state patronage. According to a special study of government employment undertaken in 1923, the national bureaucracy more than tripled in size between 1903 and 1922. The figures presented in Table 34, which were drawn from this study, indicate that employment opportunities grew especially rapidly in teaching and the autonomous institutions.[47] Taken together these two categories accounted for

TABLE 33

ARGENTINA: DISTRIBUTION OF NATIONAL GOVERNMENT
EXPENDITURES, 1905-1922
(Percentages)

Year	Public Works	Public Debt	Defense	Pensions	Administration	Salaries	Total
1905	31.2	25.3	11.7	1.8	14.0	15.9	99.9
1906	17.4	21.6	11.1	3.3	24.1	22.4	99.9
1907	13.3	20.8	12.3	3.5	25.7	24.4	100.0
1908	13.6	21.4	12.4	3.7	24.8	24.1	100.0
1909	24.2	14.4	12.7	2.6	28.8	17.2	99.9
1910	22.7	15.3	20.6	2.4	19.1	20.0	100.1
1911	23.2	15.6	19.7	3.0	19.4	19.1	100.0
1912	18.4	18.3	16.7	3.2	20.1	23.2	99.9
1913	17.3	19.9	14.7	3.6	20.7	23.8	100.0
1914	17.7	19.2	12.6	3.5	22.5	24.4	99.9
1915	16.7	20.5	12.8	4.3	23.0	22.6	100.0
1916	8.5	22.3	13.2	4.2	27.4	24.4	100.0
1917	4.3	24.0	13.0	4.9	31.3	22.5	100.0
1918	3.9	28.1	13.7	5.6	29.3	19.3	99.9
1919	3.8	29.7	14.5	4.2	27.2	20.7	100.1
1920	5.8	23.0	15.2	3.6	31.5	20.9	100.0
1921[a]	6.8	22.4	16.5	3.9	25.2	25.2	100.0
1922[a]	8.5	20.4	15.3	2.5	25.4	28.0	100.1

SOURCE: Argentina, *Los gastos públicos*, pp. 6-7.

NOTE: Figures exclude expenditures of autonomous institutions and for years 1918-1921 transfers from previous years. Figures may not total 100 due to rounding.

[a]Estimates.

approximately 35 percent of total national government employment in 1922, as compared to only 17.5 percent in 1903. Moreover, these figures suggest that the increase in the proportion of national expenditures allocated to salaries between 1905 and 1922 was even greater than previously indicated, because the autonomous institutions were not funded through the ordinary budget. The total expenditures of these institutions—which in the

1920s included the Consejo Nacional de Educación, Ferrocarriles de Estado, Banco de la Nación, Obras Sanitarias, and Banco Hipotecario—amounted to approximately $89 million paper pesos in 1922 or 12.7 percent of total spending.[48] Assuming that the average salary paid by the autonomous institutions and the regular branches of the administration was roughly the same, it can be estimated that at least 35 percent of all funds spent by the national treasury and the autonomous institutions in 1922 were allocated to salaries.[49]

Table 34 also provides evidence that, as in Chile, state education expanded rapidly during the initial stages of party competition. The number of teaching personnel increased 522 percent between 1903 and 1922. Figures on student enrollments tend to confirm this trend. Between 1910 and 1930 the number of primary school students doubled. As in Chile, however, opportunities for secondary and higher education grew even faster.[50] The precise role played by the national government in these trends is difficult to assess, because education was financed partially by special funds not included in the national budget. Nevertheless, Table 35, which provides a partial and rather rough guide to the distribution of expenditures between 1910 and 1926, does show that the expenditures of the Ministry of Justice and Public Education increased very rapidly relative to those of other government departments after 1910.[51]

Two other government departments also increased their spending with exceptional rapidity between 1910 and 1926. Ignoring the figure for 1922, which is almost certainly erroneous,[52] the Ministry of the Interior's expenditures doubled in this period as did those of the Ministry of Finance, while total government expenditures increased only 80 percent.[53] As in the case of Chile, these increases may be related to the expansion of public employment and the public debt. Expenditures on pensions also increased rapidly, confirming a trend indicated previously.

Two other notable trends indicated by Table 35 are the declining importance of expenditures on agriculture and public works. Allocations to the Ministry of Agriculture, which theoretically constituted a prime source of support for agricultural as distinct from pastoral interests, averaged $17.9 million pesos in the

TABLE 34

ARGENTINA: NATIONAL GOVERNMENT PERSONNEL, 1903 and 1922

	1903	1922	Percent Increase
1. Administration	5,544	23,535	324
2. Post and telegraph	5,872	20,949	256
3. Teaching	4,179	25,982	522
4. Police	8,046	13,898	72
5. Military	19,097	40,487	112
6. Autonomous institutions[a]	4,000[b]	28,005	600
Total	46,738	152,856	227

SOURCE: Argentina, Dirreción General de Estadística de la Nación, *Personal de los servicios públicos desde 1903 hasta 1923*, Informe No. 3, Serie A, No. 1, 1923, p. 5.

[a]Excluding teaching personnel.

[b]Approximate figure.

years before 1916 as compared to $19.0 million between 1916 and 1927. Its share of public expenditures consequently declined over time, indicating that relatively disadvantaged farm groups did not derive much benefit from political party competition.[54] Since nonvoting immigrants made up the bulk of the farm population, this trend appears to confirm the importance of electoral channels of influence. The implications of the sharp decline in public works expenditures for the inferential analysis of political influence are less clear, although it might be argued that the development of the economic infrastructure was sacrificed to expand the Radicals' patronage system. Even in the 1926-1930 period, when the trend away from public works expenditures was reversed, public works still received a smaller proportion of government funds than in the 1905-1914 decade.[55]

One other trend worth noting is the increase in military appropriations that took place after the war. Relative to other types of expenditures, defense spending rose rapidly during the Alvear administration, reaching a figure of $213.1 million pesos in

TABLE 35

ARGENTINA: DISTRIBUTION OF NATIONAL
EXPENDITURES, 1910-1926
(Millions of paper pesos)

	1910	1912	1913	1916	1918	1920	1922	1924	1926
Congress	4.4	5.1	4.9	4.6	4.6	5.2	5.9	5.8	5.7
Interior	38.2	47.2	51.5	49.9	48.6	67.5	106.8	74.4	76.2
For. Rel.	8.9	7.4	4.9	4.6	4.4	5.9	8.1	8.0	9.0
Finance[a]	83.9	94.1	106.6	123.4	150.1	152.6	159.6	151.9	172.7
Jus. & Educ.	44.7	53.2	64.4	63.9	69.5	81.2	93.5	93.9	98.2
Defense	93.1	71.9	69.1	52.7	63.8	79.7	97.5	105.4	126.6
Agricul.	23.5	15.4	15.3	12.9	13.5	18.8	21.1	17.0	20.8
Pub. Wks.	103.2	87.8	70.9	37.2	39.6	47.4	83.6	67.4	83.1
Pensions	11.1	12.7	14.5	14.9	16.8	17.1	17.1	22.1	22.3
Other	– –	9.5	12.7	14.6	10.2	13.2	14.4	19.1	18.5
Total	411.0	404.3	414.8	378.7	421.1	488.6	607.6	464.9	633.1

SOURCE: "Comparativo, por anexo, de gastos autorizados y efectuados con imputación a presupuesto, a leyes especiales y acuerdos de gobierno, 1910-1927," Argentina, Cámara de Diputados, *Diario de sesiones*, 1928, V, 455-467.

[a]Including public debt.

1927.[56] Even by prewar standards, this figure represented a high proportion of government funds.

Unfortunately, the distribution of government expenditures during the last years of the Radical era remains obscure. The annual budgets offer no real guidance, because they were presented in an extremely unsystematic form and over time authorized a smaller and smaller proportion of public expenditures.[57] The national legislature obstructed and delayed the passage of the budget to such an extent that the old one was frequently extended into the new financial year and, as in the case of the budget of 1923, far beyond. Moreover, no single agency of government assumed responsibility for preparing the budget, so it did not necessarily fulfill or reflect the requirements of the administration. Finally, many of the autonomous institutions, although theoretically self-supporting, accumulated deficits, and special authorizations of funds were required to rescue them from bankruptcy.[58]

Argentine Government Revenues

One category of public expenditure that clearly grew rapidly in the 1926-1930 period was the national public debt. Table 36 traces the growth of revenues, expenditures, and the public debt between 1900 and 1930. During the first nine years of this period the government pursued a cautious fiscal policy: revenues increased 77 percent and the public debt was reduced. But from 1909 onward the picture was increasingly one of financial disequilibrium. With the single exception of 1920, when the end of the war brought a flood of imports into the country, revenues consistently failed to cover expenditures. The deficits steadily accumulated into a large floating debt, and by 1922 the annual service on the debt absorbed 33.7 percent of national revenues.[59] During the years leading up to the war growing indebtedness was linked with heavy expenditures on public works, from which some long-term return might be anticipated. Under Radical administrations public works expenditures dwindled, and the debt grew mainly to finance ordinary administrative expenses. Although deficit financing did not begin or end with the war, disruption in international credit arrangements and trade during the 1914-1918 period provided a major impetus to this trend.

When the Radicals assumed office in 1916 public finances were in a particularly precarious state. As Table 37 shows, import duties, which were the major source of public revenue, fell quite sharply between 1913 and 1916 and continued to fall for another two years. Expenditures were cut back while attempts were made to find supplementary sources of income. Partially because genuine tax reform proposals such as that of August 1918, which called for a graduated corporate and personal income tax, were totally unacceptable to the opposition,[60] the search was not very successful, and it ended with the imposition of a tax on pastoral and agricultural exports whose prices exceeded certain fixed levels.[61] In 1918, the year the law took effect, the tax yielded a sum equiva-

TABLE 36

ARGENTINA: THE GROWTH OF NATIONAL GOVERNMENT
EXPENDITURES, REVENUES, AND THE PUBLIC DEBT, 1900-1930
(Millions of gold pesos)

Year	National Revenues		National Expenditures		Public Debt	
	Pesos	Index	Pesos	Index	Pesos	Index
1900	64.9	100	68.6	100	447.2	100
1902	65.5	101	85.3	125	435.7	98
1904	87.7	135	85.8	125	426.6	95
1906	102.0	157	118.9	174	379.6	85
1908	115.8	177	111.0	162	398.9	89
1910	135.7	209	180.9	264	490.1	110
1912	159.9	246	177.8	260	575.0	129
1914	124.2	191	184.6	269	657.8	147
1916	112.2	173	164.8	241	773.6	173
1918	145.2	224	185.2	270	891.2	199
1920	228.4	352	214.6	314	853.5	191
1922	203.8	314	270.7	396	962.5	215
1924	250.4	385	295.7	431	999.0[a]	224
1926	281.7	434	328.6	478	1100.6	246
1928	319.3	492	388.8	567	1251.3	280
1930	324.2	499	481.0	702	1517.7	340

SOURCE: Argentina, *La deuda pública*, pp. 8-9 (1900-1918); Peters, pp. 73-74 (1920-1930); expenditures as for Table 31.

[a]Approximate figure.

lent to 16.5 percent of the government's total revenues. It proved more lucrative in 1919 and 1920, but thereafter the value of agricultural exports did not rise significantly and some export duties were lowered.[62] By 1924, which was an exceptionally good year for Argentine exports, the tax yielded only 7 percent of government income. Nevertheless, because of the tax the proportion of revenues derived from customs duties remained relatively constant over time.

Some further idea of the impact of party competition on the Argentine tax system may be derived from Table 38, which compares the tax revenues of the national government in 1910 with

TABLE 37

ARGENTINA: MAJOR SOURCES OF NATIONAL GOVERNMENT
REVENUES, 1903-1930
(Millions of paper pesos)

Year	Customs Imports	Exports	Internal Taxes Direct	Indirect	Other	Total
1903	65.2	– – –	10.6	63.5	32.1	171.4
1904	91.6	– – –	11.6	49.9	35.6	188.7
1905	99.8	– – –	13.6	40.9	42.6	196.9
1906	121.4	– – –	14.1	40.0	51.3	226.8
1907	128.8	– – –	16.0	43.3	53.1	241.2
1908	136.7	– – –	16.6	45.5	56.8	255.6
1909	149.9	– – –	18.6	47.1	60.5	306.1
1910	173.0	– – –	18.8	49.3	65.0	306.1
1911	177.0	– – –	20.5	52.6	63.7	313.8
1912	188.4	– – –	22.6	58.8	68.9	338.7
1913	199.2	– – –	26.4	60.6	67.5	353.7
1914	118.4	– – –	23.3	48.6	59.8	250.1
1915	94.9	– – –	21.2	60.3	60.8	237.2
1916	104.9	– – –	21.5	54.8	59.3	240.5
1917	96.7	– – –	24.2	58.9	61.2	241.0
1918	88.5	50.9	31.8	67.3	69.8	308.3
1919	111.3	68.3	38.9	80.6	90.5	389.6
1920	160.3	96.8	44.0	91.8	101.0	493.9
1921	160.5	42.3	41.4	88.0	123.4	456.5
1922	183.1	23.2	41.8	90.4	100.4	438.9
1923	242.5	25.2	45.0	104.5	107.2	524.4
1924	256.4	39.3	60.7	83.9	137.3	577.6
1925	302.4	47.5	64.6	101.9	126.9	643.3
1926	285.9	17.7	65.1	105.4	145.2	619.3
1927	301.3	11.4	66.2	108.0	171.5	658.4
1928	330.1	28.3	69.0	111.8	163.7	702.9
1929	337.9	18.1	70.7	118.1	173.2	718.0
1930	281.3	9.4	69.1	106.6	155.0	621.4

SOURCE: Carlos F. Soares, *Economia y finanzas de la Nación Argentina, 1903-1913* (Buenos Aires, 1913), chart ff. p. 66; Argentina, *Memoria de la Contaduría General*, 1931, Cuadro 23, p. 53.

TABLE 38

ARGENTINA: NATIONAL TAX REVENUES, 1910 and 1924[a]
(Thousands of paper pesos)

Taxes	1910		1924	
	Pesos	%	Pesos	%
1. Land	12,809	5.0	32,425	6.6
2. Exports	– – –	– –	46,198	9.3
3. Patents	5,573	2.6	19,362	3.9
4. Imports	174,452	67.6	260,479	52.8
5. Internal excise	49,176	19.1	82,093	17.8
6. Civil, judicial, and commercial trans-actions[b]	14,378	5.2	41,165	8.3
7. Inheritance	1,610	0.6	6,878	1.4
Total	257,998	100.1	494,680	100.1

SOURCE: Argentina, Dirección General de Estadística de la Nación, *Los Impuestos y otros recursos fiscales de la nación y las provincias en los años 1910 y 1924-1925*, Informe No. 17, Serie F, No. 4, 1926, p. 50.

[a]Including tax revenues allocated to the Consejo Nacional de Educación, the Federal Capital, the territories, and the Fondo de Subsidios.

[b]Primarily stamp taxes.

1924, by which time the disruptive effects of the war had largely disappeared. The table includes all the taxes collected by the national government, even those whose proceeds were assigned to the Consejo Nacional de Educación, the Federal Capital, and the territories. Such taxes were not counted as part of the government's general revenues, but because they made up a high proportion of direct taxation they cannot be excluded from consideration without distorting the nature of the tax system.

Between 1910 and 1924 the general revenues of the national government doubled in value. Tax revenues also doubled in this period, so the proportion of revenues derived from taxation remained relatively constant: 81.2 percent in 1910 and 78.5 in 1924.[63] The government collected its remaining revenues from a variety of state enterprises and services, including the railways, post office, port facilities, telegraphs, and the national lottery. Although the Radicals failed to introduce any basic tax reforms, the distribution of the tax burden in 1910 and 1924 did differ in terms of the relative importance of taxes placed on production and consumption. Between 1910 and 1924 the proportion of tax revenues derived from import and internal excise duties declined from 86.7 to 70.5 percent of the total, chiefly benefitting the domestic consumer. Domestic producers, on the other hand, were not well served by this decline or by the additional export tax, which amounted to about 2 percent of the total value of exports.

Table 38 also provides evidence of a shift towards heavier direct taxation. Relative to 1910 inheritance tax revenues increased 325 percent and property taxes 150 percent. But this tendency was minor and could not have had any significant impact on the distribution of wealth. If provincial taxation is taken into consideration, the overall picture remains much the same. Between 1910 and 1924/25 the proportion of provincial tax revenues that were collected from taxes on land, agriculture, industry, the professions, and various civil, judicial, and commercial transactions all declined; taxes on inheritance and consumption, on the other hand, became increasingly important. Yet, because the provinces collected only 20.2 percent of total public tax revenues in 1910 and 28.9 percent in 1924/25,[64] the overall incidence of public taxation shifted in the directions indicated by Table 38. A slight increase in the relative importance of direct taxation accompanied a major shift in the tax burden from consumption to production.

How these tax changes actually affected various groups in Argentine society remains uncertain, because the tax system was only one variable affecting the situation and at times it worked in opposition to other aspects of government policy. Nevertheless, it appears that the relative reduction in import duties coupled with the agricultural export tax, which favored the domestic consumption of meat and cereals over exports, benefitted popular-sector groups in Argentina by stabilizing prices and increasing real wages. Between 1913 and 1930 the cost of living rose more slowly in Argentina than in most other countries.[65] Partially as a result, real wages, which fell sharply during the war, rose steadily after 1919 as did the wage share of the GDP. Between 1914 and 1925-29, real wages increased 40 percent, while per capita GDP grew only 26 percent.[66] Government monetary and exchange policies favored price stability as well. In contrast to Chile, the monetary supply expanded in line with gold stocks. After the war the peso did depreciate with respect to other world currencies, but taking the 1914-1929 period as a whole, it was one of the world's more stable currencies.[67]

Commercial Policy

The decline in the proportion of government revenues derived from import duties raises a number of important questions about the nature of Argentine commercial policy and its differential social impact. Much as in the Chilean case, a variety of observers have argued that the Argentine government pursued a free trade policy throughout the 1916-1930 period and levied duties on imported goods solely to raise revenues.[68] The supposed lack of a protectionist policy, in turn, has been taken as an indicator of the political weakness of local industrial groups vis-à-vis rural exporters and foreign interests.[69] In view of the immigrant origins of entrepreneurs, the small size of local industrial establishments, and the importance of foreign capital and rural exports to the economy as a whole, this interpretation sounds highly plausible. Nevertheless, it fails to square with available evidence.

Beginning in the 1870s the Argentine congress passed a series of tariff laws that were designed explicitly to encourage domestic industry, both in the littoral and interior regions of the country. A tariff law that went into effect in 1906 introduced major revisions in these laws and established a schedule of duties that remained in force throughout the Radical era with only a few legislative modifications.[70] As indicated by Table 39, the tariff levels established by this law measured up favorably to those of most industrialized countries in the world in the pre-1930 period. The same is true if only manufactured imports are considered. A 1927 League of Nations study revealed that the average Argentine tariff on a selected list of manufactured commodities, although lower

TABLE 39

IMPORT DUTIES AS A PERCENTAGE OF TOTAL IMPORTS FOR A
SELECTED LIST OF COUNTRIES, 1913 AND 1925

	1913	1925		1913	1925
Argentina	17.7	15.1	Germany	8.2	4.8
Australia	16.5	18.5	Italy	9.6	8.3
Belgium	1.6	3.2	Spain	14.8	23.6
Canada	17.1	15.1	United Kingdom	5.7	9.6
Chile	17.2	15.4	U.S.A.	17.7 (1912-13)	13.2
France	8.8	3.3		14.9 (1913-14)	— —

SOURCE: League of Nations, Economic and Financial Section, *Tariff Level Indices* (Geneva, 1927), p. 21; Chile, *Anuario estadístico*, 1925, VI, 14, 66.

than that of the USA, Spain, and Poland, exceeded that of the majority of countries in Western Europe.[71] In addition, the structure of import duties favored industrial development. Raw materials were generally admitted duty free or at lower rates than finished products.[72] In short, Argentine commercial policy in the years 1916-1930 cannot legitimately be characterized as "free trade" or used to support assertions that industrialists lacked political influence. Like Chile, Argentina adopted a commercial policy favorable to industrial development long before the 1930s, although in the Argentine case this policy emerged prior to the development of a competitive political system.

The changes that did occur in Argentine commercial policy after 1916 largely reflect the failure of congress to respond to rising world prices. Argentine tariffs were fixed in accordance with a nominal scale of values, and the ratio of total import duties to the total tariff value of imports remained relatively constant from 1906 until the late 1920s. But as prices rose during the war in response to factors such as the high cost of shipping, the discrepancy between nominal tariff values and real prices grew, and import duties were in effect lowered. During the war little incentive existed for congress to revise tariff values. Shortages of imported materials and credit, not foreign competition, were crippling local industries. The situation changed after the war, and in both 1920 and 1923 protectionist forces successfully pressed for legislation designed to bring *aforo* or tariff values more closely into line with world prices. Despite these revisions, a gap between real and nominal values persisted until the late 1920s, and tariffs never regained prewar levels. From 1920 to 1929 import duties as a percentage of the real value of total imports averaged 13.5 percent as compared to 19.7 percent during the 1905-1914 period.[73]

Comparisons between 1909 and 1927 indicate that some important changes in the structure of tariffs accompanied this decline in tariff levels. In 1909 the tariff revenues collected on all categories of imports averaged 21.7 percent of the real value of total imports.[74] For most foodstuffs and beverages the percentage was considerably higher. For example, import duties as a percentage of the real value of imports exceeded the average 21.7 percent figure in the case of the following categories of goods: spices and condiments (62.2), vegetables and cereals (26.2), substances for infusion and hot beverages (28.0), animal foodstuffs (40.2), flour, macaroni, fancy breads, etc. (32.5), and wines (65.7). In contrast, for certain categories of manufactured imports, such as electrical machinery and metal manufactures, duties as a percentage of the real value of imports were lower than the average 21.7 percent figure.

The situation was rather different in 1927. Revenues collected as a percentage of imports indicate that tariffs remained high for many categories of food and drink imports, but others fell well below the average tariff level. For example, whereas duties as a pecentage of the real value of all imports averaged 15.5 in 1927, the percentage in the case of animal foodstuffs equalled only 14.1. Moreover, duties on most foodstuffs and beverages had dropped more than those on other products, as a percentage of both the real and tariff value of imports. Concomitantly, duties as a percentage of both the real and nominal value of selected manufactured imports, such as paper, metal, and electrical manufactures, had risen above average levels. The difference between duties collected on raw materials and manufactured products also increased over time, creating a tariff structure more favorable to industrial development. In the case of imports of iron and steel, for example, statistics on duties collected as a percentage of imports show duties were lower for manufactures in 1909 than for raw and semi-finished products. The reverse was true in 1927.[75]

Import duties as a percentage of imports represents a rather crude measure of protection, and it is possible that changes in the composition of imports within broad import categories account for some of these apparent shifts in tariff structure. Nevertheless, the contrasts between 1909 and 1927 indicate that on the whole commercial policy between 1916 and 1930 became more favorable to industrialists and domestic consumers at the expense of importers and producers of foreign manufactures. Sharp drops in duties collected as a percentage of both the nominal and real value of food and beverage imports indicate that the shifts in tariff structure also worked against the interests of producers in the rural and interior regions of Argentina, including the traditionally favored wine industry.

This assessment of the differential social impact of changes in commercial policy does not necessarily conflict with Carl Solberg's analysis of tariff politics in the 1916-1930 period, even though Solberg concluded that commercial policy, both before and after 1916, was molded to suit the needs of cattle producers and the Sociedad Rural.[76] Since no major revision of tariff legislation emerged from the Argentine congress between 1916 and 1930, considerable continuity did characterize commercial policy over time. Furthermore, with the notable exception of the sugar tariff issue, which ended in a victory for consumer groups concerned with inflation, the major pieces of tariff legislation adopted between 1916 and 1930 secured the support of the Sociedad Rural and Conservative legislators. In the immediate postwar period, when the Radical government faced serious revenue problems and the real incidence of tariffs had fallen to relatively low levels, the Radical party also supported protectionist legislation. Thereafter, Radical administrations lent little support to protectionist policies, and partially because of the importance of regional conflicts, proposals for changes in tariff policy left Radicals in the legislature thoroughly divided. The Socialists, who represented a more coherent set of regional and class interests, unanimously opposed the protectionist measures adopted between 1916 and 1930. Unlike the Chilean Democrats, they viewed even industrial protection as an assault on working-class interests.[77]

Partially because of the failure of the Socialists to marshall a majority of votes against protectionist legislation, Solberg concluded that rural-producer interests triumphed over those of urban consumers. But *relative to the pre-1916 period*, policy did not change in directions that favored rural producers over industrial or even consumer interests. The decline in the incidence of tariffs associated with rising world prices placed protectionist forces in a defensive position. They sought a restitution of lost privileges and backed legislation that represented an acceptable compromise among disparate protariff interests in the face of strong and increasingly vociferous opposition. The element of compromise must be stressed, because as in Chile commercial legislation was shaped by a complex logrolling process involving very specific sets of interests rather than broad conflict among sectoral, regional, or class interests. Until the late 1920s, when the threat of British protectionism led cattle exporters to favor bilateral treaties lowering tariff barriers, the Sociedad Rural participated in this process and joined the Unión Industrial and other producer groups in supporting the ensuing legislation; but the tariff bills passed by the legislature did not necessarily represent an optimal outcome from the perspective of the Sociedad Rural or any other group interested in protection. Consequently, evidence that the Sociedad Rural supported the winning coalition on most congressional floor votes dealing with the tariff issue between 1916 and 1930 provides no basis for assuming that it successfully pushed for a restoration of the status quo ante or shifted commercial policy, relative to the pre-1916 period, in directions favored by cattle producers. The Unión Industrial also supported protectionist legislation, and the laws passed between 1916 and 1930 might just as plausibly be construed as a victory for industrialists. Indeed, the analysis of the tariff structure points strongly in favor of the latter conclusion and suggests that the alignment of congressional forces on tariff votes provides a somewhat misleading basis for drawing inferences about changes in commercial policy and their differential social impact. Not surprisingly, commercial policy between 1916 and

1930 reflected the demands of cattle exporters, who constituted the most powerful producer group in Argentine society; but the evidence also shows that party competition led to shifts in commercial policy corresponding to the interests of consumers and industrialists rather than rural exporters.

Exchange Policy

The central thrust of Argentine exchange policy was rather different. The Argentine peso was convertible to gold from 1899 to 1914, when a variety of difficulties associated with the outbreak of war led the government to declare peso inconvertibility. This exchange policy lasted until August 1927 when the peso returned to par, curbing a tendency towards peso appreciation. In the intervening years the peso fluctuated against its gold parity and other world currencies, and excepting the 1971-1920 period of balance-of-payments surpluses, the currency depreciated in value relative to 1916. Thus exchange policy apparently promoted both export and import-competing activities at the expense of importers and those remitting profits abroad. During the one period in which the government took no action to check the appreciation of the peso, there was little threat of foreign competition, but a great deal to be said in favor of a measure that promoted price stability.

Indices of real devaluation with respect to the United States and Great Britain, which take into account relative price levels, are presented in Table 40. They indicate that the Radical governments' exchange and monetary policies more than offset declining tariff rates and thus improved the competitive position of all domestic producers relative to 1914. Drawing conclusions about the relative political influence of different groups from this evidence, however, represents a hazardous undertaking. Devaluation might be attributed to the pressures of industrialists, rural exporters, or even to factors beyond the control of Argentine policy makers. The causal relationships are even more complex with respect to real devaluation, which was a function of exchange policy and the cost of living in Argentina relative to other countries. The latter factor obviously cannot be related solely to policy decisions made in Argentina. Assessing the real social impact of

TABLE 40

ARGENTINA: INDICES OF EXCHANGE RATES AND
REAL DEVALUATION, 1914-1929
(1914 = 100)

| | Exchange Rates | | Real Devaluation | |
	Paper Pesos per U.S. Dollar	Paper Pesos per U.K. Pound	Toward U.S.	Toward U.K.
1914	100	100	100	100
1915	101	99	95	113
1916	100	98	94	123
1917	96	94	91	122
1918	95	93	83	110
1919	97	88	105	118
1920	108	80	114	106
1921	133	105	142	141
1922	117	107	139	139
1923	123	115	151	145
1924	124	112	150	139
1925	105	104	134	134
1926	104	104	138	135
1927	100	100	131	127
1928	100	100	131	127
1929	101	101	132	126

SOURCE: Díaz Alejandro, pp. 297, 298.

exchange policy is equally problematic. Not only did commercial policy shift in a somewhat contradictory direction, but real wages rose substantially in Argentina after 1919, undercutting the apparent benefits of exchange policy for domestic producers. Devaluation theoretically benefits domestic producers because it is assumed that their costs, including wages, increase more slowly than the prices of exported or imported goods. Rising real wages call into question the validity of this assumption in the Argentine case, particularly with respect to import-competing industries that depended heavily on imports of raw materials and machinery.

In summary, the analysis of fiscal, monetary, and exchange policies in the Argentine case yields a set of somewhat ambiguous conclusions about the impact of party competition on the distribution of policy costs and benefits. In some areas of policy it is hard to pinpoint the groups that gained most from government policy, much less draw inferences about political influence. Nevertheless, the overall pattern of policy change was very different from that emerging in Chile after the introduction of a competitive system. Whereas in Chile policy shifts highly beneficial to socioeconomic elites followed the introduction of competitive party politics, in Argentina no major changes of this type occurred. Argentine policy makers may have failed to introduce fundamental tax reforms or mount any straightforward attack on the distribution of wealth; but, in contrast to their Chilean counterparts, they did not actually cut taxes on wealth and property. Instead, the Argentine tax system became moderately more progressive over time, reducing the tax burden on consumers. Similarly, while protectionist forces shaped Argentine commercial policy after 1916, consumer groups also made some headway. In Chile, on the other hand, consumers lost ground to producer groups. The two countries differed even more markedly with respect to exchange and monetary policies. In Chile a rapidly depreciating peso advantaged socioeconomic elites at the expense of popular-sector interests. The differential social impact of Argentine exchange policy not only remains far more ambiguous, but the bias towards a depreciated exchange rate was modest in comparison to Chile. As a whole the 1916-1930 period in Argentina was characterized by a stable currency, and with the exception of the war years, real wages rose relatively steadily. In short, unlike Chile, groups at the upper end of the socioeconomic continuum in Argentina reaped no major gains from the changes in fiscal, commercial, exchange, and monetary policies that followed the emergence of a competitive party system.

Within the framework of these contrasts, certain similarities between Argentine and Chilean policy can be identified. In both countries changes in spending patterns enlarged opportunities for public education and employment. Particularly notable was the trend towards the swelling of the state bureaucracy, which provided a means of satisfying the growing patronage demands of party leaders. A modest shift towards increased welfare spending may also have characterized both countries, but the limitations of Argentine budgetary data make this unclear. General similarities in fiscal policy formation, however, are quite evident. In both countries fiscal policies appear to have been designed with a view towards short-term political considerations. Hence the public debt mounted merely to finance ordinary administrative expenses, bureaucratic growth, and the related expansion of patronage channels.

These similarities and differences between public policy in Argentina and Chile are consistent with the evidence derived from the analysis of elite social backgrounds. In the case of Argentina, patterns of both political recruitment and policy formation suggest a lessening of elite control over political outcomes and a reduction in political inequality. In the case of Chile, on the other hand, changes in who benefitted from policy as much as trends in who made policy point toward the consolidation of elite control over the state. Nevertheless, the review of fiscal, monetary, and exchange policies leaves open a number of important questions, particularly since the manipulation of the socioeconomic environment through progressive taxation, exchange policy, and other such measures represents a relatively recent technique of government control. To obtain a more explicit idea of the orientations of policy makers in Chile and Argentina during the first decades of the twentieth century a broader range of government policies must be considered. Major conflicts among social groups in both countries developed over regulatory and symbolic policies that are not directly reflected in government budgets or exchange rates.

CHAPTER VII

CHILEAN AND ARGENTINE LEGISLATION

Legislative records provide additional evidence of the divergent impact of party competition in Argentina and Chile. Laws are policy statements of symbolic significance, even though they do not always describe the informal and often undocumented acts that shape public policy. Laws also capture dimensions of public policy that are not manifested in allocative decisions. The right of workers to organize and strike, the regulation of hours and working conditions, the obligation of employers to assume responsibility for work injuries, and restrictions on foreign investment—all of these issues were resolved in Argentina and Chile by decisions altering the preexisting distribution of policy costs and benefits; yet decisions of this type were not directly reflected in government budgets. The legislative records of Argentina and Chile consequently supply information that is important for assessing the impact of party competition. As inventories of the major authoritative decisions affecting broad social groups, such records supplement the preceding analysis of policy outputs and make it possible to obtain a comprehensive overview of public policy in the years following the introduction of party competition.

Two general concepts are useful in assessing the legislative records of Argentina and Chile during the initial period of party competition. The first is the *scope* of government policy. Insofar as party competition enhanced the political influence of groups at the middle or lower end of the socioeconomic spectrum, one might expect to see evidence of growing government control over society, at least with regard to the range of private activities brought within the purview of the state. Lower-class groups in Western Europe and North America have sought historically to use the influence afforded them by the vote in such a manner; and although the expansion of state control in particular historical situations may be seen as a response to military, ideological, or other imperatives, the argument that party competition reduces power differentials in a society is hollow unless it is conceded that political influence derives significance from and is directed toward the modification of private power relationships. To take some concrete examples, urban workers in both Chile and Argentina demanded that the state expand its control over the economy by regulating hours, wages, and working conditions. Similarly, tenant farmers in Argentina sought wider state intervention to compensate for their weak bargaining position vis-à-vis rural landholders. A key issue is the extent to which such relatively disadvantaged groups were able to limit the sphere of private decision making by enlisting the support of the government in their socioeconomic struggles.

Related to the question of scope is what may be called the *focus* of policies: the particularity or generality of specific decisions. In an influential essay on public policy, Theodore J. Lowi drew attention to the differences between "distributive" decisions, which are highly individual, specific in impact, and capable of an almost infinite amount of disaggregation, and others—"regulative" and "redistributive"—which establish general criteria and affect broad groups or categories of individuals.[1] Despite the difficulties encountered in the use of Lowi's typology,[2] two very interesting ideas emerge from it. The first is that there is a rough developmental sequence ranging from very particularistic policies of a "pork-barrel" variety to more general ones having a wider social impact. The second is that different types of power relationships, structures of demand, and decision-making units are related to different kinds of political outputs. Lowi's analysis suggests that insofar as party competition encourages political leaders to respond to the preferences of a broader spectrum of society, the *types* of decisions made by authorities will also change. A particularistic, patronage type of approach to policy making theoretically will give way to a more catholic one; concomitantly, decisions will relate increasingly to broad social categories or have a wider focus. The change may be conceptualized as a consequence of shifts in both political demand and political support markets. In a competitive system policy makers presumably must think in terms of the needs of social groups rather than just those of influential individuals or firms.[3]

This analysis of legislation passed in Chile and Argentina following the development of party competition consequently focuses on two general and related questions. To what extent did decision makers respond to a wider variety of social concerns, enlarging the scope of government in the interest of the less privileged? Is there evidence that decisions increasingly were made with reference to broad social groups rather than on an ad hoc, particular, and piecemeal basis?

To organize the subsequent discussion, legislation has been divided into four general substantive areas: health, education, and welfare; industry and commerce; agriculture; and civil liberties. The legislative records of the Argentine and Chilean governments in these four areas are summarized in a series of tables that appear in succeeding pages. The tables are based entirely on offical and quasi-official compilations of laws and legislative bulletins, and they include virtually all laws of a general character relating to health, labor, education, welfare, industry, commerce, agriculture, or civil liberties passed between 1912 and 1930 in the case of Argentina and 1892-1924 in the case of Chile. Laws passed in response to military intervention in the terminal years have been excluded. In cases of doubt the tables tend to err in the direction of inclusiveness, but many laws that by accumulation affected interclass or intersectoral relationships have been omitted.

In both countries the legislature granted tariff exemptions for particular categories of goods, authorized pensions for specific families and individuals, awarded concessions to private railroad companies and other firms, and passed special laws subsidizing hospitals, schools, orphanages, and asylums. The sheer volume of such distributive legislation is impressive and in itself an interesting piece of evidence. Table 41, which provides data on the number and relative importance of distributive laws in randomly selected years, shows that laws of this type accounted for an extremely high proportion of legislative decisions. The proportion remained high over time in Chile, where the party system encouraged a piecemeal, distributive approach to decision making; but in Argentina a decline in legislation having an extremely particular focus occurred during the 1920s.

In addition to the variety of laws classified in Table 41, the subsequent analysis also excludes laws relating to state finances and the monetary system. The volume of legislation of this type also reached considerable proportions, particularly in Chile, where the legislature was constantly passing budgetary supplements, considering proposals to increase the monetary supply, and authorizing new municipal bond issues. The omission of these laws and those of a pork-barrel variety is justified chiefly on the grounds that their cumulative impact has been explored in the previous discussion of monetary, fiscal, and exchange policies. This argument does not pertain to franchises and certain other concessions of privilege, and in a more detailed and limited study of public policy they might warrant further consideration. With a few exceptions, they have been ignored here for purely practical reasons.

SOCIAL POLICY

The first general area of legislation to be explored is social policy, broadly construed to include welfare, health, housing, education, and labor policy. Table 42 summarizes the major pieces of legislation passed in this area during the 1891-1924 period in Chile. Considering the length of this period, the variety of demands and proposals presented to the legislature, and the policies that were being implemented in Western Europe at this time, of which Chileans were fully aware,[4] the record is hardly imposing. Nonetheless, the legislature did depart from previous policy and adopt a few positive measures.

Perhaps the most notable was the 1906 law on worker housing: not a new idea, since such legislation had been proposed as far back as 1887,[5] but the first case of positive government action on behalf of the lower class in Chile. The author of this project was Francisco Huneeus, a Conservative businessman with interests in

TABLE 41

DISTRIBUTIVE LAWS AS A PERCENTAGE OF ALL
LEGISLATION PASSED IN SELECTED YEARS

	Chile							
	1892	1893	1902	1905	1908	1909	1912	1922
Pensions and grati- fications	18.6	18.7	17.8	36.6	24.1	12.0	41.0	30.4
Franchises, tax exemptions & special conces- sions	5.9	18.7	4.8	12.7	8.4	6.7	6.7	6.3
Public works	1.0	4.7	8.1	1.6	6.0	9.3	6.0	5.2
Subsidies	– –	– –	1.6	3.8	8.4	– –	0.7	1.2
Other	2.0	– –	1.6	7.9	8.4	16.0	4.5	10.4
Total	27.5	42.1	33.9	62.6	55.3	44.0	58.9	53.5
(No. of distrib. laws)	(28)	(63)	(21)	(39)	(46)	(33)	(79)	(93)

	Argentina						
	1905	1906	1912	1915	1918	1925	1927
Pensions and grati- fications	50.0	25.9	46.7	85.5	90.2	– –	– –
Franchises, tax exemptions & special conces- sions	7.7	10.1	6.0	0.5	0.4	– –	11.1
Public Works	17.2	18.7	9.5	1.2	0.4	20.0	11.1
Subsidies	3.6	2.9	5.0	– –	0.4	10.0	– –
Other	3.1	7.9	7.5	3.1	0.4	30.0	5.6
Total	81.6	65.5	74.7	90.3	91.8	60.0	27.8
(No. of distrib. laws)	(319)	(91)	(149)	(378)	(261)	(6)	(5)

SOURCE: Anguita, Vols. III and IV; Chile, Consejo de Estado, *Recopilación*, Vol. X; Argentina, Cámara de Senadores, *Diario de Sesiones*, 1905-1927.

both mining and electrical companies, whose declared purpose was to promote the construction of hygenic and cheap housing for the working class. To oversee this activity, the law provided for the formation of a Consejo Superior de Habitaciones, whose members included two presidents of labor organizations (nominated by the Chilean national president), the intendant of Santiago, a representative of the church, and political appointees. In addition to overseeing construction work, the council was charged with inspecting existing housing and empowered to issue repair and demolition orders. Buildings that satisfied its inspectors were to be exempted from taxes and certain charges, such as water rates. The law also authorized the executive to spend $600,000 pesos to provide state employees with low-cost housing.

The ostensibly proworking-class housing law thus contained benefits for a variety of social groups, and the provisions relating to tax exemptions were probably implemented with more enthusiasm than any others. In 1910 the social critic Alejandro Venegas wrote:

> With regard to the construction of housing for workers, I am afraid the thing remains on paper. I believe that up to now nothing positive has been done, and it would not be surprising if most of the funds assigned for this purpose were left unspent and had to be returned to the treasury.[6]

In 1911 the government's Labor Office reached a similar conclusion about the ineffectiveness of the law.[7] Expenditure data also indicate that little money was actually devoted to working-class housing. After salaries and administrative expenditures had been covered, sums such as the $36,000 gold pesos allocated to the housing council in 1920 allowed for little in the way of construction. The legislature ignored these deficiencies throughout the parliamentary period, but they received attention in a series of decree laws on housing shortly after the military intervention of 1924.[8]

Other laws representing government action on behalf of the working class were more strictly regulatory in character: the laws of 1907 and 1917 limiting the working week to six days, the so-called "Ley de Sillas" enjoining owners of commercial establishments to provide a sufficient number of chairs and a period of rest for their employees, the 1916 law placing responsibility for

TABLE 42

CHILE: SOCIAL LEGISLATION, 1892-1924

Law No.	Date	Major Provision
4325[a]	1 Sept. 1892	Establishing Consejo Superior de Higiene Pública and Instituto de Higiene
1838	20 Feb. 1906	"Habitaciones para obreros": provision and inspection of working-class housing
1990	26 Aug. 1907	"Descanso dominical": six-day week in commerce, industry and mining (obligatory for women and children only)
2498	1 Feb. 1911	Savings bank and retirement pensions for state railway employees (extended by law #3074 of 29 March 1916)
2675	26 Aug. 1912	Protection of destitute children
2923	21 Aug. 1914	Funds to assist unemployed workers with food and transport (one of a series of laws of this type: e.g., #2946, 18 Nov. 1914; #3379, 17 July 1919; #3812, 29 Nov. 1921; #3890, 11 Oct. 1922)
2951	25 Nov. 1914	"Ley de Sillas": regulation of working conditions in commercial establishments
3092	24 Apr. 1916	Establishing technical school in Valparaíso
3133	4 Sept. 1916	Antipollution law aimed at industry
3170	27 Dec. 1916	Work-related injuries: liability rests with employer
3186	13 Jan. 1917	Employers responsible for providing child care facilities and rest periods in all factories employing over 50 women
3321	5 Nov. 1917	"Descanso dominical obligatorio": extending coverage of #1990

Table 42 (*Continued*)

Law No.	Date	Major Provision
3365	19 Apr. 1918	Creating industrial schools for study of nitrate production in Antofagasta and Iquique
3379	10 May 1918	Reorganizing social security system for state railway employees (estab. by #2498 and #3074)
3385	22 May 1918	Sanitary Code: establishing administrative bodies to regulate and inspect public health conditions
3654	26 Aug. 1920	Compulsory primary education
3915	9 Feb. 1923	Maximum weight fixed for loads carried by workers
3997	2 Jan. 1924	Extending coverage of #3379

SOURCE: Anguita, Vols. III, IV; Chile, Consejo de Estado, *Recopilación*, Vols. VIII-XI; René Feliú Cruz, comp. *Indice general sinóptico de leyes, decretos leyes y decretos con fuerza de ley dictados desde el 2 de enero de 1913 hasta el 13 de abril de 1936, con los decretos supremos que les fijan textos definitivos y reglamentarios*, 3 vols. (Santiago, 1937-1940).

NOTE: Table excludes legislation passed under military pressure after September 1924.

[a]*Diario Oficial* number.

industrial accidents on the employer, and the statute of 1917 obliging owners of workshops and industrial establishments employing more than fifty women to provide nursery facilities. Few of these laws were really enforced, and many were modified to make them more effective after the military intervened in 1924.[9]

Other regulatory measures applied only to specific groups of workers. Railwaymen profited from several laws granting state pensions, as well as a decree of 1919 that regulated working conditions on the state railways. Nitrate workers were also singled out for special attention. Apart from organizing official inquiries into the conditions of work in the nitrate pampa, the legislature responded to the problem of unemployment in the North in the post-1914 period by passing a series of temporary relief laws that provided workers with food and transport to other regions of the country. During the 1913-1924 period the government also issued decrees regulating the use of explosives in mines, the conditions of work in the nitrate fields, and the transport of workers on the state railways—all of which were designed with a view toward the prevention of accidents and maintenance of health. Other decrees provided for the formation of a Labor Office within the Ministry of Industry and Public Works and established a limited basis for state intervention in the conciliation and arbitration of labor conflicts.[10]

Apart from the laws of 1892 and 1918 extending state responsibility for public health conditions, the only other notable piece of social legislation was that of August 1920, which fulfilled a very old Liberal and Radical demand for compulsory primary education. Perhaps the most interesting thing about this law is its late date. The Argentine legislature had passed a similar law in 1884. Compulsory education had also been a principle theme of the Chilean Congreso Pedagógico of 1889, which was sponsored by the Balmaceda administration and attended by legislators and government ministers.[11] The timing of the compulsory education law therefore suggests that party competition delayed, rather than encouraged, positive state action in the field of primary education.

All other health and educational measures were extremely particularistic in focus: a characteristic, as noted previously, of much legislation in this period. Two laws, Nos. 3092 and 3365, establishing technical schools have been included in Table 42. In addition to these the legislature approved many individual educational subsidies as well as special allocations to control epidemics.

To put this record of social legislation into perspective, it is worth considering some of the proposals that were presented to the legislature but not passed: limitations on the length of the working day, broad regulation of female and child labor, minimum wage legislation, obligatory payment of salaries in cash, state arbitration and conciliation of labor disputes, a comprehensive labor code, social security legislation, and the formation of departments of labor and social security.[12] Significantly, virtually all of these proposals did become law on September 8, 1924—at the insistence of the military.[13] Hence again the evidence indicates that inter-party competition impeded, rather than promoted, state action on behalf of subordinate groups in Chile.

Argentina

Table 43 summarizes the social legislation passed by the national legislature in Argentina between 1912 and 1930. Overall groups at the lower end of the socioeconomic spectrum gained far more than in Chile, even if the same cut-off date is used. The formation of a department of labor, the control of rents, the regulation of labor conditions, and the extension of pension rights all went beyond the actions taken in Chile. At the same time there are some interesting parallels between social legislation in the two countries. Between 1905 and 1920 legislatures in both Chile and Argentina established a social security system for railway workers, altered the law relating to work injuries, accepted some responsibility for low-cost housing and destitute children, limited the length of the work week, and took steps to regulate female and child labor. These similarities point to the importance of factors other than regime change: notably, cultural diffusion and labor unrest. The twenty-year interval between the emergence of competitive party systems in the two countries strengthens this interpretation. Even before the development of party competition on a national scale, the Argentine legislature passed laws granting workers in the Federal Capital one rest day a week (No. 4661 of September 6, 1905) and regulating the employment of minors (No. 5291 of October 14, 1907). The latter law also included more restrictive provisions relating to the employment of female and child labor in the Federal Capital. Both of these oligarchical reform measures reflected awareness of social policy developments in other parts of the world. They also represented attempts at containing political challenges from below, although strictly speaking neither law can be described as a preemptive state initiative. By 1905 the Argentine ruling elite faced pressure from an increasing disruptive trade union

TABLE 43

ARGENTINA: SOCIAL LEGISLATION, 1912-1930

Law No.	Date	Major Provision
8999	30 Sept. 1912	Establishing national department of Labor
9085	18 June 1913	Providing for indemnification of employees of Ministry of Public Works in cases of work injury
9104	12 Aug. 1913	"Descanso dominical": extending coverage of #4661 that applied to Federal Capital to national territories
9148	25 Sept. 1913	Creation of public employment agencies
9677	5 Oct. 1915	Providing for cheap public housing in Federal Capital and national territories
9688	11 Oct. 1915	Work-related injuries: liability rests with employer
10505	8 Oct. 1918	Regulation of home employment
10650	30 Apr. 1919	Retirement pensions for railroad employees
10861	27 Sept. 1919	Creating national university
10903	21 Oct. 1919	"Patronato de menores": protection of abandoned children
11110	11 Feb. 1921	Retirement pensions for all employees of private utility companies (electricity, light, etc.)
11156	19 Sept. 1921	Rent controls (extended by #11231 and #11318 to 30 Sept. 1925)
11173	13 Oct. 1921	"Hogar ferroviario": special state mortgage loans to railroad employees (modifying #10650)

Table 43 (*Continued*)

Law No.	Date	Major Provision
11178	14 Oct. 1921	Minimum salary for government employees
11232	1 Nov. 1923	Retirement pensions for bank employees
11278	10 Nov. 1923	Regulating salary payments—to be paid fully in cash
11289	28 Nov. 1923	Social security for workers in merchant marine, newspaper, industrial and commercial establishments (suspended by #11358, 20 Sept. 1926)
11317	30 Sept. 1924	Regulation of female and child labor
11320	29 May 1925	Regulation of working hours in commercial establishments (vetoed)
11338	9 Sept. 1926	Prohibition of night work in bakeries, confectioneries, and similar businesses
11471	1 Oct. 1928	Retirement pensions for state employees working at home
11544	12 Sept. 1928	Eight-hour day, 48 hour week (excepting domestic and agricultural workers)
11570	25 Sept. 1929	Legal procedures for application of social legislation: placing burden of proof on defense in cases of possible infraction
11575	5 Dec. 1929	Retirement pensions for bank employees: extending coverage of #11232 and reforming pension system

SOURCE: Rocha, Vols. I-XVIII; Argentina, Cámara de Senadores, *Diario de sesiones*, 1912-1930; Jerónimo Remorino et al., comps., *Anales de legislación argentina: Complemento años 1889-1919* (Buenos Aires, 1954); idem, *Anales de legislación argentina: Complemento años 1920-1940* (Buenos Aires 1953).

movement as well as electoral competition from the Socialists in the Federal Capital, the district to which the two reform laws mainly applied.

The significance of cultural diffusion as a source of policy change is further emphasized by the similarities that exist among Latin American countries in the timing of the adoption of social security programs. For example, between 1911 and 1924 not only Argentina and Chile, but Uruguay, Cuba, Bolivia, Panama, Brazil, Ecuador, Peru, Colombia, Venezuela, Costa Rica, and El Salvador first adopted laws relating to work injuries.[14] In the overwhelming majority of these cases, the introduction of this social welfare legislation occurred under authoritarian rather than competitive rule.

Apart from the 1915 law protecting workers in cases of injury, probably the most important pieces of social legislation passed in Argentina during the 1912-1930 period were those of September 1924, which extended the scope of the 1907 law regulating female and child labor, and September 1928, which regulated the length of the working day. The law extending social security coverage to most urban workers (No. 11289) met opposition from both labor and employers' groups and was revoked within a short space of time. The other laws listed in Table 43 represent a more piecemeal approach to social issues, either because they were temporary measures, such as the law of 1921 freezing rents, or because they only applied to selective groups of workers.

The rent control act was one of several steps taken during the first Irigoyen administration to contain the rise in the cost of living. During the war the government issued a series of decrees restricting the export of flour, sugar, metals, chemicals, fuels, and other raw materials to prevent national shortages and maintain price stability.[15] Since the Argentine cost of living actually rose quite gradually by international standards, there is some reason to rate this price control policy a positive achievement.

As in Chile, the Argentine legislature singled out railwaymen for special treatment on numerous occasions, mainly because of their capacity to disrupt the economy and the political vulnerability of foreign-owned railway companies. In 1917, after the Senate refused to consider legislation regulating working conditions on the railways, the Irigoyen government issued a decree that established a 10 percent increase in salaries and reduced the working day to eight hours.[16] The laws of April 1919 and October 1921 established a social security system for railroad employees and special lending facilities for the purchase of housing. None of these measures was very palatable to the railway companies, particularly since what the *Review of the River Plate* described as the "onerous conditions imposed by the Government" were coupled with controls on railway tariffs.[17]

Bank and public utility employees, the majority of whom worked for foreign-owned firms, also received special treatment through laws Nos. 11110, 11232, and 11575. Another group of workers that benefitted from public policy was that composed of government employees for whom a minimum salary was established in 1921, raising the pay of those at the lowest end of the salary scale 50 percent.[18]

Other significant pieces of social legislation include the law establishing the Comisión Nacional de Casas Baratas, which initiated the work of providing low-cost housing for workers in the Federal Capital and national territories; law No. 11338 of 1926, which protected certain categories of workers from night employment; and law No. 10505 of 1918, which regulated the working conditions and wages of dispersed employees such as seamstresses. The latter law obliged employers to keep a register of their workers, and the Department of Labor was authorized to establish municipal salary commissions at the request of workers to fix minimum salaries.

In the field of education, legislation provides little evidence of a new policy approach. Virtually the only law passed was that of September 17, 1919, establishing the Universidad del Litoral. One reason for this inaction was the strong record of educational reform that had been achieved by Argentina between 1880 and 1912. By the standards of Chile and most other Latin American countries, the state school system was well developed. Nevertheless, it still had many shortcomings.[19] These were recognized both by Irigoyen, who pressed for the expansion of primary education, and by Alvear, who presented a comprehensive reform bill to the legislature in 1923; but the legislature took no action.[20] In their positive response to student demands, however, Radical leaders did play a supporting role in educational reform at the university level.[21]

To evaluate the Argentine legislative record in the general field of social policy, some further consideration should be given to other policies proposed by Radical administrations but not implemented. Although the central concern here is legislation, inaction brings to light negative kinds of policy decisions and provides a standard against which positive measures may be assessed. In the Argentine case, there is a further reason for widening the scope of the analysis to include a broader variety of evidence: namely, the relative importance of the executive branch in that country. In Chile the administration changed constantly due to cabinet shuffles, and the executive branch in general enjoyed a "low profile," making it difficult for contemporaries and historians alike to obtain information about its policy orientation or even to ascribe much importance to it. In Argentina, on the other hand, there was one prominent and influential government spokesman— the president. He largely determined the chief political issues of the day, shaped much of the legislation considered by congress, exercised a decisive influence over its implementation, and established the tone of the entire national government. Since as much satisfaction may develop from the symbolic fulfillment of demands as from any other source, statements of policy intentions, policy proposals, and other actions of the Argentine executive, which may have convinced the public that certain interests and needs were being served, are of some relevance to the present discussion.

Ricardo Caballero explicitly underlined the importance of the president's attitude towards the popular sector in 1925, when he sought to defend the work of the Irigoyen administration in a Senate debate. Irigoyen's policies, he claimed, created new hope for the workers.

> Whether this hope was realized or not scarcely affects the value of the social concepts . . . I will say that the recognition of an unacknowledged right in the slow process of human evolution is worth as much as its realization . . . Where did a conflict develop between labor and capital that did not find him [Irigoyen] on hand? What part of the country did not send committees of workers and producers soliciting his intervention

and advice? Haven't we ourselves witnessed that the doors of the presidential office were as open to workers as to men of privilege? And the large newspapers of the republic, didn't they state in confirmation of what I have said . . . that shortly after Dr. Irigoyen ceased to be president of the republic there was no longer a bad odor in Government House because the workers had ceased gathering in the president's office?[22]

Caballero was pointing to the importance of leadership style, access, verbal encouragement, and other types of associated outputs that contributed to a greater *sense of representation* of subordinate group interests. Regardless of the social origins of Radical party leaders or the tangible benefits that various groups derived from Radical party control over the government, it cannot be doubted but that in this specialized sense of the term the government represented the interests of less advantaged groups more completely than any of its predecessors or successors up until the Peronist era.

The Irigoyen administration originally proposed most of the measures listed in Table 43, including those passed between 1922 and 1928, and by its own standards they amounted to only a partial success. The legislature blocked many social projects that would have expanded the scope of government, including bills providing for the conciliation and arbitration of labor disputes, the recognition and regulation of trade unions, the protection of workers in the national territories, a comprehensive labor code, and a minimum salary.[23] Particularly after 1918 the administration made a point of emphasizing its commitment to social justice, and near the end of his first term Irigoyen did his best to convince the public that government policy had in fact favored less privileged groups. In his official message of 1922, he asserted that the efforts of the government "have constantly tended to alleviate the sufferings of the masses" by promoting equitable solutions to conflicts between labor and capital, increasing real wages, shortening working hours, reducing unemployment, decreasing strike activity, and equalizing the distribution of wealth.[24] Most of these claims had substance. Improvements in the real wages of Argentine workers have been documented in the previous chapter. In asserting that the number of strikes had decreased, Irigoyen was using statistics rather selectively,[25] but in any case the lessons to be learned about government policy from the number of strikes are ambiguous.

Much more important is the government's attitude toward labor organizations and strikes—an area of some controversy. On the one side may be cited the interventions of Radical governments, both at the provincial and national levels, on behalf of striking workers. Sympathy for organized labor is also evident in Irigoyen's negative reaction to the request that the government use the military to break the railroad strike of 1917:

> Is this the solution you bring to the government of your country? Is this the measure you come to propose to the government that has arisen from the very soul of democracy, after thirty years of predominance and privilege? Understand, gentlemen, that privilege is finished in this country and from now on the armed forces will not stir except to defend their honor and integrity. The government will not use force to destroy this strike, which signifies the expression of neglected grievance.[26]

On the other hand, the government occasionally did resort to military and police repression to cope with disruptive strike action. The packinghouse workers' and tenant farmers' strikes of 1917 as well as the uprising of pastoral laborers in Patagonia in the early 1920s are cases in point. The best-known example, however, is the "Semana Trágica" of January 1919, which began with a strike of workers at the Vasena metallurgical factory and rapidly developed into a general strike, involving considerable violence and the intervention of the police and military. Yet, as David Rock has argued on the basis of a rather detailed analysis, these episodes of repression constitute the exception rather than the rule. They largely reflect the intense pressures placed on the government by elites concerned with "foreign agitation" and labor unrest in the postwar period.[27]

The Radicals' ideal was the reconciliation of social conflicts, equilibrium and harmony between classes: a policy that was neither prolabor nor procapital.[28] This policy proved difficult to pursue in the atmosphere of social crisis that followed World War I, particularly since the Radical party's base of political support was so socially heterogeneous. The government's labor policy therefore vacillated considerably over time in response to political pressures. Electoral considerations initially led the Irigoyen administration to support organized labor in the Federal Capital, where the UCR faced serious competition from the Socialists. This policy provoked the formation of an employers' association, the National Labor

Association, in 1918. The following year witnessed the emergence of the highly nationalistic, antilabor, and antileftist Liga Patriótica Argentina, which rivalled the UCR in terms of organizational strength and political resources.[29] Faced with these new organizational pressures, the Radical government modified its initial policies, but it continued to attempt to woo working-class support. The balance struck between the interests of workers and propertied groups shifted somewhat under the Alvear administration, which did not press for any major pieces of new legislation with lower-class interests in mind; but relative to previous governments, which had been frankly hostile to labor interests, invoking the military to intimidate strikers almost as a matter of routine, and even post-1930 ones, whose orientations were usually anything but popular, social policy throughout the 1916-1930 period was quite favorable to less privileged groups, even if the symbolic satisfaction of demands is not considered.

Shifts in policy at the provincial level of government, where major responsibility for social policy in Argentina rested, also need to be taken into account. In many provinces major changes in policy that benefitted groups at the lower end of the socioeconomic continuum followed the emergence of a competitive party system. In 1918, for example, the legislature in Mendoza passed laws limiting the working day to eight hours, regulating female and child labor, establishing minimum wages, creating a provincial labor office, and providing pensions for teachers. After 1916 similar legislation also emerged in San Juan. These policy changes underline the differing impact of party competition on social policy in Chile and Argentina.[30]

CIVIL LIBERTIES

Related to the question of social policy is that of governmental respect for civil liberties. With one exception no major pieces of legislation were passed in this area in either country. The exception is the rarely invoked Chilean Law of Residence of December 12, 1918 (No. 3446), which was directed against foreign agitators and revolutionaries—the counterpart of the Argentine law of November 1902.[31] In the Argentine case the absence of positive legislative action is significant. Neither the 1902 law nor the "social defense" law of June 1910, which was directed against anarchists, was repealed. Moreover, the Argentine Radicals utilized both these laws in the postwar period.[32]

Other omissions point towards a more positive record of respect for civil liberties. Between 1900 and 1912 the Argentine legislature had passed four laws suspending civil liberties to deal with labor agitation and, in 1905, a Radical revolution. Another state of siege was not approved by the legislature until 1932. After Irigoyen was deposed and imprisoned on the island of Martín García, he stressed this point in one of the series of letters he wrote defending his political record:

> . . . never, not in any case or circumstance, was anyone arrested, nor a newspaper suspended, nor a state of siege established; neither was the slightest coercive measure taken, notwithstanding the copious amount of rebelliousness, abuse, and insolence directed against the government.[33]

This claim was somewhat exaggerated, because the government of Irigoyen did resort to repression in dealing with labor unrest; but on balance Radical governments displayed considerable respect for civil liberties. Despite the fears aroused by the Russian revolution, even the Communist party enjoyed de facto freedom of operation in Argentina until 1930.[34]

The Chilean record was not too different. In addition to the 1918 law mentioned above, the government declared a five-month state of siege in response to postcivil war tensions in 1893. Another, lasting seventy days, was declared in February 1919 to deal with labor unrest in the North. The latter piece of legislation points to the one significant policy difference between the two countries in the area of civil liberties: state intervention in labor conflicts involved repression far more consistently in Chile than in Argentina. In the latter country the policy response of authorities to the demands of organized labor might be called "benevolent neutrality;" in the Chilean case a more appropriate description might be "malign neglect" combined with occasional brutality.[35] A long series of bloody clashes between workers and Chilean military and police forces punctuated the 1891-1924 period. During the Iquique strike of 1907 alone, government forces massacred at least 1,000 persons. By way of comparison, the death toll resulting from the infamous "Semana Trágica" in Argentina is usually estimated at a figure around one hundred. Yet the attacks of the Chilean government on organized labor fell short of a policy of systematic persecution. Partially because of cabinet instability, repression was applied only intermittently. In addition, trade unions and other groups pressing the claims of workers reaped real gains from the respect that governments showed for traditional civil liberties during the parliamentary period. Again, even the Communists, who were harshly repressed during the Ibáñez era, enjoyed freedom of association.[36]

RURAL POLICY

Particularly sharp differences between Chile and Argentina emerge in the area of rural policy. The rural sectors of both countries at the turn of the century were characterized by major inequalities. Despite the growth of party competition, Chilean policy makers never directly addressed this issue. Until 1919 agrarian reform even failed to secure a place on the political agenda.[37] Setting to one side a series of laws on southern colonization that were highly particularistic in character, Chilean legislative activity in the area of rural policy consisted chiefly of projects encouraging irrigation. Law No. 2953 of December 9, 1914, in particular, which established general regulations for the organization and financing of irrigation projects, provided a major impetus to expanding the area of land under irrigation. Otherwise government policy towards the rural sector can be characterized as one designed to maintain the status quo.

In contrast, rural policy aroused great controversy in Argentina, and important policy changes followed the development of party competition. Radical governments did not totally abandon the "hands-off" policy of previous administrations, which had deferred to powerful pastoral interests; but the needs of the relatively disadvantaged farm community received greater attention.

Table 44 summarizes the legislation passed between 1912 and 1930 that directly affected Argentine rural interests. Perhaps the most striking feature of this legislative record is that virtually all of the measures aimed at assisting and promoting agriculture rather than stock-raising. Far from demonstrating that one set of rural producers was favored over another, this emphasis reflects the fact that farmers, facing highly unstable prices and other difficult economic conditions, demanded more positive government assistance than ranchers. The interests of the two groups only came into direct conflict with respect to the law regulating rural contracts (No. 11170). This law was one of the two major pieces of rural legislation passed after 1916, and it represented something of a triumph for agriculturists, who had long clamored for protection against the burdensome and short-term contract conditions that large landowners were able to impose. Law No. 11170 attempted to address farmers' demands by fixing a minimum contract period of four years, by relieving farmers of the obligation to purchase equipment and supplies from or sell crops to particular parties, and by guaranteeing farmers compensation for property improvements.

The second important rural measure was the Homestead Law of 1917, which offered farmers a free plot of land ranging from 20 to 200 hectares. Given the depletion in the supply of fertile public land, the law's value was more symbolic than real; but, as with the law regulating rural contracts, it marked a real departure from previous government policy. The same is true of law No. 10676 increasing agrarian credit facilities, which up to this time had been severely restricted, and laws Nos. 11380 and 11388 promoting agricultural cooperatives. Most of the other measures listed in Table 44 were designed to cope with temporary emergencies, such as grain bag and seed shortages or insect invasions.

The legislative record outlined in Table 44 was inadequate by the standards of both the Irigoyen and Alvear administrations, not to mention the Federación Agraria Argentina (FAA). From 1917 on Irigoyen had drawn attention to the plight of the tenant farmer and the problems created by inequalities in land distribution. He had also proposed a variety of corrective measures to the legislature. One of these was the law regulating rural contracts, which like many of his social proposals was designed to eliminate conflict or, as he put it, to "procure a real and effective solidarity between the interests of proprietors and farmers."[38] With the exception of the reform of the state mortgage bank and the Homestead Law, his other suggested reforms all died in the legislature: the formation

TABLE 44

ARGENTINA: RURAL LEGISLATION, 1912-1930

Law No.	Date	Major Provision
10247	11 Sept. 1917	Seed grains exempted from import duties
10284	25 Sept. 1917	Homestead law: grants of public land to colonists
10278	27 Sept. 1917	Emergency acquisition of burlap sacks and twine for agricultural harvest
10403	6 Aug. 1918	Acquisition of seed for farmers
10676	22 Sept. 1919	Reform of national mortgage bank to ease agricultural credit facilities
10777	25 Sept. 1919	Emergency acquisition of burlap sacks and twine
11109	2 Feb. 1921	Temporary exemption from customs duties of wool and hide exports
11170	28 Sept. 1921	Regulation of rural contracts
11203	26 Apr. 1923	Acquisition of seed for farmers
11212	6 Sept. 1923	Acquisition of seed for farmers
11280	20 Nov. 1923	Emergency appropriation of funds for destruction of locusts
11380	30 Sept. 1926	Loans to agricultural cooperative societies
11388	20 Dec. 1926	Agricultural cooperatives: legal recognition and definition
11563	18 Sept. 1929	Providing for pastoral census

SOURCE: As for Table 43.

of rural arbitration boards to settle contractual disputes, the promotion of agricultural cooperatives through tax exemptions, the creation of a National Agricultural Bank to increase credit facilities for tenant farmers, and an emergency 50 percent reduction in rural land rents that he proposed in 1922 to relieve the burdens created by falling market prices.[39] Other actions also indicated that the Irigoyen government repudiated past policy, particularly the encouragement which that policy had given to unequal land distribution. Irigoyen urged provincial governors not to sell provincial land in the usual large lots on the grounds that this practice encouraged the formation of large estates and retarded progress.[40] In a decree of April 21, 1917, which called for the retrieval of public lands that were held in lots over 20,000 hectares in size or farmed by tenants, the president sought to remedy past abuses even more directly.[41]

By no stretch of the imagination was the Alvear administration hostile to ranching interests or large landholders, but it too recognized the need for reforms and introduced legislation to subdivide lands, promote colonization, and regulate rural contracts.[42] To some extent the failure of the legislature to support these measures reflected the temporary return of favorable market conditions for agricultural produce in the middle 1920s and the associated decline in rural stagnation and unrest. But more fundamentally, the proposals failed because the Radical party included conservative rural interests and was thoroughly divided on questions of rural reform. This problem was particularly obvious after 1928. The world-wide depression in agriculture severely affected Argentina, but all proposals for government action fell victim to the political wrangles that prevented the Senate from even convening in 1930.

The legislation, administrative proposals, and policy actions described above all failed to satisfy organized farmers, who were by 1930, if not before, thoroughly disillusioned with parliamentary democracy.[43] In retrospect it is also evident that a great deal more might have been done to alleviate farmers' difficulties. The Radicals' failure to implement any program of land reform or even to provide support for one until 1924 is a leading example. Still, at the risk of sounding like an apologist for the Irigoyen and Alvear governments—and the danger is far from remote, given the unflattering and often condemnatory assessments that have been made of Radical government policy in this field—several considerations must be kept in mind. First, the farmers' grievances emerged in response to many factors beyond the control of government, such as massive crop failures, shipping shortages during World War I, and low agricultural prices during the early and late 1920s. Second, in terms of legislation the government did more to meet the demands of agriculturists than any government in Argentina up until the time of Perón, and even Perón steered clear of basic rural reforms. Obviously, the problem here is to find a standard by which to judge government policy. One observer's "marginal innovation" may be another's "fundamental reform." Previous government policy may be too generous a yardstick; but it does provide an objective and realistic standard as well as the appropriate basis for assessing the policy impact of party competition. Third, the efforts of the Radical administrations to alter the rural status quo were also exceptional by cross-national standards. In most other South American countries rural reform only became a serious political issue in the 1950s.[44] Finally, the overwhelming majority of farmers were unnaturalized citizens with no voice in elections. The failure of government policy to reflect more fully the interests of the farm community thus confirms rather than confutes the importance of the vote in holding decision makers responsible to subordinate groups in Argentina. Taking into account as well the xenophobia that prevailed in the ranks of the Radical and other parties, perhaps what is most surprising about Argentine government policy towards the rural sector in the 1912-1930 period is its responsiveness—not lack of responsiveness—to the demands of farmers. Even allowing for the economic importance of agriculture and the political support that farmers received from other groups, notably commercial interests in the cereal belt, the political realities of the country were hardly favorable to the recognition of farmers' needs.

COMMERCIAL AND INDUSTRIAL POLICY

Turning to legislation affecting commerce and industry, Table 45 summarizes the major measures adopted in Chile between 1892 and 1924. Again the evidence shows that minimal policy change occurred in response to party development and electoral competition. This finding is somewhat surprising, because by the turn of the century Chileans had begun to perceive the disadvantages of foreign economic penetration and were analyzing the lopsided economic relationships between developed and underdeveloped countries in terms that sound remarkably familiar to the modern ear.[45] By this time too national industry had made real progress and was better placed to demand governmental support. Tariff policy provides evidence of both these trends. Yet in other areas of public policy relating specifically to commerce and industry, legislative records show little sign of policy innovation.

Virtually all of the measures listed in Table 45 were designed to promote and protect domestic industry, but basically they perpetuated a tradition of special concessions, privileges, and subsidies dating back at least as far as the Bulnes administration.[46] Only the laws of 1917 and 1922, promoting the Chilean merchant marine, established a broader nationalistic policy, and these legislative measures, which had been debated in various forms since 1892, were never fully implemented.[47] The only other laws deserving special mention are those relating to nitrate production. These laws reflect the disastrous effects of the postwar collapse of the nitrate market for the economy as a whole, and while they might be seen as a step toward greater state control over a critical sector of the economy, essentially they were emergency measures and ones designed to rescue foreign firms at that.

What is particularly striking about Table 45 is the almost complete absence of laws regulating and controlling industry and commerce. The government created opportunities and distributed benefits—little more. One omission warrants particular mention and that is the lack of legislation significantly expanding government control over banking. The laws of 1904 and 1912 only underline the very weak control that the state exercised over the economy at this time. The absence of a central bank made the government particularly vulnerable, and the money supply was frequently expanded merely to rescue over-extended private institutions from collapse. Balmaceda had proposed positive state action to remedy this problem, but strong resistance from private

TABLE 45

CHILE: COMMERCIAL AND INDUSTRIAL LEGISLATION 1892-1924

Law No.	Date	Major Provision
1533	10 July 1902	Special premiums to encourage manufacture of sulfuric acid
1665	4 Aug. 1904	Concessions of public land to encourage electrical power industry
1712	19 Nov. 1904	Regulation of financial operations of insurance firms
1768	31 Oct. 1905	Special premiums, profit guarantees, and concessions for establishment of an iron and steel plant awarded to a particular firm
1855	13 Feb. 1906	Bonuses to encourage domestic sugar production
1949	24 June 1907	Subsidies to promote national fishing industry (extended by #3315, 21 Sept. 1917 and #3490, 24 Jan. 1919 for 10 years)
2654	12 May 1912	Establishing Caja de Emisión to regulate the volume of currency in circulation
2918	12 Aug. 1914	Advance payments to nitrate producers to encourage them to continue operations (one of a long series: e.g., laws #2969, 3006, 3101, 3299, 3409, 3666, 3795, and 3917)
3219	29 Jan. 1917	Protection of national merchant marine (also #3841, 6 Feb. 1922, reserving the coastal trade for Chilean vessels)
3386	31 May 1918	Commission to study problems of nitrate industry
3607	14 Feb. 1920	Caja de Crédito Popular: small loans and savings bank

SOURCE: As for Table 42.

banking interests left the Chilean government in a very real sense the victim rather than the master of the economy. Significantly, a central bank and a general banking law appeared in 1925 immediately following the collapse of the parliamentary system.[48]

Argentina

By the turn of the century the Argentine government exercised much greater control over the economy than did the Chilean government, and the legislature passed several measures between 1912 and 1930 that increased state control even further. The exclusion of most laws with an extremely narrow focus from the two tables summarizing industrial and commercial policies unfortunately minimizes the contrast between the two countries. While the Chileans remained preoccupied with distributing privileges to private firms, Argentina was moving in a very different direction toward the regulation of trade and commerce and the expansion of the public sector.

The Chilean approach had much in common with nineteenth-century Argentine policy, which had attempted to stimulate economic development through grants of special exemptions and privileges. To encourage the meat industry, for example, the Argentine congress had passed a series of laws between 1868 and 1900 offering prizes to the inventor of the best system of preserving meat, tariff exemptions to specific meat-packing firms for imports of machinery, bonuses for the promotion of beef and mutton exports, and guaranteed profits of 5 percent per annum to meat-exporting companies.[49] A few further laws of this type were passed between 1900 and 1912. Laws Nos. 4163 and 7844 of December 29, 1902 and September 30, 1910 granted customs exemptions to meat-packing firms, and law No. 8864 of February 27, 1912 offered a bonus for the establishment of a packing house in Entre Rios. After 1912, however, state subsidies to trade and industry virtually disappeared. In the wake of the introduction of party competition, the government sought instead to regulate and bring under its control the single most important industry in the country—meat-packing.

The first law of this type authorized the investment of public

funds for the installation of a meat-packing plant in the Federal
Capital, and it was adopted in the interest of consumers as well as
small ranchers. Law No. 11227 sought to extend government control over the meat trade itself, fixing maximum prices for sales
destined for internal consumption and minimum prices for export,
while laws Nos. 11226 and 11210 aimed at eliminating abuses
such as price-fixing, which deprived breeders—especially small
ones—of fair prices. In practice these laws had little impact.
Despite the opposition of the Sociedad Rural, Alvear succumbed
to pressure from packers and suspended the minimum price provisions of No. 11227; the maximum price provisions were never
implemented. The construction of the municipal meat-packing
plant was delayed until 1928-1929, while the attempt to control
the North American trusts that dominated the meat industry
proved notoriously abortive. Nevertheless, public opinion did
encourage the government to take symbolic actions in the interest
of consumers and domestic producers.[50]

A tendency towards the expansion of government control over
the economy is also evident in the case of law No. 10350, regulating the sale of agricultural products abroad. This law fixed
minimum prices for the sale of grains and was designed partially
to defend the economic interests of small and scattered rural producers in the international market.

To some extent both law No. 10350 and the legislation on
beef reflected the growth of strong nationalistic sentiments in
Argentina. The politics of petroleum provide further evidence of
this trend, although, as in the case of the beef industry, a more
nationalistic oil policy was directed against North American,
rather than British, companies and posed no basic threat to local
elites concerned with protecting their export markets. Where
British interests were involved, government policy exhibited less
economic nationalism, especially in the late 1920s. A notable case
in point is the D'Abernon agreement of 1929, whereby the Argentines granted major trade concessions to the British.[51]

Apologists for the Irigoyen administrations have written a great
deal about the petroleum issue, often obscuring the significant
fact that state intervention in this area was not the result of a one-
man war against foreign interests and plutocrats, but the out-

TABLE 46

ARGENTINA: COMMERCIAL AND INDUSTRIAL LEGISLATION
1912-1930

Law No.	Date	Major Provision
10350	25 Jan. 1918	Trade agreement with England and France; fixing minimum prices and offering credits for purchase of cereals
10606	30 Sept. 1918	Reserving coastal trade for national ships and providing subsidies for the promotion of the national merchant marine
11205	19 July 1923	Investment of public funds to install meat-packing plant in Federal Capital
11210	24 Aug. 1923	Illegality of trusts and monopolies in trade and industry
11226	3 Oct. 1923	Control of meat trade: outlawing monopolies, price-fixing, invidious distinctions between sellers; requiring registration of traders with Ministry of Agriculture
11227	3 Oct. 1923	President to fix minimum prices for meat sales destined for export; maximum prices for domestic consumption
11228	3 Oct. 1923	Requiring sales of meat on a peso per kilogram basis

SOURCE: As for Table 43.

growth of a series of actions dating back to President Figueroa Alcorta's decision to reserve the Comodoro Rivadavia area to the nation in 1907. At the same time, Irigoyen was the first national leader to seize upon the petroleum issue and bring it to the forefront of national debate, and his policy proposals generated considerable controversy. Indeed, state involvement in oil production has remained a source of political conflict in Argentina up until the present day, largely because it has symbolized commitment to national economic independence.

From the beginning of his first presidency, Irigoyen was pre-occupied with the development of a state-run oil industry. On December 11, 1916 he sent a message to congress requesting the allocation of funds for the exploitation of the Comodoro Rivadavia site, and this proposal was followed by many others, none of which secured legislative approval. Frustrated in his efforts to secure legislation, Irigoyen established a state petroleum agency, Yacimientos Petrolíferos Fiscales (YPF), by decree in 1922. His successor, Alvear, pursued a similar policy and requested additional financial support and legislation, but the two presidents disagreed over the extent to which the state should monopolize oil production. During 1927 this issue absorbed considerable debating time in the Chamber of Deputies. Anti-Personalists, Conservatives, and many Socialists rejected the idea of a state monopoly in favor of mixed state and private exploitation, and they succeeded in blocking any further nationalization measures in the Senate. Irigoyen continued to press the issue during his second administration, but with no success.[52]

Nationalism also influenced state policy regarding transport industries. Law No. 10606, listed in Table 46, sought to promote the development of a national merchant marine by reserving coastal shipping to Argentine vessels and by providing subsidies for naval construction. No legislation affected the British-owned railroads beyond that explored in the section on social policy, but government policy, particularly during the first Irigoyen administration, became less favorable to foreign firms than during the pre-1912 period. When private railway companies that had been granted concessions by previous administrations found it difficult to fulfill their contracts during the war, Irigoyen seized upon their failure and revoked some concessions by decree. The president attempted to clarify his position on the issue of foreign control in a 1920 message to congress, which accompanied his veto of a bill selling a portion of the small state-owned railway system to private interests. Irigoyen stated that Argentina ought to imitate the more progressive countries of the world and expand the economic role of the state, particularly in public service industries. Even though the Irigoyen administration actually accomplished little in the way of wresting control of the nation's railway system from foreign interests, its popular nationalism was very new. Until 1922 the national administration adopted a decidedly prolabor and anticapital position on the important issues of labor conflict and rate increases, and even after that date the British railways remained in a highly defensive position.[53]

The idea of economic diversification through deliberate state action also gained ground over time. Yet while Irigoyen pointed to the need to increase Argentina's industrial independence,[54] no new proposals or measures emerged during the 1912-1930 period, beyond the revisions of the tariff laws discussed in the previous chapter. The only other concrete economic proposal of importance made by the national administration was the creation of a new central banking institution: a proposal that died in the legislature during Irigoyen's first administration.[55]

In summary, while Chilean commercial and industrial policy continued to emphasize the distribution of benefits to specific firms and individuals, Argentine policy makers abandoned the traditional pork-barrel approach in favor of policies expanding state control in the interest of broad social groups. The tangible accomplishments of the Radicals in this area were few and far between. Moreover, the government formulated a new policy only with respect to two basic industries, meat-packing and petroleum. In these two areas, however, there is clear evidence of a new policy orientation—one, which in the case of the meat trade, took the interests of consumers explicitly into account.

THE LEGISLATIVE RECORDS IN COMPARATIVE PERSPECTIVE

Contrasts in the legislative records of Argentina and Chile buttress the findings of the preceding chapter. In every major area, Argentine public policy exhibited more support for less privileged groups than Chilean policy. Argentine policy also changed more profoundly after the introduction of competitive party politics. The scope of policy expanded in favor of non-elites, augmenting state control over society. Likewise, the focus of Argentine government policy shifted away from purely distributive types of decisions in favor of regulative and redistributive policies affecting broad social groups. In Chile, on the other hand, the scope and focus of public policy only changed conspicuously after the collapse of the parliamentary system. These divergences in the impact of party competition are evident from longitudinal data on legislation having a particularistic focus as well as from the analysis of laws passed in all major areas of government activity.

In the area of social policy, legislative records supply evidence of innovation in both countries, but the growth of social protection was much slower in Chile than in Argentina. Most of the key social reforms introduced in Chile during the parliamentary period had been adopted in Argentina even before the development of party competition. In fact, one of the most fundamental Chilean reforms—the compulsory education law of 1920—had been introduced in Argentina as early as 1884. After 1916, when an Argentine president was first elected through competitive elections, the gap between the two countries in the field of social policy widened. This trend was only reversed in 1924, when the Chilean military pushed through the reforms that Alessandri and many others regarded as fundamental. In other words, party competition appears to have braked rather than promoted the expansion of social protection in Chile. Marked changes in social policy, as well as effective implementation of social legislation, occurred in response to military intervention rather than party competition.

Those changes that did take place in Chilean social policy prior to 1924 can be viewed as symbolic responses to cultural diffusion and labor unrest, rather than as consequences of party competition. The law limiting the work week to six days, for example, was first introduced in congress after the Valparaíso riot of 1903 and finally passed after the 1907 general strike in Santiago.[56] The importance of cultural diffusion as a source of policy innovation is emphasized by the parallels between Argentine and Chilean social policy in the pre-1916 period, as well as by the similarities across Latin America in the timing of the adoption of social reform legislation.

In the case of Argentina, stronger evidence exists that party competition led to the introduction of social policies favorable to groups at the lower end of the socioeconomic continuum. The regulation of hours, wages, and working conditions was more extensive in Argentina, social security coverage was also more comprehensive, and during the Irigoyen administrations authorities frequently championed lower-class interests. At the same time, a real gap existed between rhetoric and action. The legislature shelved many of Irigoyen's most important proposals, and the government occasionally resorted to repression in dealing with strikes. Overall, however, the departures from previous policy were more marked than in Chile and the social protection of less privileged groups more extensive.

Legislative records show similar contrasts between Argentina and Chile in the area of industrial and commercial policy. In the case of Chile, there was no expansion of state control over the economy and no shift away from the distributive approach of the past. After the introduction of competitive party politics, the Chilean government continued to concentrate on allocating privileges to particular firms, rather than on regulating and controlling industry and commerce. In contrast, the Argentine government's approach in the area of commercial and industrial policy changed over time in favor of a new emphasis on state regulation and control. The efficacy of the tentative steps that were made in this direction can be legitimately questioned; but the expansion of the state petroleum industry, the regulation of the meat-packing trade, the law against trusts and monopolies, and the establishment of a publicly owned meat-packing plant involved a new regulative and nationalistic policy approach. Overall, Argentine policy makers exercised much greater control over the economy than their Chilean counterparts.

The contrasts between the two countries are even more obvious in the area of rural policy. Again, the annals of Argentine legislation provide far more evidence of policy change. In relation to their demands and needs Argentine farmers received an inadequate amount of state support and protection; but they gained some ground after 1916. Two general pieces of legislation addressed the needs of farm interests, and one of them directly modified private property relationships. Radical governments also gave some attention to the problem of land distribution. The Chilean government, on the other hand, undertook virtually no action in the field of rural policy; it basically ratified the status quo.

Even in the area of civil liberties, important differences emerge between the policies pursued in the two countries. Legislation allowing summary deportation of dissidents and agitators remained on the books in Argentina, but, unlike Chile, the legislature did not pass new legislation of this type or approve a suspension of civil liberties to cope with labor unrest. Overall, Argentine authorities displayed significantly more tolerance for strikes and other forms of labor protest than their Chilean counterparts. At the same time, the record of both countries in preserving the liberal freedoms of speech, press, and assembly was consummate by the standards of both previous and later regimes. Since respect for civil liberties amounts to a defining characteristic of competitive regimes, this finding is not surprising; but neither is it insignificant. Even if opportunities for the exercise of civil liberties vary with the social position of citizens, the vigor and strength of lower-class protest against the status quo depends at least partially on the possibilities that exist for organization and propaganda.

In conclusion, the review of legislation provides evidence that the emergence of party competition led to a marked increase in the variety of social interests represented in the policy-making process in Argentina, but not in Chile. Chilean policy remained highly particularistic and exhibited no marked tendency toward the expansion of government control in the interest of less privileged groups. The collapse, rather than the inauguration of a competitive party system, led to major changes in government policy. The few innovations in Chilean social policy that did occur during the 1891-1924 period represented responses to cultural diffusion and labor unrest and remained largely symbolic. In contrast, Argentine policy shifted away from highly particularistic decision-making patterns and displayed a tendency toward the expansion of state control and the modification of private power relationships on behalf of the less privileged.

CHAPTER VIII

THE EFFECTS OF REGIME CHANGE

The emergence of competitive party systems in Chile and Argentina in the years leading up to World War I reflected the extraordinary success of the European economic and political ventures that reshaped the nineteenth-century world. As exporters of "munitions and mutton," Chile and Argentina became integrated into the expanding world market and their societies were rapidly transformed. The resulting pressures for change in existing political arrangements led to the adoption of European political models under conditions that seemed highly favorable to future development along a pluralist path. Liberal democratic institutions were nearing the height of their international prestige. Moreover, by the standards of the period, Chile and Argentina were highly prosperous and modernized. Citizens and foreigners alike regarded the two countries as outposts of modern European civilization rather than as members of the relatively impoverished collection of nations that we refer to today as the Third World.

Despite these apparently auspicious beginnings, liberal democratic institutions in both Chile and Argentina had succumbed to military rule by 1930. The two countries were also similar in that the collapse of competitive politics was associated with a major reversal in the established pattern of export-oriented development. The key difference between the two cases is that after an eight-year period of political instability—a period that witnessed the dictatorship of Carlos Ibáñez (1927-1931) as well as the short-lived "Socialist Republic" of 1932, Chilean parliamentary institutions were reconsolidated in a remarkably durable form. Apart from Australia, New Zealand, and the North Atlantic nations, Chile is the only nation in the world to have consistently selected its political leaders by competitive elections throughout the 1932-1973 period. Even by European standards, Chile compiled an exceptional record of adherence to constitutional norms. As Régis Debray once observed, until 1973 many European countries, including France, looked like banana republics in comparison to Chile.[1]

The long-term fate of democratic institutions in Argentina differed significantly. The 1916-1930 period still remains the longest extended period of liberal democratic rule in Argentine history. Indeed, party competition determined political outcomes in only ten of the fifty years following the overthrow of the Irigoyen administration. As a result, Argentina has achieved a reputation as one of the least stable and least democratic countries in Latin America, even though it also has ranked consistently as the most industrially developed and socially modernized country on the continent. The political distinctiveness of Argentina, often described as the "Argentine paradox," has revolved around this failure of political developments to measure up to the expectations created by high levels of socioeconomic modernization. In short, whereas political stability and careful adherence to democratic constitutional norms distinguished Chilean politics in the decades following the breakdown of the parliamentary system, Argentina became conspicuous for continuing military rule and political instability. Even after the military coups of the 1970s installed rather similar regimes in the two countries, this long-term contrast in political development continued to create important differences between Chilean and Argentine politics.

Efforts to explain these contrasting and equally unusual patterns of political development typically have focused on events before 1890 or after 1930, rather than on the initial period of party competition. In the Argentine case, emphasis has been placed on the post-1930 period, especially the legacy of the Peronist era; explanations of Chilean political distinctiveness, on the other hand, usually hark back to the early and mid-nineteenth century.[2] Consequently, the significance of the experiences of the

1890-1930 period for understanding political contrasts between the two countries has been neglected.

The historiography of the 1890-1930 period is partially to blame. Most historians have viewed the regime changes that inaugurated the Chilean parliamentary period and Argentine Radical era less as major political watersheds than as adjustments in established patterns of political development. According to the Chilean historian Alberto Edwards Vives, for example, "No period in the history of Chile was more conservative. Things were the same in 1918 as in 1891."[3] Argentine historians have similarly argued that the 1912-1930 period did not mark a real break with the past.[4]

These assessments reflect the very real continuities that characterized Chilean and Argentine politics over time. The emergence of party competition did not fundamentally alter the preexisting structure of political conflict in either country. The multipolar framework of competition survived in Chile, while in Argentina the basically bipolar struggle between "ins" and "outs" was reestablished after 1916. Important continuities also characterized patterns of leadership selection and policy formation over time. Despite the development of a competitive system, socioeconomic elites in both countries retained privileged access to political office and a dominant voice in the upper house of the legislature. Similarly, no radical transformation of public policy followed the development of party competition, partially because economic prosperity lent respectability to long-standing policy formulas and created few incentives for major reforms. Hence political authorities in both countries concentrated on providing short-term political payoffs, rather than on pursuing a distinctive set of long-range goals.

An emphasis on continuities over time and similarities between the two countries, however, distorts historical reality and leads to misleading assessments of the 1890-1930 period. As David Rock has argued with specific reference to Argentina,[5] elements of continuity between the periods before and after the development of competitive regimes do not necessarily mean that political authorities in post-1891 Chile or post-1912 Argentina merely continued what had gone before or responded to issues in the same manner as their predecessors. Nor do continuities mean that the

first periods of political party competition in the two countries
were unmarked by deep political conflicts. At an historical distance such conflicts may be seen as minor tussles, just as most
policy alterations, particularly when measured by late twentieth-
century standards of social reform and state planning, may be dismissed as "mere tamperings."[6] The perspective of contemporaries,
which needs to be taken into account to explain the collapse of
competitive party systems in the two countries, was often rather
different. But perhaps most important, an emphasis on continuities
obscures important contrasts between the effects of party competition in Chile and Argentina—contrasts that are essential for understanding the diverging political paths taken by the two countries
since 1930.

ENVIRONMENTAL INFLUENCES, PARTY COMPETITION,
AND POLITICAL OUTCOMES

In the Chilean case, data on political recruitment and public
policy contradict the proposition that party competition produces
changes in the distribution of power favorable to less privileged
social groups. Far from equalizing political opportunities, the
shift to a competitive system in Chile initially strengthened the
odds favoring the recruitment of legislators from upper-class backgrounds. During most of the parliamentary period, Chile's socioeconomic elite directly controlled a higher proportion of legislative seats than in the years immediately preceding or following the
1891-1924 era of competitive politics.

Similarly, public policy during the parliamentary period reflected the interests of the socially privileged more blatantly than
under the presidency of Balmaceda or any post-1924 government.
Almost all proposals for changing the existing distribution of
policy costs and benefits fell victim to cabinet instability, while
issues such as agrarian reform even failed to secure a serious place
on the political agenda. Yet the benefits accruing to a narrow
privileged elite were not merely a function of policy inertia. Both
changes and continuities in Chilean public policy during the
parliamentary era served upper-class interests. Hence direct taxes
were reduced, while revisions in tariff and monetary policies

assisted large landowners and businessmen at the expense of the average citizen.

Policy shifts favoring the privileged more than offset any benefits received by groups at the middle or lower end of the socioeconomic spectrum through modest advances in social legislation or increased spending on education and social welfare. Moreover, those few policy changes that did address popular-sector needs can be explained in terms of factors such as cultural diffusion, rather than party competition. Chileans were acutely aware of the growth of social protection in Europe and of their standing among "civilized" nations. Hence in adopting social reforms, policy makers were not necessarily responding to pressures created by party competition; as the parallels that existed between Argentine and Chilean policy before the introduction of competitive politics in Argentina emphasize, similar social legislation was emerging throughout Latin America at the time—even in highly authoritarian political settings.

Factors other than party competition also influenced policies favoring better-endowed private actors in Chile. The expansion of nitrate exports and the associated increase in nitrate tax revenues, for example, created conditions favorable to tax reductions. Policy outcomes, such as inflation and devaluation, were shaped even more directly by factors other than government behavior. Yet, on the whole, the analysis of politics in the parliamentary era suggests that the relationship between party competition and public policy, far from being tenuous in Chile, was very strong in the sense that electoral competition allowed powerful private interests to consolidate their control over the state.

Before 1891 public policy could and occasionally did diverge from the preferences of powerful private-sector elites; likewise, wealthy and socially prestigious individuals, notably those belonging to Conservative landowning families, could be and were excluded from policy-making positions. After 1891 both of these possibilities waned. The introduction of a competitive system and the related reduction in the national administration's ability to control political outcomes meant that patterns of political recruitment and public policy formation came to reflect more faithfully the highly skewed distribution of resources in civil society. Literate, male citizens gained a vote and hence a voice in public affairs; but that voice did not find an audience among the privileged who dominated both the electoral process and congressional debate. The issue is not just one of institutional change. Had congress played a weaker role vis-à-vis the Chilean president, the interests of the many might conceivably have received a little more attention. On the other hand, political outcomes would still have responded to the demands and interests of the upper class, which controlled a highly disproportionate share of political resources. Under the conditions prevailing in Chile, the introduction of a competitive system strengthened, rather than diluted, the correlation between socioeconomic status and political power.

The political experience of Chile in the 1891-1924 period thus has major theoretical implications. It demonstrates that the interests of the many are not necessarily served by party competition. Depending on the scope of political participation and the structure of political conflict, party competition may fail to equalize access to political power and even have negative consequences for less privileged social groups.

Although this line of analysis runs counter to key assumptions about political democracy, it will not appear anomalous to the many historians who have seen the fall of Balmaceda as a tremendous coup for oligarchical interests and as a major reversal in the trend toward increased state autonomy. Nor is the combination of liberal democratic institutions and oligarchical political outcomes one that is unfamiliar to scholars of other Latin American countries or historical periods. The combination is also evident, for example, in the modern politics of Ecuador, Peru, and Colombia: countries in which military regimes have posed more of a threat to established elites than competitive ones. In such cases competitive political arrangements have shared two fundamental similarities with those of Chile during the parliamentary period: political competition has not been structured along well-defined lines and the scope of political participation has been limited.

Given the socioeconomic structure of Chile, the probability of more positive state action on behalf of less privileged groups under a different kind of regime cannot be considered high. Yet the possibility of such an outcome cannot be dismissed entirely.

The argument on this point must necessarily be tentative, speculative, and based on potentially controversial counterfactual assumptions; yet the experience of many countries, including Chile and Argentina, indicates that cultural diffusion combined with anticipatory, preemptive, and cooptive strategies frequently gives rise to policy innovations under noncompetitive regimes. It is certainly striking that many basic reform proposals in Chile were passed and implemented after 1924 in response to military intervention—not party competition. The fact that Balmaceda threatened vested interests before 1891 by advocating measures such as the consolidation of state control over banking is also worth consideration.

The argument that party competition in Chile impeded policy reform favorable to less privileged groups can also be developed along more general lines. In a competitive system political authorities respond to societal pressures; hence both Marxist and liberal accounts of decision making in liberal democracies assume that policy outcomes reflect the distribution of political resources in civil society. In a noncompetitive system this assumption becomes more problematic, since political authorities may enjoy considerable autonomy and implement policies in the absence of or in spite of pressures from below. In other words, although nitrate workers or primary school teachers would not have had more influence under a noncompetitive regime, large landowners or mining elites might well have had less, enhancing the possibility of state action in the interests of the former. Under the conditions prevailing in Chile, a noncompetitive regime was a necessary, albeit insufficient, condition for the development of policies that diverged from the preferences of the upper class.

The historical experience of other world regions offers support for these speculations. Gaston Rimlinger's comparative study of the growth of social legislation in the United States, Germany, France, Britain, and the Soviet Union, in particular, points to the possibility of a negative correlation between regime competitiveness and the development of social welfare policies. Rimlinger concluded, "In the countries studied, the more democratic governments were slower to introduce social protection than the authoritarian and totalitarian governments."[7] In the former public policy responded to the relative strength, organization, and representation of social interests; in the latter authorities were free to pursue their own goals and the interests of the state could take precedence. The relatively early and rapid development of social welfare legislation in Germany, which adopted health, accident, and old age insurance during the 1880s, is a case in point.

Rimlinger also found that ideas about class relations were important and that social protection developed more slowly in countries where liberalism and individualism flourished than in countries where paternalism retained a strong influence.[8] This proposition is of some relevance because while liberalism and individualism had their advocates in Chile, notably among the "old guard" of the Radical party, a very strong tradition of paternalism persisted—one that is evident in the programs of the Conservative party as well as the Liberal administration of Alessandri. In view of this tradition, the argument that public policy in Chile would have been equally, if not more, favorable to less privileged groups under a noncompetitive regime appears particularly plausible. Only with regard to civil liberties would the outlook for subordinate groups have been worse.

At the very least, the negative consequences of party competition for subordinate groups would have been limited under a different regime. It is difficult to imagine any government responding to upper-class demands and interests more consistently than Chile's parliamentary regime. It was precisely this responsiveness that produced political outcomes contrary to the interests of the many.

In the Argentine case, the evidence points in a very different direction. There the development of a competitive party system led to a rapid and dramatic change in the social composition of the political elite as well as important policy shifts. Social protection became more extensive than in Chile, government policy fostered price stability rather than inflation, the real wages of workers increased both absolutely and as a proportion of national income, tentative efforts were made to control and regulate industry, changes in the tariff structure favored consumer interests, and some attention was even given to the problem of rural reform. As in Chile, opportunities for education and public employment also expanded in the wake of the shift toward a competitive system.

Considering the question from another perspective, Argentine public policy brought few positive gains to powerful socioeconomic interests, such as reductions in direct taxation. There was a slight real devaluation of the Argentine peso, which theoretically tended to benefit powerful exporting interests as well as industrialists, but this trend can be attributed at least partially to factors beyond the control of Argentine policy makers. Even more important, the rise in real wages undermines the argument that devaluation represented a positive gain.

Altogether the approach of authorities was much more energetic than in Chile, where public policy was characterized mainly by the distribution of benefits or by inaction that left decisions in the hands of powerful private interests. Public policy in Argentina may not have posed a serious threat to the socioeconomic status quo, but there was at least some expansion of the scope of government control in the interests of the less privileged, some expression of sympathy for the urban working class, and a few instances of action directly threatening upper-class interests. The rural contract law, rent control legislation, and meat policy are cases in point. The efficacy of these latter measures may be legitimately questioned; but with the exception of meat policy, which brought two powerful sets of interests into collision, a cynical interpretation would be farfetched. Hence in the case of Argentina, the argument that the introduction of a competitive party system worked against the interests of less privileged groups can be rejected.

Disposing of the argument that party competition played no role in the implementation of policies favoring groups at the middle or lower end of the socioeconomic spectrum in Argentina is more difficult. Nevertheless, setting aside policy outcomes such as the advance in real wages, which may plausibly be explained in economic terms, the link between party competition and policy shifts favorable to less privileged groups appears far stronger than in Chile, primarily because advances in social protection were not just isolated or symbolic concessions. Taking into account government policy in other fields, statements of policy intentions, and the general political situation, it would be difficult to argue that the Argentine government acted merely out of paternalism or in response to a world-wide recognition of the need for broader state action in the social field, even though it may have been influenced by these factors. In the case of Argentina everything points in the direction of a real redistribution of political power, including the negative reaction of conservative interests to the country's experiment with competitive party politics.

The cross-national comparison between Chile and Argentina supports the conclusion that regime change was an important intervening variable accounting for shifting patterns of political recruitment and public policy formation in each country. Cultural diffusion provided an important impetus to policy change, especially in the field of social legislation; but the geographical propinquity of the two countries and the near identity of the time periods studied mean that diffusion cannot explain the policy contrasts between Chile and Argentina. Assessing the extent to which shifting patterns of political recruitment and public policy in each country reflected socioeconomic rather than political changes presents greater difficulties; but again the cross-national comparison points to the importance of political variables. Chile and Argentina were experiencing very similar processes of socioeconomic change, such as rapid urbanization and export-oriented growth; yet patterns of political recruitment and public policy in the two countries shifted in nearly opposite directions. Underlying socioeconomic conditions provide a basis for understanding this contrast, but the similarities between the socioeconomic changes taking place in Chile and Argentina suggest that intranational or longitudinal variations in public policy and political recruitment cannot be explained simply in terms of shifting environmental conditions.

THE VARIABLE IMPACT OF PARTY COMPETITION

Two factors—the scope of political participation and the structure of political conflict—explain the varying impact of party competition in Chile and Argentina. Because of differences in these factors, authorities had more incentive to search for lower- and middle-class support in Argentina than in Chile, and the needs and interests of the less privileged accordingly received greater attention. Viewing the question from a slightly different perspective, parties representing conservative interests exercised more influence in Chile, where electoral competition from parties representing middle- and lower-class groups remained weak until the end of the parliamentary period.

The contrast in the scope of political participation is brought out by electoral statistics. Partially because of variations in suffrage regulations, a higher percentage of the population voted in the Argentine elections of 1916 than in any Chilean election until the 1950s. But the question is not just one of the size of the electorate. The relative independence of voters must be taken into account. Because of socioeconomic conditions, Chilean elites exercised considerable control over the electorate. This control was particularly evident in rural areas, but the severe social inequalities and related attitudes of deference that shaped class relationships in Chile also affected the quality of electoral participation elsewhere. The situation differed in Argentina, where rural elites had to contend with relatively independent farmers, rather than a mass of deferential and apolitical peasants, and where the sheer pace and magnitude of social change undermined rigid class distinctions.

The structure of political conflict in Argentina was also more conducive to the introduction and implementation of policies beneficial to non-elites. The Chilean multiparty system did not clarify choices; it confused them. Almost every important policy issue cut across party lines, giving rise to cabinet instability and the formation of governments on the basis of particular interest and material gain, rather than general issues. These tendencies left voters without any effective means of holding decision makers responsible for policy outputs and discouraged the expansion of electoral participation. The structure of political conflict in Chile also worked against the representation of popular interests by impeding policy innovation and reform. Public inertia left the field completely open to powerful private decision makers, whose resources became more, rather than less, useful under the parliamentary system. In Argentina electoral alternatives were much more clearly defined, because of the previous pattern of development as well as legal regulations governing the system of representation. Consequently, the vote was a more meaningful sanction and the incentives to participate in elections far stronger than in Chile.

To link these findings with previous research on the impact of party competition, it is interesting that the level of competition alone was not an important factor. Indeed, if anything, its relationship to public policy and the level of political participation was just the opposite of that posited in previous policy studies. The closely balanced strength of parties in Chile, for example, discouraged policy innovation. This study also demonstrates the importance of looking at regulatory and symbolic policies. It is in this realm that the consequences of regime change were most palpable, no doubt because economic and other environmental factors imposed the fewest constraints on decision makers. A government's resource base directly limits its capacity to allocate funds for welfare, but the same cannot be said with regard to the recognition of civil liberties or the expression of sympathy for lower-class groups. Because as much satisfaction may flow from symbolic as tangible allocations, this study thus underlines the true enormity of the leap from findings that *levels* of competition do not explain variations in *levels* of public expenditure or taxation to the proposition that political system characteristics do not explain variations in public policy.

The divergent impact of party competition in Chile and Argentina also provides a basis for understanding the contradictory findings of the comparative policy literature. As this study shows, the consequences of party competition (and presumably lack of competition) may vary widely across cases. This finding points not to the irrelevance of political variables, but to the importance of deflating the concepts that have guided research to take into account more theoretically appropriate regime characteristics. In the case of competitive regimes, the relevant variables are the scope of participation and structure of political conflict.

CONCLUSION: PARTY COMPETITION, POLITICAL OUTCOMES,
AND PATTERNS OF DEVELOPMENT

This book began with the question, How did party development and electoral competition affect the struggle for power in Chile and Argentina? Its findings, which show that under some conditions party competition fails to shift political outcomes in a more egalitarian direction, contradict assumptions that have guided comparative research for several decades. The analysis of political outcomes during the 1890-1930 period also challenges existing interpretations of Chilean and Argentine history. Far from representing periods of continuity that are unimportant for understanding long-term development contrasts, the Argentine Radical era and Chilean parliamentary period left deep marks on political life in the two countries.

In the Chilean case, the emergence of a relatively well-institutionalized party system did not result in a more equitable distribution of power, nor did it enhance the capacity of the state to adapt to or direct change. Yet the 1891-1924 period cannot be dismissed as a do-nothing era of merely formal democracy or corrupt, oligarchical rule. The emergence of parties with a popular base, the institutionalization of norms of freedom of expression and opposition, and the rise of the political left and the trade union movement—all these developments took place under conditions favorable to the consolidation of upper-class control over the state. The political experience of the parliamentary period thereby established the basis for Chile's peculiarly strong tradition of constituutional democracy—a tradition that is central to any analysis of modern Chilean politics, including the election and overthrow of Salvador Allende. The emergence of a competitive party system in Argentina, on the other hand, resulted in a substantial diffusion of power in the short run, but at the expense of future development along a pluralist path.

These contrasts between Chile and Argentina emphasize the theoretical significance of variations in the timing, sequence, and pace of political change.[9] In Chile organized electoral competition emerged under conditions highly favorable to elite acceptance of liberal democracy. Parties developed relatively early, gradually, and before the growth of pressures for mass political participation. In Argentina, on the other hand, a system of protoparty competition did not precede the formation of full-blown parties, and an extended suffrage was introduced virtually overnight into an oligarchical regime. Partially as a result, the Argentine upper class found it much more difficult to adjust to party competition than its Chilean counterpart and developed no strong commitment to liberal democratic institutions. When the depression struck the country, elites seized the opportunity to oust the Radicals and end Argentina's initial experiment with competitive party politics. Since 1930 conservative groups in Argentina have continued to question the legitimacy of liberal democracy and have provided a key source of support for military intervention.

In contrast to the Argentine case, the first competitive party regime in Chile collapsed in response to reformist, rather than conservative, pressures. Particularly after the events of the 1924-1932 period, which demonstrated the unreliability of the military as a bastion against reformist and revolutionary pressures, Chilean socioeconomic elites supported the return to liberal democratic institutions. It took a major rupture of Chile's socioeconomic order before privileged groups withdrew that support in the 1970s.

In short, the success of Chilean and Argentine socioeconomic elites in controlling political outcomes after the introduction of a competitive regime not only differed significantly, but that difference had major implications for the long-term viability of liberal democracy in the two countries. If a single lesson is to be drawn from the complex evidence concerning the introduction of competitive party politics in the two countries, it is that the consolidation of liberal democratic institutions depends not upon their effectiveness in equalizing the distribution of political power, but upon their acceptability to the propertied and powerful.

NOTES

Introduction

1. In the case of Latin America, most research has cast considerable doubt
    upon the relevance of regime differences for explaining variations in poli-
    cy performance. Yet these results remain controversial. For a summary
    and critique of the literature see Karen L. Remmer, "Evaluating the
    Policy Impact of Military Regimes in Latin America," *Latin American
    Research Review*, XIII, no. 2 (1978):39-54. Research in other political
    contexts has also tended to minimize the significance of national institu-
    tional arrangements for explaining political outcomes. See, for example,
    Frederic L. Pryor, *Public Expenditures in Communist and Capitalist
    Nations* (Homewood, Ill., 1968); Harold L. Wilensky, *The Welfare State
    and Equality: Structural and Ideological Roots of Public Expenditures*
    (Berkeley, 1975); and Joel G. Verner, "Socioeconomic Environment,
    Political System, and Educational Policy Outcomes: A Comparative
    Analysis of 102 Countries," *Comparative Politics*, XI (January 1979):
    165-187. Nevertheless, there are notable exceptions, such as Richard
    Gunther's recent study *Public Policy in a No-Party State: Spanish Plan-
    ning and Budgeting in the Twilight of the Franquist Era* (Berkeley,
    1980), which argues that the absence of a competitive regime in Spain
    during the 1960s and early 1970s biased public policy towards middle-
    and upper-class interests. The literature on policy formation at the sub-
    national level also indicates that party competition and other political
    variables are relatively unimportant for explaining political outcomes.
    But again, a few studies contradict these findings, and the debate over
    the relevance of party competition remains far from closure. For a review
    of this literature that discusses its potential applicability to cross-national
    analysis see Richard I. Hofferbert, "State and Community Policy Studies:
    A Review of Comparative Input-Output Analysis," in *Political Science
    Annual*, Vol. III, ed. James A. Robinson (Indianapolis, 1972), pp. 3-
    72. For other literature reviews see Herbert Jacob and Michael Lipsky,
    "Outputs, Structure, and Power: An Assessment of Changes in the Study
    of State and Local Politics," *Journal of Politics*, XXX (May 1968):
    510-538; and John H. Fenton and Donald W. Chamberlayne, "The Litera-
    ture Dealing with the Relationships between Political Processes, Socio-
    economic Conditions and Public Policies in the American States: A
    Bibliographic Essay," *Polity*, I (Spring 1969):388-404. Recent sub-
    national level studies of the link between political variables and public
    policy include R. Kenneth Godwin and W. Bruce Shepard, "Political
    Processes and Public Expenditures: A Re-examination Based on Theories
    of Representative Government," *American Political Science Review*,
    LXX (December 1976):1127-1135; David R. Morgan and John P. Pelis-
    sero, "Urban Policy: Does Political Structure Matter?" ibid., LXXIV
    (December 1980):999-1006; Michael S. Lewis-Beck, "The Relative
    Importance of Socioeconomic and Political Variables for Public Policy,"

ibid., LXXI (June 1977):559-566; Edward T. Jennings, Jr., "Competition, Constituencies, and Welfare Policies in American States," ibid., LXXIII (June 1979):414-429; Eric M. Uslaner, "Comparative State Policy Formation, Interparty Competition, and Malapportionment: A New Look at 'V.O. Key's Hypothesis,' " *Journal of Politics*, XL (May 1978):409-432; Virginia Gray, "Models of Comparative State Politics: A Comparison of Cross-Sectional and Time Series Analysis," *American Journal of Political Science*, XX (May 1976):235-256; and Richard Winters, "Party Control and Policy Change," ibid., XX (November 1976): 597-636. See also Howard Leichter, "Comparative Public Policy: Problems and Prospects," in *Policy Studies Review Annual*, Vol. I, ed. Stuart S. Nagel (Beverly Hills, 1977), pp. 138-150 for a discussion of the limited range of inferences that may be drawn from sub-national level comparative policy studies.

2. See, for example, the introduction of Joseph La Palombara and Myron Weiner (eds.), *Political Parties and Political Development* (Princeton, 1966), where the emergence of political parties is described as a "useful institutional index of political development" (p. 7). See also Samuel P. Huntington, *Political Order in Changing Societies* (New Haven, 1968). Huntington attaches a great deal of importance to party development and argues that the "distinctive institution of the modern polity . . . is the political party" (p. 89).

3. Most studies of party development have focused on individual nations; others have emphasized comparisons in the process of party development rather than its impact on policy or other political outcomes.

4. For literature on the policy impact of diffusion and the problems it raises for comparative research see Virginia Gray, "Innovation in the States: A Diffusion Study," *American Political Science Review*, LXVII (December 1973):1174-1185; Jack L. Walker, "The Diffusion of Innovations Among the American States," ibid., LXXI (June 1977):441-447; David Collier and Richard E. Messick, "Prerequisites versus Diffusion: Testing Alternative Explanations of Social Security Adoption," ibid., LXIX (December 1975):1299-1315; David Klingman, "Temporal and Spatial Diffusion in the Comparative Analysis of Social Change," ibid., LXXIV (March 1980):123-137; Marc Howard Ross and Elizabeth Homer, "Galton's Problem in Cross-National Research," *World Politics*, XXIX (October 1976):1-28.

5. This term is normally reserved for the countries that participated in the first wave of industrialization, such as Great Britain. Their developmental experiences are contrasted with those of the "late developers" and "late, late developers." For literature emphasizing the timing of development see Alexander Gerschenkron, *Economic Backwardness in Historical Perspective* (Cambridge, Mass., 1962); Glaucio Ary Dillon Soares, "The New Industrialization and the Brazilian Political System," in *Latin America: Reform or Revolution?* ed. James Petras and Maurice Zeitlin,

Political Perspectives Series (Greenwich, Conn., 1969), pp. 186-201; Karl de Schweinitz, Jr., "Growth, Development, and Political Modernization," *World Politics*, XXII (July 1970):518-540; Philippe C. Schmitter, "Paths to Political Development in Latin America," in *Changing Latin America: New Interpretations of Its Politics and Society*, ed. Douglas A. Chalmers, Proceedings of the Academy of Political Science, vol. XXX (New York, 1972), pp. 83-105; James R. Kurth, "Patrimonial Authority, Delayed Development, and Mediterranean Politics," paper prepared for Annual Meeting of the American Political Science Association, New Orleans, September 1973.

6. Gino Germani, "Estrategia para estimular la mobilidad social," in *La industrialización en América Latina*, ed. Joseph A. Kahl (Mexico, 1965), pp. 294-295. Estimates of per capita income in Argentina and Chile at the outbreak of World War I are discussed below in Chapter II.

7. The concept "fragment" is explored in Louis Hartz, ed., *The Founding of New Societies* (New York, 1964). See also Barry M. Schultz, "The Concept of Fragment in Comparative Political Analysis," *Comparative Politics*, I (October 1968):111-125.

8. In addition to the studies cited in note 1 above, see Margaret Daly Hayes, "Policy Consequences of Military Participation in Politics: An Analysis of Tradeoffs in Brazilian Federal Expenditures," in *Comparative Public Policy: Issues, Theories, and Methods*, ed. Craig Liske, William Loehr, and John McCamant (Beverly Hills, 1975), pp. 21-52; Robert W. Jackman, "Politicians in Uniform: Military Governments and Social Change in the Third World," *American Political Science Review*, LXX (December 1976):1078-1097; R.D. McKinlay and A.S. Cohan, "A Comparative Analysis of the Political and Economic Performance of Military and Civilian Regimes," *Comparative Politics*, VIII (October 1975):1-30; idem, "Performance and Instability in Military and Nonmilitary Regime Systems," *American Political Science Review*, LXX (September 1976): 850-864; Eric A. Nordlinger, "Soldiers in Mufti: The Impact of Military Rule upon Economic and Social Change in the Non-Western States," *American Political Science Review*, LXIV (December 1970):1131-1148; Philippe C. Schmitter, "Military Intervention, Political Competitiveness and Public Policy in Latin America: 1950-1967," in *On Military Intervention*, ed. Morris Janowitz and J. van Doorn (Rotterdam, 1971), pp. 425-506; Benjamin A. Most, "Authoritarianism and the Growth of the State in Latin America: An Assessment of Their Impacts on Argentine Public Policy, 1930-1970," *Comparative Political Studies*, XIII, 2 (1980): 173-203. See also David Collier, ed., *The New Authoritarianism in Latin America* (Princeton, 1979), which also raises important questions about the relationship between regime type and public policy.

9. In the case of Latin America, even scholars using bureaucratic-authoritarian, historical-materialist, and other theoretical frameworks emphasizing socioeconomic constraints on political actors have oriented their

research around questions of regime change and consolidation. See, for example, Göran Therborn, "The Travail of Latin American Democracy," *New Left Review*, no. 113-114 (January-April 1979):71-109; and Guillermo O'Donnell, *Modernization and Bureaucratic-Authoritarianism: Studies in South American Politics*, reprint ed. (Berkeley, 1973).

10. Robert A. Dahl, *A Preface to Democratic Theory* (Chicago, 1956); idem, *Polyarchy: Participation and Opposition* (New Haven, 1971), pp. 17-32; Seymour Martin Lipset, *Political Man* (Garden City, N.Y., 1963), p. 27; idem, "Party Systems and the Representation of Social Groups," in *Political Parties: Contemporary Trends and Ideas*, ed. Roy C. Macridis (New York, 1967), pp. 40-74; V.O. Key, Jr., *Southern Politics* (New York, 1949), pp. 304-307; Kenneth Prewitt and Alan Stone, *The Ruling Elites: Elite Theory, Power, and American Democracy* (New York, 1973), pp. 233-236; Walter Dean Burnham, *Critical Elections and the Mainsprings of American Politics* (New York, 1970).

11. While this consequence of party competition often receives minimal attention in the theoretical literature, it is emphasized by scholars concerned with leadership selection. See, for example, Lester G. Seligman et al., *Patterns of Recruitment: A State Chooses Its Lawmakers* (Chicago, 1974), pp. 32-34, 189; Lester E. Seligman, "Political Parties and the Recruitment of Political Leaders," in *Political Leadership in Industrialized Societies*, ed. Lewis J. Edinger and Donald D. Searing (New York, 1967), pp. 294-315.

12. See, for example, Willis D. Hawley, *Nonpartisan Elections and the Case for Party Politics* (New York, 1973); Kenneth Prewitt, *The Recruitment of Political Leaders: A Study of Citizen-Politicians* (Indianapolis, 1970).

13. Key, p. 304.

14. See, for example, David Robertson, *A Theory of Party Competition* (London, 1976); Morris P. Fiorina, *Representatives, Roll Calls, and Constituencies* (Lexington, Mass., 1974); Michael Margolis, "From Confusion to Confusion: Issues and the American Voter (1956-1972)," *American Political Science Review*, LXXI (March 1977):31-43; James H. Kuklinski, "Representativeness and Elections: A Policy Analysis," ibid., LXXII (March 1978):165-177.

15. See Robert Burrowes, "Theory Sí, Data No! A Decade of Cross-National Research," *World Politics*, XXV (October 1972):120-144. The problems in the selection of variables and operational indicators that have beset comparative quantitative research are particularly evident in the field of policy analysis. Characteristics of the political system that can be readily translated into numerical terms, such as the level of party competition, have been emphasized at the expense of theoretically relevant variables, such as the structure of party competition. Similarly, the comparative policy literature has concentrated on explaining variations in government expenditures and revenues and virtually ignored symbolic and regulatory policies involving such issues as the right of workers to organize and

strike, minimum wages, land reform, and the appointment of minority members to government posts. This emphasis is obviously theoretically unsound, since regulatory and symbolic policies create serious conflicts among social groups and affect who benefits most from government and at the expense of whom. For a further discussion of these issues as they relate to the study of regime impact in the Latin American context, see Remmer, pp. 44-50.

16. See, for example, Francis G. Castles, "The Impact of Parties on Public Expenditure," in *The Impact of Parties: Politics and Policies in Democratic Capitalist States,* ed. idem, (Beverly Hills, 1982), pp. 21-96.

17. This point has been emphasized with specific reference to the study of policy by Marsha Chandler, William Chandler, and David Vogler, "Policy Analysis and the Search for Theory," *American Politics Quarterly,* II (January 1974):108. See also Gray, "Models of Comparative State Politics," pp. 235-256.

18. See, in particular, Eric A. Nordlinger, "Political Development: Time Sequences and Rates of Change," *World Politics,* XX (April 1968):494-520. See also fn. 5, supra.

19. O'Donnell, pp. 1-48 provides a good summary of the weakness of this literature with specific reference to Latin America.

20. "Party Development and Party Action: The American Origins," *History and Theory,* III (1963):91-120; *Political Parties in a New Nation: The American Experience 1776-1809* (New York, 1963); "Party Development and the American Mainstream," in *The American Party Systems: Stages of Political Development,* ed. William N. Chambers and Walter D. Burnham (New York, 1967), pp. 3-32.

21. This definition of democracy is a paraphrase of the classic definition provided by Joseph A. Schumpeter, *Capitalism, Socialism and Democracy,* 3rd ed. (New York, 1962), p. 269.

Chapter I

1. There are a large number of works on this early period of national independence, including Domingo Amunátegui y Solar, *Pipiolos y pelucones* (Santiago, 1939); Agustín Edwards MacClure, *The Dawn* (London, 1931); Alberto Edwards Vives, *La organización política de Chile (1810-1833)* (Santiago, 1943); Luis Vitale, *Interpretación marxista de la historia de Chile,* 3 vols. (Santiago, 1967-1971), III. The most comprehensive treatment of the period in English is Simon Collier, *Ideas and Politics of Chilean Independence, 1808-1833* (Cambridge, England, 1967). On the nature of the conservative *pelucón* tendency see also Simon Collier, "Conservatismo chileno, 1830-1860. Temas e imágenes," *Nueva historia,* II, no. 7 (1983):143-163.

2. For an analysis of the many issues involved see José Luis Romero, *A History of Argentine Political Thought* (Stanford, Calif., 1963). See

228 Notes to Pages 10-14

also Miron Burgin, *The Economic Aspects of Argentine Federalism, 1820-1852* (Cambridge, Mass., 1946), which examines the relationship of economic interests to the conflict; and Leonardo Paso, *Historia del origen de los partidos políticos en la Argentina (1810-1918)* (Buenos Aires, 1972), pp. 20-213, which provides a general history of political conflicts in the post-independence period.

3. Julio César Jobet, *Ensayo crítico del desarrollo económico-social de Chile* (Santiago, 1955), p. 33.

4. The society was founded in 1850, and although it survived less than a year, Marxist historians attach a great deal of importance to it. The society not only led the first significant public campaign for civil liberties and electoral freedom in Chile, but one of its founders, Santiago Arcos Arlegui, was a student of the French social utopians who emphasized the importance of economic realities and proposed a division of landed property to bring about political democracy in Chile. See ibid., pp. 37-40.

5. See Alberto Edwards Vives, *El gobierno de don Manuel Montt, 1851-1861* (Santiago, 1932); Benjamín Vicuña Mackenna, *Historia de los diez años de la administración de don Manuel Montt*, 5 vols. (Santiago, 1862-1863); and Luis Vitale, *Los guerras civiles de 1851 y 1859 en Chile* (Concepción, 1971), pp. 5-35.

6. The dispute developed over the dismissal of two canons who appealed to the supreme court to revoke the action of the clerical authorities. The latter refused to submit themselves to the jurisdiction of civil authority. For useful summaries of this affair see J. Lloyd Mecham, *Church and State in Latin America: A History of Politico-Ecclesiastical Relations*, rev. ed. (Chapel Hill, N.C., 1966), pp. 209-210 and Edwards Vives, *El gobierno*, pp. 173-250.

7. Vitale, *Los guerras civiles*, pp. 37-74.

8. Alberto Edwards Vives and Eduardo Frei Montalva, *Historia de los partidos políticos chilenos* (Santiago, 1949), p. 57. This book includes two separate studies: the first by Edwards, "Bosquejo histórico de los partidos políticos chilenos" (pp. 9-111), was initially published in 1903 and covers the 1833-1891 period; the second by Frei takes the study up to 1938. On the minority position of the Montt government, see also Collier, "Conservatismo chileno," p. 156.

9. For accounts of this revolt see Edwards Vives, *El gobierno*, pp. 250-320 and Vitale, *Los guerras civiles*, pp. 37-74.

10. The Radicals date their origins back to the late 1850s when a group of liberals organized the Asamblea Constituyente to press for the reform of the 1833 constitution. The actual organization of the party can be traced back to 1863 when the first Radical assembly was founded in Copiapó.

11. Edwards Vives and Frei, p. 65.

12. In particular, the liberals sought to secularize cemeteries, separate church and state, establish civil marriage requirements, and abolish the ecclesi-

astical *fuero*. Further differences arose over the issue of state control of education. See Mecham, p. 211; Fredrick B. Pike, *Chile and the United States, 1880-1962* (Notre Dame, Indiana, 1963), p. 19.

13. See, for example, the figures on election results presented in Ricardo Donoso, *Las ideas políticas en Chile* (Mexico, 1946), pp. 408-435.

14. Francisco Antonio Encina, *Historia de Chile*, 20 vols. (Santiago, 1922), XIX, 63-64.

15. The Radicals are a possible exception. Peter G. Snow, for example, has argued that the Radicals were basically composed of segments of the newly emerging middle class. *Radicalismo chileno: Historia y doctrina del partido radical* (Buenos Aires, 1972), p. 21. See also John J. Johnson, *Political Change in Latin America* (Stanford, Calif., 1958), p. 72. If "wealthy bourgeoisie" is substituted for "middle class," this proposition is acceptable, but there is very little evidence to suggest that there were any real barriers to prevent men of wealth from becoming assimilated into the upper class. In 1873, for example, Manuel Antonio Matta, the Radicals' "early guiding spirit," was elected president of the Club de la Unión, one of Chile's most exclusive social organizations. Pike, p. 18.

16. Mecham, p. 211.

17. Edwards Vives and Frei, p. 84.

18. Encina, *Historia*, XIX, 48-49.

19. Ibid., XIX, 56.

20. Edwards Vives and Frei, p. 115.

21. The Radicals were exceptional in this regard. From the beginning they were committed to a program of specific constitutional reforms that were designed mainly to limit the power of the president and provide for a greater measure of electoral freedom. See Snow, pp. 19-20.

22. The election of 1876 is of particular interest in this connection, because for the first time in Chile both presidential candidates campaigned around the country expounding political programs. The opposition, which banded together under the Liberal-Democratic label to support the candidacy of Benjamín Vicuña Mackenna, led the way in this development. The platform that formed the basis of Vicuña Mackenna's campaign, however, was essentially that of an individual candidate. When Vicuña Mackenna was defeated, the Liberal-Democratic grouping dissolved. Edwards Vives and Frei, p. 81; Donoso, *Las ideas políticas*, pp. 426-427.

23. Snow, p. 31.

24. To simplify matters the term *liberales disidentes* is used here to refer to all the liberals who opposed or took an independent stance vis-à-vis the governments of the Liberal Republic: the *liberales reformistas* who fought in the election of 1870; the *liberal-democrático* group which backed Vicuña Mackenna in the election of 1876; the *liberales sueltos* or *doctrinarios* who broke with Santa María in 1885; and the *mocetones* or

nacionalizados, led by Isidoro Errázuriz Errázuriz, who followed the political lead of the Nationals.

25. Encina, *Historia,* XIX, 43.

26. Ibid., p. 42.

27. Chile, Congreso Nacional, Cámara de Diputados, *Boletín de las sesiones ordinarias de la Cámara de Diputados,* 7 July 1888, p. 566 (cited hereafter as Chile, Cámara de Diputados, *Sesiones ordinarias*).

28. Donoso, *Las ideas políticas,* p. 426.

29. For example, in 1881 Santa María was selected to succeed Pinto and was "nominated" by the Radicals, Liberals, and Nationals in separate conventions.

30. Armando Donoso, *Recuerdos de cincuenta años* (Santiago, 1947), p. 210.

31. Abdón Cifuentes, *Memorias,* 2 vols. (Santiago, 1936), I, 147.

32. Ibid., pp. 148-150.

33. Fernando Campos Harriet, *Historia constitucional de Chile* (Santiago, 1956), p. 477.

34. Cifuentes, II, 122-124.

35. This reform gave voters the right to cast their votes for one person or for as many different candidates as there were deputies to be elected in each district.

36. For discussions of these reforms see Atilio A. Borón, "La evolución del régimen electoral y sus efectos en la representación de los intereses populares: El caso de Chile," *Revista latinoamericana de ciencia política,* II (December 1971):395-431; R. Donoso, *Las ideas políticas,* pp. 409-431; Campos Harriet, pp. 475-484; Ricardo Salas Edwards, *Balmaceda y el parlamentarismo en Chile,* 2 vols. (Santiago, 1925), Vol. I; Domingo Amunátegui y Solar, *El progreso intelectual y político de Chile* (Santiago, 1936), pp. 132-139.

37. On the importance of violence and fraud under Santa María see Edwards Vives, p. 86; Encina, *Historia,* XX, 14.

38. Encina, *Historia,* XIX, 116 cites the case of an independent Liberal who had the support of over 70 percent of the voters in the Department of Loncomilla. The administration resorted to every possible type of fraud to prevent his election there, but had him elected from the Department of Puchacay where he was a complete stranger. See also José Miguel Yrarrázaval Larraín, "Las elecciones de 1888," *Boletín de la Academia Chilena de la Historia,* XXI, no. 50 (1954), 71-87.

39. Cifuentes, II, 279-280; Encina, *Historia,* XIX, 116.

40. Chile, Cámara de Diputados, *Sesiones ordinarias,* pp. 565-566.

41. For discussions emphasizing the constitutional issues see Julio Bañados Espinosa, *Balmaceda, su gobierno y la revolución de 1891,* 2 vols. (Paris, 1894); Encina, *Historia,* Vols. XIX, XX, passim; Pedro Montt, *Exposition of the Illegal Acts of the Ex-President Balmaceda, which Caused the Civil War in Chile* (Washington, D.C., 1891); Salas Edwards, Vols. I, II, passim.

42. Hernán Ramírez Necochea, *La guerra civil de 1891: Antecedentes económicos* (Santiago, 1943); Jobet, *Ensayo*, pp. 76-106. See also M.H. Hervey, *Dark Days in Chile: An Account of the Revolution of 1891* (London, 1891). For an appraisal of the evidence supporting this interpretation see Harold Blakemore, "The Chilean Revolution of 1891 and Its Historiography," *Hispanic American Historical Review*, VL (August 1965):393-421; idem, *British Nitrates and Chilean Politics, 1886-1896: Balmaceda and North* (London, 1974); Julio Heise González, *Historia de Chile: El período parlamentario, 1861-1925*, 2 vols. (Santiago, 1974-1982), I, 69-132; José Miguel Yrarrázaval Larraín, *La política económica del Presidente Balmaceda* (Santiago, 1963).

43. Jobet, p. 103.

44. Ibid., pp. 81, 83; Alejandro Venegas [Dr. J. Valdés Cange], *Cartas al Excelentísimo Señor Don Pedro Montt sobre la crisis moral de Chile en sus relaciones con el problema económico de la conversión metálica* (Valparaíso, 1909).

45. Pike, pp. 44-45, 321n. For an extended discussion of Balmaceda's banking policies, which discounts their importance in the civil war, see Yrarrázaval Larraín, *La política económica*, pp. 57-112. Yrarrázaval Larraín points out that supporters of metallic conversion fought on both sides in the civil war.

46. Edwards Vives and Frei, p. 82.

47. The Conservatives strongly supported a plan devised by Manuel José Yrarrázaval to establish autonomous local governments that would assume control over many of the functions of the national government. See Amunátegui y Solar, *El progreso*, p. 135.

48. Encina, *Historia*, XX, 61.

49. Edwards Vives and Frei, pp. 94-95.

50. Lía E.M. Sanucci's excellent study, *La renovación presidencial de 1880* (La Plata, 1959), discusses the background to this agreement in some detail (pp. 13-23).

51. Félix Luna, *Yrigoyen* (Buenos Aires, 1964), p. 35.

52. Gabriel del Mazo, *El Radicalismo: Ensayo sobre su historia y doctrina*, 2 vols. (Buenos Aires, 1957-1959), I, 15. The Republican program is reprinted in Leandro Alem, *Leandro Alem: Mensaje y destino*, 8 vols. (Buenos Aires, 1955-1957), V, 309-310.

53. Sarmiento tried to persuade both Roca and Tejedor to withdraw their candidacies in his favor to avoid a violent conflict. Letters relating to this effort are reprinted in Sanucci, pp. 181-194.

54. Ibid., pp. 113-114.

55. Oscar E. Cornblit, Ezequiel Gallo (H.), and Alfredo A. O'Connell, "La generación del 80 y su proyecto: Antecedentes y consecuencias," in *Argentina, sociedad de masas*, ed. Torcuato S. DiTella et al., 3rd ed. (Buenos Aires, 1966), p. 43; Luis V. Sommi, "Estudio preliminar," in *La política económica argentina en la década del 80*, ed. idem (Buenos Aires, 1955), p. 22.

56. Ibid.
57. Natalio R. Botana, *El orden conservador: La política argentina entre 1880 y 1916* (Buenos Aires, 1977), pp. 65-116.
58. José Nicolás Matienzo, *El gobierno representativo federal en la República Argentina*, 2nd ed. (Madrid, 1917), pp. 221-222; Angel Carrasco, *Lo que yo ví desde el 80: Hombres y episodios de la transformación nacional* (Buenos Aires, 1947), p. 80.
59. Matienzo, p. 201.
60. Vicente C. Gallo, *Por la democracia y las instituciones: Propaganda cívica, 1891-1921* (Buenos Aires, 1921), p. 147. See also the tables presented by Botana, pp. 158-160.
61. In the congressional debate on the Saenz Peña law of November 15, 1911, Manuel Peña drew attention to this development: "Before 1880 the president of the nation needed the support of the provincial governors; that was his source of power. After 1880 a notable change in this situation took place; after 1880 the provincial governors needed the support of the president of the republic because he had increased his powers of protection and influence." Argentina, Ministerio del Interior, Subsecretaría de Informaciones, *Las fuerzas armadas restituyen el imperio de la soberanía popular,* 2 vols. (Buenos Aires, 1946), I, 112.
62. Del Mazo, I, 16.
63. This dependence virtually gave presidents the power to install and depose governors. To cite one interesting example: in March 1888 the Governor of Córdoba, who was a supporter of Roca, requested federal intervention after he was ousted by a provincial revolt. President Juárez refused the request and his brother, Marcos Juárez, was installed as governor. Ismael Bucich Escobar, *Historia de los presidentes argentinos* (Buenos Aires, 1934), p. 235.
64. In 1880 the income of the national government was $19,594,306 gold pesos. By 1890 the figure was $73,150,856 gold pesos. Argentine Republic, Comisión Nacional, *Tercer censo nacional levantado el 1 de junio de 1914,* 10 vols. (Buenos Aires, 1916-1919), X, 386.
65. In his study of Radicalism, del Mazo alludes to the importance of the bank and quotes *La Prensa* of 12 April 1891 as asking, "When the change of a provincial governor is scheduled, what person is in the forefront of the political negotiations?" The answer was, "The director of the Banco Nacional!" (I, 16).
66. Argentina, *Tercer censo,* 1914, X, 405.
67. See, for example, the denunciation of the Comité Nacional de la Unión Cívica Radical, "Manifiesto del Comité Nacional, al reorganizarse," 29 February 1904, reprinted in del Mazo, I, 325. See also Romero's unflattering assessment of the *unicato,* pp. 188-192.
68. Del Mazo, I, 40 estimates that scarcely 2 percent of the population voted in the presidential election of 1880. For more precise figures on electoral participation see Botana, pp. 189-195.

69. *A través de la República Arjentina: Diario de viaje* (Santiago, 1890), pp. 145-146.

70. Ibid., p. 213.

71. "Las elecciones del domingo" as quoted in Ezequiel Ortega, *"Quiera el pueblo votar?" Historia electoral argentina, desde la Revolución de Mayo a la Ley Sáenz Peña, 1810-1912* (Bahia Blanca, 1963), p. 519. See also ibid., pp. 513-518; del Mazo, I, 101-104, Carrasco, p. 39, who describes the violence associated with elections in the Federal Capital during the 1890s; and the speech given by Carlos Pellegrini before the Chamber of Deputies on 9 May 1906, *Pellegrini 1846-1906: Obras,* ed. Agustín Rivero Astengo, 5 vols. (Buenos Aires, 1941), IV, 377-388.

72. König, p. 144.

73. Argentina had "no use for abstract ideas or immortal principles; its chief ambition being above all to sell its corn and cattle and to enrich itself. Behind the agitation of the political parties there is no other object than this: to share in the exploitation of the country and enjoy its wealth." Albert B. Martinez and Maurice Lewandowski, *The Argentine in the Twentieth Century,* trans. Bernard Miall, 3rd ed. (London, 1911), p. 63. This theme crops up frequently in contemporary literature.

74. January 9, 1886 as quoted in Ortega, p. 418.

75. Juárez pointed to this situation as a mark of success in his 1888 presidential address. "In no part of the country are there any organized oppositions, established parties or political circles which consider themselves excluded from public affairs . . . " Miguel Juárez Celman, *Message of the President of the Republic on Opening the Session of the Argentine Congress,* (Buenos Aires, n.d.), p. 36.

76. The literature on this subject is vast. The following are among the most useful sources: Jorge W. Landenberger and Francisco M. Conte, eds., *Unión Cívica: Su origen, organización y tendencias* (Buenos Aires, 1890); del Mazo, Vol. I; Alem, Vol. VII; Hipólito Irigoyen, *Hipólito Yrigoyen: Pueblo y gobierno,* ed. Instituto Yrigoyeneano, 12 vols. (Buenos Aires, 1956), Vol. II.

77. Landenberger and Conte, p. 7.

78. See "Exposición del Doctor Aristóbulo del Valle," 1 December 1890, printed in ibid., pp. 199-222; Dr. F.A. Barroetaveña, "Reseña histórica de la Unión Cívica," in ibid., p. lxiv. See also the letter from Alem to Barroetaveña, reprinted in ibid., pp. lxi-lxiii.

79. Coronel Julio Figueroa attributed the defeat to the failure of the revolutionary leaders to take the offensive. "Exposición del Coronel Julio Figueroa," 24 September 1890 reprinted in ibid., pp. 223-228. See also in the same volume "Exposición del Coronel Mariano Espina," pp. 229-230; and the reports of General Campos to Alem, 28 July 1890, p. 195 and 31 July, pp. 233-238; Coronel Espina to Campos, 30 July 1890, pp. 240-241; Mayor Day to Campos, 30 July 1890, pp. 241-243; Mayor O'Connor to Alem, 1 August 1890, pp. 243-245. For other documents

and accounts see Alem, VII, 47-105; Olegario Becerra, "Interpretación radical de la revolución del 90," *Revista de Historia*, No. 1 (1er trimestre, 1957), pp. 52-55; Roberto Etchepareborda, *La revolución argentina del 90* (Buenos Aires, 1966); Luis Sommi, "La estructura económico-social de la Argentina en 1890," *Revista de Historia*, No. 1 (1er trimestre, 1957), pp. 18-35; *The July Revolution 1890 in Buenos Aires*, 2nd ed. (Buenos Aires, 1890); Horacio Zorraquín Becú et al., *Cuatro revoluciones argentinas* (Buenos Aires, 1960); and Jorge Abelardo Ramos, *Revolución y contrarrevolución en la Argentina*, 2nd ed. (Buenos Aires, 1961).

Chapter II

1. Chile, Oficina Central de Estadística, *Anuario estadístico de la República de Chile*, 1918, Vol. VI: *Hacienda*, p. 64.
2. Ibid.
3. Chilean Legation (London), *Resumen de la hacienda pública de Chile desde 1833 hasta 1914* (London, 1915) p. 94.
4. Pike, p. 33.
5. Ibid., p. 35, quoting from the January 22, 1880 edition of the paper.
6. See Humberto Fuenzalida Villegas, "La conquista del territorio y la utilización de la tierra durante la primera mitad del siglo XX," in *Chile*, ed. Humberto Fuenzalida Villegas et al. (Buenos Aires, 1946), pp. 11-34.
7. For an analysis of this development see Thomas F. O'Brien, Jr., "Chilean Elites and Foreign Investors: Chilean Nitrate Policy, 1880-82," *Journal of Latin American Studies*, II (May 1979):101-121.
8. "The Role of Government in the Resource Transfer and Resource Allocation Process: The Chilean Nitrate Sector, 1880-1930," in *Government and Economic Development*, ed. Gustav Ranis (New Haven, 1971, pp. 193-195.
9. Oscar Muñoz Gomá, *Crecimiento industrial de Chile, 1914-1965*, Publicaciones del Instituto de Economía y Planificación, no. 105 (Santiago, 1968), p. 26. Markos J. Mamalakis, *The Growth and Structure of the Chilean Economy: From Independence to Allende* (New Haven, 1976), pp. 4-6 presents identical estimates for the 1915-1924 period as well as a discussion of reasons for rejecting the lower growth estimates of Marto E. Ballesteros and Tom E. Davis, which are presented in "The Growth of Output and Employment in Basic Sectors of the Chilean Economy, 1908-1957," *Economic Development and Cultural Change*, II (January, 1963):152-176. According to Ballesteros and Davis, the annual percentage rate of increase in output per capita equalled only 1.45 between 1908 and 1927.
10. Even if the Ballesteros and Davis estimate of growth between 1908 and 1927 is accurate, the contrast with recent years still holds. Ballesteros and Davis place the increase in output per capita at only 0.94 percent

between 1927 and 1940 and 0.96 percent between 1940 and 1957. Ibid., p. 172.

11. See Ricardo Couyoumdjian, "El mercado del salitre durante la primera guerra mundial y la postguerra, 1914-1921," *Historia* (Santiago), XII (1974-75):13-55; Leo Stanton Rowe, "The Early Effects of the European War upon the Finance, Commerce, and Industry of Chile," in *Preliminary Economic Studies of the War*, ed. David Kinley (New York, 1918), pp. 33-101.

12. Pedro Luis González, *Chile industrial, 1919* (Santiago, 1919) p. 52.

13. Mamalakis, "The Role of Government," p. 184. According to Marcello Carmagnani, *Sviluppo industriale e sottosviluppo economico: Il caso cileno (1860-1920)*, (Torino, 1971), pp. 15, 26, 192 these difficulties dramatically reduced Chile's capacity to import and lowered the annual rate of growth of artisan and industrial activity from 7.5 percent in the 1895-1910 period to only 2.3 percent between 1910 and 1918. For other estimates of the rate of expansion of industrial production see Ricardo Lagos Escobar, *La industria en Chile: Antecedentes estructurales* (Santiago, 1966), p. 34; Ballesteros and Davis, p. 160.

14. See, in particular, Francisco A. Encina, *Nuestra inferioridad económica* (Santiago, 1955), which was originally published in 1911; and Alejandro Venegas [Dr. J. Valdés Cange] *Sinceridad: Chile íntimo en 1910*, 2nd ed. (Santiago, 1910), pp. 12-32.

15. Carmagnani, p. 21.

16. Chile, Oficina Central de Estadística, *Anuario estadístico de la República de Chile: Industrias* (Santiago, 1911), pp. 68-69.

17. Chile, Oficina Central de Estadística, *Sinopsis estadística de la República de Chile* (Santiago, 1919), pp. 98-102. As indicated previously, Chilean industry did not expand during the war, and thus the 1918 data probably provide a reasonably accurate picture of the industrial sector at an earlier date.

18. For a more comprehensive analysis of the industrial sector and its growth over time see Carmagnani, who provides extensive data on industrial and artisan activities in Chile in the 1880-1920 period.

19. Mamalakis, "The Role of Government," p. 195.

20. For a discussion of these problems see Arnold J. Bauer, *Chilean Rural Society from the Spanish Conquest to 1930* (Cambridge, England, 1975), pp. 242-245.

21. The nitrate industry alone employed 39,653 workers in 1907, and other mining activities probably accounted for half that number again. Chile, *Sinopsis estadística*, 1919, p. 96.

22. Pedro Luis González estimated that there were approximately 70,000 industrial workers in 1908 (p. 52). A comparison of his figures for 1917 with the more detailed ones included in the *Sinopsis estadística* of 1919 indicates that his calculations include a number of very small workshops and need to be slightly deflated.

236 Notes to Pages 40-44

23. See Bauer, pp. 246-247.
24. Chilean Legation, p. 94.
25. For example, the production of wheat, which was the most important agricultural commodity, was growing slowly at the turn of the century. See Chile, Oficina Central de Estadística, *Importación, exportación y consumo de trigo en Chile, en los últimos 20 años* (Santiago, 1915).
26. Figures drawn from an analysis of the 1902 tax roll, which is presented in Enrique Espinoza, *Jeografía descriptiva de la República de Chile,* 5th ed. (Santiago, 1903). According to Carl Solberg, *Immigration and Nationalism: Argentina and Chile, 1890-1914* (Austin, 1970), p. 55, immigrants owned an even higher proportion of Chile's largest estates. See also Henry W. Kirsch, *Industrial Development in a Traditional Society: The Conflict of Entrepreneurship and Modernization in Chile* (Gainesville, 1977), pp. 66-95 and Bauer, pp. 174-214 for useful discussions of the interlocking interests of urban and rural elites in Chile.
27. See Chapter III below.
28. According to census results, total population growth equalled 0.71 percent per annum between 1885 and 1895 and 1.52 percent between 1895 and 1907. Chile, Comisión Central del Censo, *Censo de la República de Chile levantado el 28 de noviembre de 1907* (Santiago, 1908), p. 1263.
29. Approximately 30 percent of the foreigners were Bolivians and Peruvians who were incorporated with the northern nitrate territories after the War of the Pacific. Ibid., p. 1294.
30. Ibid., pp. 1270-1273, 1305; Chile, Dirección General de Estadística, *Censo de población de la República de Chile levantado el 15 de diciembre de 1920* (Santiago, 1925), p. 303.
31. Chile, *Censo,* 1907, pp. 1270-1273.
32. Bauer, passim.
33. Carlos F. Díaz Alejandro, *Essays on the Economic History of the Argentine Republic* (New Haven, 1970), p. 3.
34. According to Díaz Alejandro, by 1929 Argentina had reached a GNP per capita of around $700 U.S. dollars at 1964 prices (p. 55), and per capita GDP in 1929 was only 26 percent higher than in 1914 (p. 43). Translating these figures into 1980 U.S. dollars, using the implicit price deflator for the U.S. GNP, yields a figure of $1354. The Chilean estimate is drawn from J. Gabriel Palma, "Chile 1914-1935: De economía exportadora a sustitutiva de importaciones," *Nueva historia,* II, no. 7 (1983): p. 166. Although possibly erring slightly on the high side, this estimate is fully plausible in view of the slow growth of the Chilean economy since the 1920s as well as the exceptionally high level of per capita export earnings in the years leading up to World War I.
35. Inter-American Development Bank, *Economic and Social Progress in Latin America: 1983 Report* (Washington, D.C. 1983), p. 345.
36. According to ECLA data, foreign investment accounted for 31.8 percent of total fixed capital in the 1900-04 period. Foreign investment

quadrupled in real terms in the subsequent decade and accounted for
47.7 percent of fixed capital in 1910-14. United Nations, Economic
Commission on Latin America, *Análisis y proyecciones del desarrollo
económico*, Vol. V: *El desarrollo económico de la Argentina* (Mexico,
1959), Part I, p. 28.
37. H.S. Ferns, *Britain and Argentina in the Nineteenth Century* (Oxford,
1960), p. 397.
38. Díaz Alejandro, p. 30.
39. Argentina, Comisión Nacional, *Tercer censo nacional levantado el 1 de
junio de 1914*, 10 vols. (Buenos Aires, 1916-1919), X, 399.
40. See Gino Germani, *Política y sociedad en una época de transición* (Buenos
Aires, 1962).
41. Argentina, Comisión Directiva, *Segundo censo de la República de Argentina, mayo 10 de 1895*, 3 vols. (Buenos Aires, 1898), III, xxxi; James
R. Scobie, *Revolution on the Pampas: A Social History of Argentine
Wheat, 1860-1910* (Austin, 1964), pp. 172, 174.
42. In the Argentine case it is important to distinguish pastoral and crop-
raising activities. Following the usual practice, the term "agricultural"
in the subsequent discussion is used to refer only to the latter.
43. Díaz Alejandro, p. 5.
44. Ibid., p. 43.
45. Roberto Cortés Conde, "El sector agrícola en el desarrollo económico
argentino, 1880-1910," (unpublished paper, Centro de Investigaciones
Económicas, Instituto Torcuato Di Tella, Buenos Aires, October 1979),
pp. 10-27.
46. Díaz Alejandro, p. 6.
47. Argentina, *Tercer censo*, 1914, VIII, 134-135.
48. Ibid., VII, 53-54, 109-110.
49. Ibid., VII, 246; *Segundo censo*, 1895, Vol. III, passim.
50. Argentina, *Tercer censo*, VII, 59, 75.
51. Díaz Alejandro, p. 10.
52. According to the *Tercer censo*, 1914, VII, 108, industrial workers accounted for 12.8 percent of the economically active population in
Argentina.
53. W.G. Hoffman, *The Growth of Industrial Economies*, trans. W.O. Henderson and W.H. Chaloner (Manchester, 1958), p. 161.
54. It is virtually impossible to determine the exact size of the Argentine
rural labor force in either 1895 or 1914. Census results for these years
included a large proportion of the economically active population under
the vague occupational category *jornaleros*. The estimates presented in
Table 6 are based on the agricultural census of 1914, which shows that
2,125,870 persons (27.0 percent of the total population) were living on
agricultural and livestock holdings in Argentina in 1914. *Tercer censo*,
V, 573. To arrive at the figure of 28.7 percent presented in Table 6,
children have been eliminated from this total, and it has been assumed

that the ratio of male to female employment in the rural sector was the
same as that of the employed population as a whole. The estimate for
1895 is probably less accurate, since it is based on the assumption that
the proportion of rural workers in the census category *jornaleros* was the
same in 1895 as in 1914. It should be noted that these estimates do not
agree with those made by ECLA, cited in Guido Di Tella and Manuel
Zymelman, *Las etapas del desarrollo económico argentino* (Buenos
Aires, 1967), p. 28, which assigned 39.2 percent of the economically
active population to the agricultural sector in the years 1900-04 and
34.2 percent in 1910-14. The estimates do, however, closely match
those presented by Oscar Cornblit, "European Immigrants in Argentine
Industry and Politics," in *The Politics of Conformity in Latin America*,
ed. Claudio Véliz (London, 1967), p. 226.

55. Argentina, *Segundo censo*, 1895, Vol. II, pp. CXC-CXCIII.
56. Argentina, *Tercer censo*, 1914, Vol. IV.
57. Chile, *Censo*, 1907, p. 1294.
58. Mauricio Lebedinsky, *Estructura de la ganadería* (Buenos Aires, 1967),
    p. 21.
59. For example, in Santa Fe, the major cereal province, land values rose
    from $4.94 gold pesos per hectare in 1888 to $21.70 in 1911. Scobie,
    Revolution, pp. 51, 171.
60. Ibid., p. 89.
61. Argentina, *Tercer censo*, 1914, V, 837.
62. Ibid., pp. 309-310.
63. Ibid., VI, 679; V, 837.
64. *Segundo censo*, 1895, Vol. II, pp. CXC; *Tercer censo*, 1914, IV, 383.
65. Of the 5,233 holdings over 5,000 hectares in size listed in the census of
    1914, only 104 produced wheat or some other farm crop. *Tercer censo*,
    V, 73.
66. *El yrigoyenismo* (Buenos Aires, 1965), p. 92.
67. Argentina, *Tercer censo*, 1914, V, 3; Chile, *Anuario estadístico*, 1917-
    1918, Vol. VII: *Agricultura*, p. 20.
68. Chile, Dirección General de Estadística, *Resultados del X censo de la
    población efectuado el 27 de noviembre de 1930*, 3 vols. (Santiago,
    1931-35), I, 50. Rural was defined to include all population clusters
    less than 1,000.
69. Argentina, *Tercer censo*, 1914, V, 573.
70. Figures for the number of rural holdings are drawn from Chile, *Anuario
    estadístico*, 1917-1918, VII, 20-21; Argentina, *Tercer censo*, 1914,
    V, 3. Rural labor force estimates are based on Chile, *Censo*, 1920; Ar-
    gentina, *Tercer censo*, V.
71. Chile, *Anuario estadístico*, 1917-1918, VII, 21.
72. Solberg, *Immigration and Nationalism*, p. 15.
73. *Del Atlántico al Pacífico y un argentino en Europa: Cartas de viaje*
    (Rosario, 1890), pp. 108-109, 126-129 as quoted in Guillermo Feliú

Cruz, *Chile visto a través de Agustín Ross* (Santiago, 1950), pp. 143-145. See also Venegas, *Sinceridad*, p. 205, who similarly commented on the absence of a Chilean middle class.

74. *South America: Observations and Impressions* (London, 1912), p. 341.
75. Germani, "Estrategia," pp. 294-295.
76. Alieto A. Guadagni, "La estructura ocupacional y el desarrollo económico de Chile," (unpublished paper, Centro de Investigaciones Económicas, Instituto Torcuato Di Tella, Buenos Aires, October 1965).
77. Argentina, *Segundo censo*, Vol. II, p. CLXXIII.
78. Argentina, *Tercer censo*, 1914, I, 170.
79. Chile, *Censo*, 1920, p. 303.
80. Altogether 76.2 percent of the country's literate population lived in the littoral area as compared to 63.6 percent of its total population. Argentina, *Segundo censo*, 1895, Vol. II, p. CLXXIII.

Chapter III

1. For the text of these laws see Ricardo Anguita, comp. *Leyes promulgadas en Chile desde 1810 hasta el 1 de junio de 1913*, 5 vols. (Santiago, 1912-1913), III, 120-138, 194-207. For a study that attributes major importance to the law strengthening local government see Arturo Valenzuela, *Political Brokers in Chile: Local Government in a Centralized Polity* (Durham, N.C., 1977), pp. 193-220. See also Agustín Correa Bravo, *Comentarios y concordancias de la ley de organización de las municipalidades del 22 de diciembre de 1891*, 3rd ed. (Santiago, 1914) for an extensive analysis of the 1891 law. An appendix to this study offers a discussion of the reforms in local government introduced by Law 2960 of 18 December 1914.
2. Federico G. Gil, *The Political System of Chile* (Boston, 1966), p. 49.
3. Pike, p. 87.
4. See, in particular, José Antonio Alfonso, *Los partidos políticos de Chile* (Santiago, 1902?); idem, *El parlamentarismo i la reforma política en Chile* (Santiago 1909); Guillermo Subercaseaux, *Estudios políticos de actualidad* (Santiago, 1914).
5. Quoted in Pike, p. 92.
6. Taking into account all cabinet changes, except those resulting from simple ministerial substitutions and interim appointments, one hundred forty-three cabinets served during the period, an average of 4.3 per year. The number of major cabinet changes was considerably smaller, although no consensus exists as to the precise total. For example, whereas Encina, *Historia*, XX, 342 counts eighty different ministries between December 1891 and December 1920, excluding partial changes of government, Valenzuela, *Political Brokers*, p. 202 arrives at a total of seventy-one for the same period. Nevertheless, most observers agree that an unusual degree of cabinet instability characterized the 1891-1924 period. A

notable exception is Heise González, *Historia*, pp. 286-287 who presents
data to show that a pattern of ministerial instability developed before
1891 and that the rotation of cabinet officials was even more rapid after
1924 than before. The difficulty is that Heise González' data fail to take
into account the growth in the size of the cabinet, which included only
four posts in 1861 as opposed to twelve in the 1941-1951 period. The
number of ministerial posts changing hands over time consequently provides a misleading indicator of cabinet instability. To avoid controversy
over how much change needs to occur before a shift in ministers counts
as a total or partial cabinet change, it may be noted that the Ministry of
the Interior changed hands thirty-two times between September 1861
and August 1891: an average of 1.1 ministers per year, excluding ministerial substitutions and interim appointments. The average was nearly
identical during the 1932-1958 period, when the Ministry of the Interior changed hands thirty-two times for an average of 1.2 per year. In
contrast, between December 1891 and September 1924 the number of
changes equalled ninety-eight, an average of 3.0 per year. These calculations are based on Luis Valencia Avaria, ed., *Anales de la República*,
2 vols. (Santiago, 1951), I.

7. Luis Palma Zuñiga, *Historia del partido radical* (Santiago, 1967), pp. 63-
   64 reprints the program.
8. Snow, pp. 23, 28.
9. Luis Galdames, *Valentín Letelier y su obra, 1852-1919* (Santiago, 1937),
   pp. 291-293.
10. Ibid.
11. Palma Zuñiga, p. 65 quoting *La convención radical de 1888*, pp. 16-17.
12. Encina, *Historia*, XIX, 54.
13. Palma Zuñiga, p. 97. See also pp. 84-86, 95-96; Galdames, *Valentín
    Letelier*, pp. 366-381.
14. Palma Zuñiga, p. 98-99.
15. Ibid., pp. 127-130.
16. Rafael Luis Gumucio, *El partido conservador* (Santiago, 1911), p. 19.
17. Ibid., p. 20.
18. Encina, *Historia*, XIX, 117-118.
19. See, for example, Chile, Congreso Nacional, *Boletín i actas de las sesiones
    celebradas por el Congreso Nacional en 1906 con motivo de la elección
    de Presidente de la República* (Santiago, 1906).
20. Armando Donoso, interview with Enrique Mac-Iver, p. 139; Alberto
    Edwards Vives, *La fronda aristocrática*, 6th ed. (Santiago, 1966), p. 178;
    Manuel Rivas Vicuña, "Recuerdos electorales de 1918," *El Mercurio*
    (Santiago), 17 January 1924, reprinted in Manuel Rivas Vicuña, *Historia
    política y parlamentaria de Chile*, ed. Guillermo Feliú Cruz, 3 vols.
    (Santiago, 1964), II, 398-401; Encina, *Historia*, XX, 341; Guillermo
    Feliú Cruz, *Chile visto a través de Agustín Ross* (Santiago, 1950), p. 11;
    Pike, p. 88; Luis Galdames, *A History of Chile*, trans. Isaac Joslin Cox

(Chapel Hill, N.C., 1941), p. 368; René Millar Carvacho, *La elección presidencial de 1920* (Santiago, 1981), pp. 162-173.

21. Pellegrini, III, 497, letter sent to *La Nación* (Buenos Aires) from the United States, 6 January 1905.
22. Valenzuela, *Political Brokers*, p. 205.
23. Palma Zuñiga, p. 79.
24. Ibid., pp. 115, 127.
25. Hernán Ramírez Necochea, *Historia del movimiento obrero en Chile* (Santiago, [1956]), pp. 214-215.
26. Feliú Cruz, pp. 126-128; Encina, *Historia*, XIX, 55.
27. Jordi Fuentes and Lía Cortés, *Diccionario político de Chile* (Santiago, 1967), p. 147.
28. See Jorge I. Barría Serón, *Los movimientos sociales de Chile desde 1910 hasta 1926* (Santiago, 1960), pp. 373-374 for the Socialist Labor party's list of grievances against the Democrats.
29. For a more comprehensive account of these developments see Peter DeShazo, *Urban Workers and Labor Unions in Chile, 1902-1927* (Madison, 1983); idem, "The Valparaíso Maritime Strike of 1903 and the Development of a Revolutionary Labor Movement in Chile," *Journal of Latin American Studies*, II (May 1979):145-168; Barría Serón; Ramírez Necochea, *Historia*; Alan Angell, *Politics and the Labour Movement in Chile* (London, 1972); Julio César Jobet, *Recabarren: Los orígenes del movimiento obrero y del socialismo chileno* (Santiago, 1955).
30. Julio Heise González, *La constitución de 1925 y las nuevas tendencias político-sociales* (Santiago, 1951), p. 98 estimates that labor organizations included approximately 55,000 members in 1910. DeShazo, *Urban Workers*, who emphasizes the absence of reliable data on trade union membership for the 1891-1925 period, cites figures of 65,136 for 1909 and 91,609 for 1912-13 (p. 130).
31. See Gonzalo Izquierdo Fernández, "Octubre de 1905: Un episodio en la historia social chilena," *Historia* (Santiago), XIII (1976):55-96; Thomas C. Wright, "Origins of the Politics of Inflation in Chile, 1888-1918," *Hispanic American Historical Review*, LIII (May 1973):239-259.
32. See DeShazo *Urban Workers*, especially pp. 146-178. According to DeShazo, more strikes occurred in 1919 than in any year up until the 1950s (p. 164).
33. Arturo Valenzuela, *The Breakdown of Democratic Regimes: Chile* (Baltimore, 1978), p. 117n cites the 270,000 figure, which is drawn from the U.S. Bureau of Labor Statistics, *Bulletin*, no. 461 (October 1928). Most evidence suggests, however, that Chilean trade unions greatly exaggerated their membership in this period. DeShazo, *Urban Workers*, pp. 195-200 dismisses figures that place union membership over 200,000 in the mid-1920s as gross overstatements based on guesswork and suggests that even in Santiago union membership failed to account for more than 15 percent of the total work force. See also James O. Morris, *Elites,*

Intellectuals, and Consensus: A Study of the Social Question and the Industrial Relations System in Chile, Cornell International Industrial and Labor Relations Report, no. 7 (Ithaca, N.Y., 1966), p. 94.

34. See DeShazo, *Urban Workers,* pp. 201-210.

35. For the program adopted at this meeting see Barría Serón, pp. 374-375.

36. Rollie Poppino, *International Communism in Latin America: A History of the Movement, 1917-1963* (Glencoe, Ill., 1964), p. 68.

37. Ricardo Cruz-Coke, *Geografía electoral de Chile* (Santiago, 1952), p. 53.

38. Maurice Duverger, *Political Parties: Their Organization and Activity in the Modern State,* trans. Barbara and Robert North, 2nd ed., rev. (London, 1959), p. 228.

39. Edwards Vives and Frei, pp. 11-12.

40. Conservatives could be astonishingly frank about this manipulation. Julio Subercaseaux Browne, a well-connected Conservative who entered politics in the early 1890s at a time when he was involved in banking, pointed out in his memoirs that his family could dispose of the votes of some 3,000 *inquilinos* living on their estates: "Such was the electoral influence the bank possessed before its clients." "Reminiscencias," *Boletín de la Academia Chilena de la Historia,* XXVIII (Segundo semestre, 1961):239-240. See also Julio Heise González, "El caciquismo político en el período parlamentario, 1891-1925," in *Homenaje a Guillermo Feliú Cruz* (Santiago, 1973), pp. 537-575.

41. Pending the installation of new municipal governments in accordance with the 1891 Law of Municipalities, the electoral reform law of August 1890 placed authority for the registration of voters and supervision of elections in the hands of the largest seven taxpayers in each subdelegation. Subsequently, locally elected officials (*alcaldes* and *regidores*) were to assume these functions. The electoral reform laws of 20 October 1892 (No. 4352), 4 September 1893 (No. 4612), 18 January 1894 (No. 4720), and 22 February 1896 (No. 5340) altered these provisions and left some of the electoral responsibilities assigned to local officials in the 1890 law in the hands of committees of large taxpayers. After the electoral reform laws of 21 February 1914 (No. 2883), 4 June 1914 (No. 2893), and 12 February 1915 (No. 2983), which provided for a complete renewal of electoral registers every nine years and excluded municipal officials from the administration of the electoral process, the authority assigned to large taxpayers for the registration of voters and supervision of elections expanded considerably. For the text of the electoral law which emerged from these changes see Chile, Consejo de Estado, *Recopilación de leyes por orden numérico arreglada por la secretaría del Consejo de Estado* (Santiago, 1914-1925), VIII, 190-240.

42. See the debate on the 1906 elections in Tarapacá, 13 June 1906, Chile, Cámara de Diputados, *Sesiones ordinarias,* particularly the comments of Oscar Viel Cavero, pp. 119-120 and Luis Izquierdo, p. 162.

43. Significantly, the Conservatives strongly opposed the reform that eliminated local government control over the electoral process. In contrast, the Radicals and Democrats, who drew support from a more popular set of political forces, favored a more centralized system of electoral administration. See Rivas Vicuña, III, 562-565; I, 292-294, 398-399, 461; Galvarino Gallardo Nieto, *La Liga de Acción Cívica i los partidos políticos* (Santiago, 1912), pp. 25-26.
44. Valentín Letelier, *La lucha por la cultura* (Santiago, 1895), p. 210.
45. Gumucio, p. 10.
46. Convención Conservadora, *Ideas para la convención: Programa y estatutos, preséntalos a la convención un grupo de conservadores de Valparaíso* (Valparaíso, 1901). See also *El Mercurio* (Santiago), 2 October 1918, p. 15 for a report on the Conservative convention of 1918. At the latter convention the party's efforts to broaden its base of popular support even included a move to nominate a member of the working class to the national legislature from Santiago. The assembly of that province proposed, "that it is necessary to define officially the democratic concept of the party to shelter it from all criticism or charges to the effect that it is an oligarchic party."
47. Gumucio, p. 10.
48. Germán Urzúa Valenzuela, *Los partidos políticos chilenos* (Santiago, 1968), p. 57.
49. It should be noted, however, that the legislative branch of the party was not completely unified even after 1901. In a speech before the Senate in 1911 Arturo Besa, a National, referred to a Liberal Democratic faction led by Juan José Latorre, a naval officer who had supported Balmaceda: "On various occasions we were invited to join this bloc in opposition to the faction led by Señor Sanfuentes." Chile, Congreso Nacional, Cámara de Senadores, *Boletín de las sesiones ordinarias de la Cámara de Senadores*, 16 August 1911, p. 511. On divisions within the party during the last decade of the parliamentary period see Horacio Aránguiz Donoso, Ricardo Coudyoudmjian Bergamali, and Juan Eduardo Vargas Cariola, "La vida política chilena 1915-1916," *Historia*, VII (1968):15-89.
50. See, for example, Edwards Vives and Frei, p. 178.
51. Sanfuentes retired from politics in 1920 at the end of his presidential term. The Liberal Democratic party survived until 1932 when it united with other liberal groups.
52. Edwards Vives, *La fronda*, p. 177.
53. Partido Liberal-democrático, *Carta política del Señor Ismael Pérez Montt* (Santiago, 1903), p. 29.
54. See, for example, *El Mercurio* (Santiago), 1 December 1914, p. 11; 10 December 1914, p. 9.
55. Between September 1901 and September 1902 the thirty-eight member executive committee met forty-nine times; the directorate ten times. Partido Liberal-democrático, p. 28.

56. See Luis Antonio Vergara's account of Sanfuentes' conflict with the majority of Liberal Democratic legislators in 1907 in Cámara de Senadores, *Sesiones ordinarias*, 9 August 1911, pp. 476-479.

57. Ibid., 16 August 1911, p. 510.

58. Rivas Vicuña, I, 137.

59. It should be noted that this was one of the very few occasions when the Conservative party suffered a definite split.

60. *El Mercurio* (Santiago), 11 December 1914, p. 11. Reports on the Radical party at this time indicate, in contrast, that there was not only popular participation in party affairs at the local level, but real competition in the nomination of candidates. Ibid., 1 December 1914, p. 10.

61. Rivas Vicuña, I, 145.

62. Fuentes and Cortés, p. 276.

63. "Convención Liberal," *El Mercurio* (Santiago), 16 September 1919, p. 15.

64. See Borón, pp. 410-422.

65. Palma Zuñiga, p. 110.

66. Paul S. Reinsch, "Parliamentary Government in Chile," *American Political Science Review*, III (November 1909):518.

67. Some contemporaries argued that it was completely sterile. See, for example, Guillermo Subercaseaux, *Estudios políticos*, passim.

68. Alfonso, *Los partidos políticos*, p. 36.

69. See the debate on this issue during July 1898 in Chile, Cámara de Diputados, *Sesiones ordinarias*, pp. 317ff., particularly the comments of Enrique Mac-Iver, who led the Radical opposition to a new law of emission (pp. 321-334), and on the other side the comments of Liberal Democrats such as Roberto Meeks (pp. 390-401). In the voting which followed on July 20 the Conservatives, Liberals, Nationals, and Liberal Democrats tended to support a new emission, while the Radicals and Democrats were solidly opposed (p. 457).

70. On 23 July 1895, for example, fifty-one deputies supported a resolution favoring monetary stability. Ibid., p. 567.

71. Ibid., 14 July 1897, p. 493.

72. Ibid., 12 July 1897, p. 453.

73. For an extended discussion of the rise of the "social question" and the political response it generated see Morris. See also Jorge Gustavo Silva, *Nuestra evolución político-social (1900-1930)* (Santiago, 1931).

74. Gumucio, pp. 38-39. See also Luis A. Undurraga's speech on the social issue of 12 July 1923 in Chile, Cámara de Diputados, *Sesiones ordinarias*, pp. 667-671, 673-675; Morris, pp. 121-143.

75. Feliú Cruz, pp. 132-133. The most comprehensive project for social reform introduced in the Chilean legislature before Alessandri assumed office was sponsored by Conservative Senators. Their bill, submitted on 2 June 1919, included provisions to regulate hours of work, protect female and child labor, and ensure wages payments were made in cash.

In addition, the bill would have fully involved the state in trade union activities and labor conflicts. See Chile, Cámara de Senadores, *Sesiones ordinarias*, 2 June 1919, pp. 40-46.

76. Feliú Cruz, pp. 132-133; Pike, pp. 116-117; Morris, p. 149.

77. *La constitución de 1833 en 1913* (Santiago, 1913), p. 683.

78. *Memorias de ochenta años*, 2nd ed., 2 vols. (Santiago, 1936), II, 75. See also the comments of Arturo Besa, Chile, Cámara de Senadores, *Sesiones ordinarias*, 16 August 1911, p. 510.

79. *Political Brokers*, pp. 204-209.

80. See Rivas Vicuña, I, 140.

81. See, in particular, the comments of Arturo Alessandri Palma, *Recuerdos de gobierno*, I (Santiago, 1952), 61-66; idem, *Parlementarisme et régime presidentiel*, trans. Jacqueline Ch. Rousseau (Paris, 1930), pp. 33-34; Germán Riesco, *Presidencia de Riesco, 1901-1906* (Santiago, 1950), pp. 89-155.

82. Figure for 1915.

83. In 1909 José Antonio Alfonso, *El parlamentarismo*, pp. 26-27, observed: ". . . frequently there are cases of a congressman, deputy, or senator, with a broader perspective and a greater sense of justice, who gives preference to those general interests, to questions of great national interest, and relegates to second place the merely local interests of his district. This legislator is politically dead and fails to be reelected."

84. *Memorias*, II, 203.

85. Galdames, *A History of Chile*, p. 368; Alfonso, *El parlamentarismo*, p. 24; Feliú Cruz, p. 110; Venegas, *Cartas*, p. 20; Heise González, II, 227-237; see also the comments of Malaquías Concha on the role of money in elections in Chile, Cámara de Diputados, *Sesiones ordinarias*, 7 June 1915, pp. 163-166.

86. Rivas Vicuña, II, 400. For a contemporary account of the use of funds in elections see Robert E. Mansfield, *Progressive Chile* (New York, 1913), pp. 136-137.

87. Galdames, *A History of Chile*, p. 365.

88. Poblete Troncoso, pp. 8, 55.

89. The age was reduced to twenty-one in the 1880s.

90. Borón, p. 429.

91. Sweden, *Historisk Statistik för Sverige: Statistiska Översiktstabeller* (Stockholm, 1960), pp. 268-270.

92. Chile, *Censo*, 1920, p. 303.

93. The parade of ministers, governors, intendants, and other political appointees left not only the president but many sub-secretaries and senior bureaucrats in their posts. Luis Izquierdo, *Nuestro sistema político ante el senado* (Valparaíso, 1916), pp. 68-71. See also Riesco, p. 343; Encina, *Historia*, XX, 343.

94. Alessandri's program, reprinted in Alessandri, *Recuerdos*, I, 431-439, called for institutional reforms to correct the increasingly obvious draw-

backs of the parliamentary system as well as socioeconomic measures such as tax reforms, social security legislation, monetary stability, the regulation of female and child labor, and the intervention of the state in labor disputes. See also Alessandri's message of 1 June 1921, *Mensaje leído por S.E. el Presidente de la República en la apertura de las sesiones ordinarias del congreso nacional* (Santiago, 1921). For a study focused specifically on the 1920 election see Millar Carvacho, *La elección presidencial.*

95. Arturo Olavarría Bravo, *Chile entre dos Alessandri: Memorias políticas,* 4 vols. (Santiago, 1962-1965), I, 81-82. See also I, 86, where the author describes the activities of working-class leaders after it became known that the electoral outcome was inconclusive.

96. Not only was Alessandri's conversion to the cause of social reform sudden and late (he had been a legislator since 1897), but none of his concrete proposals was the least revolutionary. Alessandri's own comments about the reception he received in the Centro Radical "Juan Castellón" in Concepción just before his nomination are revealing: "The traditional Radicals, the old guard of the party who feared my social ideas which they regarded as subversive, understood, once they listened to me, that what I was doing was precisely to defend the public order through the evolution required by the times in which we were living . . ." *Recuerdos,* I, 31. For a disparaging assessment of Alessandri see Pike, pp. 170-177, who describes his electoral program as consisting of little more than "mild palliatives." Not surprisingly, Alessandri (*Recuerdos,* I, passim) and his secretary, Olavarría Bravo (*Chile entre dos Alessandri,* I, 62-93), provide a different view. See also Ricardo Donoso, *Alessandri: Agitador y demoledor,* 2 vols. (Mexico, 1952).

97. Cruz-Coke, p. 53.

98. For an analysis of this opposition see Gertrude M. Yeager, "The Club de la Unión and Kinship: Social Aspects of Political Obstructionism in the Chilean Senate, 1920-1924," *Americas,* XXXV (April, 1979): 539-572.

99. Emilio Bello Codesido, *Recuerdos políticos* (Santiago, 1954) provides a detailed account of the collapse of the Alessandri government and the political events of the 1920s. See also Frederick M. Nunn, *Chilean Politics 1920-1931: The Honorable Mission of the Armed Forces* (Albuquerque, N.M., 1970); Clarence E. Haring, "Chilean Politics, 1920-1928," *Hispanic American Historical Review,* XI (February, 1931):1-26; René Millar Carvacho, *Significado y antecedentes del movimiento militar de 1924* (Santiago, 1974).

Chapter IV

1. Many of the movement's original supporters sought only to rid themselves of an unpopular administration. See, for example, the article by

"Arminius" entitled "Presidentes argentinos," originally published in
El Argentino, 1 July 1890, reprinted in Landenberger and Conte, pp.
177-181.

2. A manifesto to this effect, issued on 2 July 1891, is reprinted in del
   Mazo, I, 308-312.
3. Luis was the father of presidential candidate Roque Saenz Peña, who led
   a political group that represented something of a challenge to the traditional leadership of PAN. With his father in the race, Roque was forced
   to withdraw.
4. The UCR National Committee announced its reasons for not participating
   in the elections on 10 April 1892. The document is reprinted in Irigoyen,
   Hipólito Yrigoyen: Pueblo y gobierno, III, 64-69.
5. For the constitution see del Mazo, I, 312-316. On the importance of
   North American parties as models see the comments of F.A. Barroetaveña
   in Landenberger and Conte, p. 353.
6. See Irigoyen, *Hipólito Yrigoyen: Pueblo y gobierno*, II, 62-29, 79.
7. Various documents pertaining to the 1893 revolutions are reprinted
   in Leandro Alem, *Leandro Alem: Mensaje y destino*, VIII, 137-238;
   Irigoyen, *Hipólito Yrigoyen: Pueblo y gobierno*, III, 276-297.
8. Del Mazo, I, 95.
9. Comité de la Unión Cívica Radical de la Provincia de Buenos Aires to
   Comité Nacional, 29 September 1897, reprinted in Carlos J. Rodríguez,
   Irigoyen: Su revolución política y social (Buenos Aires, 1943), pp.
   112-114; see also "Abstención de 1909: Convención Nacional," 31
   December 1909 in Irigoyen, *Hipólito Yrigoyen: Pueblo y gobierno*,
   III, 81-82.
10. "Manifiesto del Comité Nacional, al reorganizarse," 29 February 1904,
    reprinted in del Mazo, I, 324, 327.
11. See Irigoyen, *Hipólito Yrigoyen: Pueblo y gobierno*, III, 298-341 and
    Hipólito Irigoyen, *Ley 12839: Documentos de Hipólito Yrigoyen:
    Apostolado cívico, obra de gobierno, defensa ante la corte* (Buenos Aires,
    1949), pp. 22-34 for some of the relevant documents.
12. Pellegrini, IV, 378.
13. Del Mazo, I, 123.
14. Pellegrini made this point in a speech before the Senate on 26 July 1901,
    Obras, IV, 429.
15. Irigoyen, *Ley 12839*, pp. 323-352 provides an account of the various
    offers that were made to him. In 1907 and 1908 a series of meetings
    between Figueroa and Irigoyen took place to discuss electoral reform.
    For Irigoyen's 1909 account of these see "Informe sobre las conferencias
    con el Presidente Figueroa Alcorta," reprinted in ibid., pp. 34-38. For a
    slightly different version see Ezequiel Ramos Méxia, *Mis memorias,
    1853-1935*, 2nd ed. (Buenos Aires, 1959), p. 251.
16. Carrasco, pp. 101-104.

17. The Governor of Buenos Aires, for example, was called to a meeting with Figueroa Alcorta on February 5 and asked to choose between "submission" or intervention. José Arce, *Marcelino Ugarte: El hombre, el político, el gobernante* (Buenos Aires, 1959), p. 251.

18. Presidential messages, reprinted in H. Mabragaña, *Los mensajes*, 6 vols. (Buenos Aires, 1910), of Luis Saenz Peña, May 1893, V, 97; Uriburu, May 1898, V, 311; Roca, May 1899, V, 348; Quintana, May 1905, VI, 113; Figueroa Alcorta, May 1907, 1908, and 1909, VI, 204, 319, 392.

19. For Saenz Peña's views on electoral reform see Roque Saenz Peña, *Escritos y discursos*, 2 vols. (Buenos Aires, 1914-1915), Vol. II, passim. See also Argentina, Ministerio del Interior, *Las fuerzas armadas*, Vol. I, which contains Saenz Peña's campaign speeches, reform proposals, and the complete legislative debate on the issue.

20. For accounts of these meetings see Irigoyen, *Ley 12839*, pp. 338-340; Ramón J. Cárcano, *Mis primeros 80 años* (Buenos Aires, 1943), pp. 297-303.

21. The complete text is reprinted in Argentina, Ministerio del Interior, *Las fuerzas armadas*, I, 304-319.

22. This point was made by the Minister of the Interior, Indalecio Gómez, in the debate on the law in the Chamber of Deputies, ibid., pp. 59-60.

23. Ramón J. Cárcano, p. 303; Carrasco, p. 177; Botana, pp. 251-345.

24. "Ecos del día," quoted in Ortega, p. 620.

25. Puiggros, pp. 38, 40.

26. Darío Cantón, *Materiales para el estudio de la sociología política en la Argentina*, 2 vols. (Buenos Aires, 1968), I, 85. This is the best available collection of materials for the study of Argentine elections.

27. F.L. Defrance, "Recent Political Evolution in Argentina," *The Quarterly Review*, CCV (January 1916), 49.

28. For concrete evidence of the importance of this distinction for understanding the structure of political conflict in Argentina after 1916 see Peter H. Smith, *Argentina and the Failure of Democracy: Conflict among Political Elites, 1904-1955* (Madison, 1974), which provides an analysis of roll call votes in the Chamber of Deputies. It should be noted, however, that Smith's data may exaggerate the extent to which purely political differences predominated over ideological concerns or other influences on legislative behavior. Roll call votes were usually optional, and limited information exists on the alignment of deputies on many crucial socioeconomic issues. A high proportion of the roll call votes recorded in the 1916-1930 period dealt with narrowly defined issues, such as the election of legislative officers, on which one might expect a high degree of partisan cohesion and polarization between government and opposition elements.

29. For a comprehensive overview of the party and its base of political support see Richard J. Walter, *The Socialist Party of Argentina, 1890-1930* (Austin, 1977).

30. Juan B. Justo, *Obras completas*, Vol. I: *La moneda* (Buenos Aires, 1937), pp. 228-229; Hobart Spalding, *La clase trabajadora argentina (Documentos para su historia -1890/1912)* (Buenos Aires, 1970), pp. 257-282.

31. Juan B. Justo, *El programa socialista del campo*, 2nd ed. (Buenos Aires, 1915), originally delivered as a speech, 21 April 1901.

32. Idem, *El impuesto sobre el privilegio*, 2nd ed. (Buenos Aires, 1928), p. 10.

33. The Italian Socialist, E. Ferri, anticipated this development in 1908. See Justo, *Obras*, I, 239.

34. On the electoral base of the Socialist party see Richard J. Walter, "Elections in the City of Buenos Aires during the First Yrigoyen Administration: Social Class and Political Preferences," *Hispanic American Historical Review*, LVIII (November 1978):595-624; idem, *Socialist Party*.

35. See "Renuncia al radicalismo," reprinted in Lisandro de la Torre, *Obras de Lisandro de la Torre*, ed. Raul Larra, Vols. I-III, 3rd ed. (Buenos Aires 1957-1958); Vols. IV-VI, 2nd ed. (Buenos Aires, 1960), I, 14-16.

36. Arce, pp. 41-52. De la Torre later wrote about his difficulties with conservative forces in the 1916 elections: letters to Dr. Robustiano Patrón Costas, 24 May 1920 and Dr. Mariano Demaria (h.), 21 January 1921, reprinted in de la Torre, V, 60-110.

37. Cantón, *Materiales*, I, 81-99; Walter, "Elections," pp. 595-624.

38. The collected works of Lisandro de la Torre provide a relatively complete guide to the party's program.

39. See de la Torre, VI, 12-16.

40. Ibid., VI, 25.

41. Arce, p. 45.

42. Ibid.

43. Cantón, *Materiales*, I, 83, 87, 89, 93, 97.

44. Ibid., I, 93-94.

45. A full record of the Irigoyen interventions together with relevant documents, speeches, debates, and newspaper editorials is presented in Irigoyen, *Hipólito Yrigoyen: Pueblo y gobierno*, Vols. V and VI.

46. The word "national" must be stressed, because provincial Radical parties often did issue programs calling for concrete socioeconomic measures such as minimum wage legislation, progressive taxation of land and income, social security benefits, and similar reforms. See, for example, "Tucumán—Convenciones Radicales," *La Prensa* (Buenos Aires), 6 February 1922, p. 8.

47. Molina to Dr. Eleodoro Fierro (Vice-President of the UCR Central Committee), 15 July 1909, reprinted in Irigoyen, *Hipólito Yrigoyen: Pueblo y gobierno*, II, 114.

48. Molina to Irigoyen, September 1909, ibid., p. 136.

49. "Manifiesto—la UCR al pueblo de la república," 26 July 1915, reprinted in ibid., III, 404-405. See also "Declaraciones de la Convención Nacional," 22 March 1916, ibid., III, 411-412.

50. In its electoral manifesto of 30 March 1916 the party declared: "La Unión Cívica Radical es la Nación misma . . ." Ibid., III, 415.

51. Celso Rodríguez, "Cantonismo: A Regional Harbinger of Peronism in Argentina," *Americas*, XXXIV (October 1977):170-201; idem, *Lencinas y Cantoni: El populismo cuyano en tiempos de Yrigoyen* (Buenos Aires, 1979); Dardo Olguín, *Lencinas: El caudillo radical, historia y mito* (Buenos Aires, 1961).

52. Smith, *Failure of Democracy*, pp. 77-80.

53. "Radicales principistas: Manifiesto al pueblo de la república," *La Prensa*, 9 February 1922, pp. 10-11.

54. Benjamin Villafañe, *Irigoyen, el último dictador*, 6th ed. (Buenos Aires, 1922), pp. 58-59.

55. Ibid., pp. 59 and 93.

56. Robert A. Potash, *The Army and Politics in Argentina, 1928-1945* (Stanford, Calif., 1969), pp. 29-54.

57. See, for example, the comments of Ramos Méxia, p. 387; Villafañe, p. 16; Puiggros, p. 79.

58. According to the *Review of the River Plate*, Alvear's candidacy was well received in all circles, even by the opposition press. "Doctor Marcelo T. de Alvear," 17 March 1922, p. 659.

59. Peter H. Smith, *Politics and Beef in Argentina: Patterns of Conflict and Change* (New York, 1969), p. 49.

60. Marvin Goldwert, "The Argentine Revolution of 1930; the Rise of Modern Militarism and Ultra-nationalism in Argentina" (unpublished Ph.D. thesis, University of Texas, 1962) explores the background to the 1930 coup in some detail. Other recent analyses include Peter H. Smith, "The Breakdown of Democracy in Argentina, 1916-30" in *The Breakdown of Democratic Regimes: Latin America*, ed. Juan J. Linz and Alfred Stepan (Baltimore, 1978), pp. 3-27; Anne L. Potter, "The Failure of Democracy in Argentina 1916-1930: An Institutional Perspective," *Journal of Latin American Studies*, XIII (May 1981):83-109; David Rock, *Politics in Argentina, 1890-1930: The Rise and Fall of Radicalism* (London, 1975), pp. 252-264; idem, "Radical Populism and the Conservative Elite, 1912-1930," in *Argentina in the Twentieth Century*, ed. idem (Pittsburgh, 1975), pp. 66-87. For a contemporary account see José María Sarobe, *Memorias sobre la revolución del 6 de septiembre de 1930* (Buenos Aires, 1957).

61. Carrasco, p. 178.

62. Speech by Vicente C. Gallo, "La unidad moral y los símbolos del radicalismo," November 1914, reprinted in V. Gallo, pp. 301-314.

63. "La obra del radicalismo: Aspectos y enseñanzas de una obra," originally published in *La revista de ciencias políticas*, January 1916, reprinted in ibid., p. 358.

64. "Machine Politics in Buenos Aires and the Argentine Radical Party, 1912-1930," *Journal of Latin American Studies*, IV (November 1972): 233-256.

65. Germani, *Política y sociedad*, p. 225.

66. Cantón, *Materiales*, I, 3-29 provides a full record of these complaints.

67. Ibid., I, 257-278 provides data on provincial elections. It should be noted that the northern region of Santa Fe was a conservative stronghold characterized by very extensive rural holdings. See Ezequiel Gallo and Silvia Sigal, "La formación de los partidos políticos contemporáneos: La UCR (1890-1916)," in *Argentina, sociedad de masas*, Torcuato S. Di Tella et al., pp. 158-160.

68. See Scobie, p. 128; Argentina, *Tercer censo*, 1914, I, 210-214; Germani, *Política y sociedad*, pp. 203-204; Oscar E. Cornblit, Ezequiel Gallo, and Alfredo A. O'Connell, "La generación del 80 y su proyecto: Antecedentes y consecuencias," in *Argentina, sociedad de masas*, Di Tella et al., pp. 25-28.

69. Argentina, *Tercer censo*, 1914, I, 212.

70. *Política y sociedad*, p. 225.

71. Roque Saenz Peña to Dr. Félix T. Garzón (Governor of Córdoba), 14 March 1912 and Dr. Salustiano F. Zavalia, 14 March 1912 in Saenz Peña, II, 131 and 134-135.

72. Solberg, *Immigration and Nationalism*, pp. 80-90, 125-127.

73. Ezequiel Gallo, *Farmers in Revolt: The Revolutions of 1893 in the Province of Santa Fe, Argentina* (London, 1976).

74. *Politics in Argentina*, p. 50.

75. José Panettieri, *Los trabajadores en tiempos de la inmigración masiva en Argentina, 1870-1910*, Facultad de Humanidades y Ciencias de la Educación, Departamento de Historia, Universidad Nacional de la Plata, Monografías y Tesis, VIII (La Plata, 1966), pp. 122-123. See also Alberto Belloni, "Las luchas obreras durante el apogeo oligárquico," in *El régimen oligárquico: materiales para el estudio de la realidad argentina (hasta 1930)*, ed. Marcos Giménez Zapiola (Buenos Aires, 1975), pp. 217-231.

76. It has been estimated that the membership of the anarchist federation FORA reached a figure of 25,000 in 1906, while the Socialists, who split with the anarchists in 1902 and formed the Unión General de Trabajo, had a following of 10,000. Autonomous unions accounted for another 10,000 workers. Samuel L. Baily, *Labor, Nationalism and Politics in Argentina* (New Brunswick, N.J., 1967), p. 195.

77. Argentina, Departamento Nacional del Trabajo, *Boletín*, no. 30 (April, 1915): p. 19.

78. Augusto da Rocha, comp., *Leyes nacionales clasificadas y sus decretos reglamentarios*, 18 vols. (Buenos Aires, 1935-1938), I, 249 (Law No. 4144).

79. Ibid., I, 250-255 (Law No. 7029).

80. Ibid., I, 257-258 (No. 4661); 271-273 (No. 5291); 285-287 (No. 8999); 299-303 (No. 9677); 331-338 (No. 9688).

81. See Baily, p. 30.

82. See Puiggros, pp. 112-123; Carl Solberg, "Rural Unrest and Agrarian

Policy in Argentina, 1912-1930," *Journal of Inter-American Studies and World Affairs*, XIII (January 1971):18-52.

Chapter V

1. National legislators, even within a single legislative body, are not equally influential, nor are they necessarily the only or even the most important decision makers in a given country. Moreover, information about the social origins and career backgrounds of political elites provides no solid basis for predicting policy orientations or political behavior. For a discussion of these issues see Geraint Parry, *Political Elites* (London, 1969), pp. 97-105; Robert D. Putnam, *The Comparative Study of Political Elites* (Englewood Cliffs, N.J., 1976), pp. 41-44; John D. Nagle, *System and Succession: The Social Bases of Political Elite Recruitment* (Austin, 1977), pp. 229-251; Lewis Edinger and Donald Searing, "Social Background and Elite Analysis: A Methodological Inquiry," *American Political Science Review*, LXI (June 1967):428-445.
2. See, for example, Lester G. Seligman et al., *Patterns of Recruitment: A State Chooses Its Lawmakers* (Chicago, 1974).
3. Suzanne Keller, *Beyond the Ruling Class: Strategic Elites in Modern Society* (New York, 1963), pp. 206-207, 292-293 summarizes this evidence and provides a list of major studies.
4. Valenzuela, *Political Brokers*, p. 194n.
5. Darío Cantón, *El parlamento argentino en épocas de cambio: 1890, 1916 y 1946* (Buenos Aires, 1966), p. 38.
6. Ibid.
7. "The Structure of Politics in Nineteenth Century Spanish America: The Chilean Oligarchy, 1833-1891" (Ph.D. dissertation, University of Notre Dame, 1973), p. 87.
8. Cantón, *El parlamento*, pp. 56-57.
9. Ibid.; Gallo and Sigal, p. 163.
10. This analysis of partisan differences is based on the same sources as Tables 18 and 19.
11. As indicated above, occupational data provide only limited information about the socioeconomic status of legislators. This problem is intensified by obstacles to the classification of legislators in a single occupational category. During the course of their lifetimes, legislators typically carried out more than one occupation. Even when biographical records provide information on the occupational roles of legislators at the time they assumed office, classification problems emerge. For example, a volume published in Santiago in 1909, *El Congreso Nacional de Chile de 1909 a 1912*, described the newly elected congress. The book listed more than one occupation for 53.1 percent of the senators and 37.9 percent of the deputies. One senator, Eduardo Charme, can be classified into four

distinct occupational categories. Although economic elites in Argentina were less frequently involved in more than one sector of the economy, biographical records indicate that Argentine legislators also carried out more than one occupation at a time. Enrique Udaondo, *Diccionario biográfico argentino* (Buenos Aires, 1938); William Belmont Parker, *Argentines of To-Day*, 2 vols. (Buenos Aires, 1920); Sociedad Inteligencia Sud Americana, *Hombres del día: El diccionario biográfico argentino* (Buenos Aires, 1917). The accuracy of the occupational classification of Argentine legislators, reported in Table 17, consequently appears questionable.

12. Smith, *Failure of Democracy*, pp. 30-31.
13. Ibid., p. 31.
14. Ibid., pp. 117-126.
15. Ibid., pp. 123-124.
16. Ibid., pp. 122-124.
17. Andre Siegfried, *Impressions of South America*, trans. H.H. and Doris Hemming (London, 1933), p. 80.
18. Mariano G. Bosch, *Historia del partido radical* (Buenos Aires, 1931), p. 214.
19. Only a few efforts of any kind have been made to investigate the social backgrounds of Chilean political elites in the late 19th and early 20th centuries. These include Bauer, pp. 215-217; Yeager, pp. 539-572; and Thomas C. Wright, *Landowners and Reform in Chile: The Sociedad Nacional de Agricultura, 1919-40* (Urbana, Ill., 1982), p. 222.
20. Venegas, *Sinceridad*, pp. 44-47. See also George McCutchen McBride, *Chile: Land and Society* (New York, 1936), p. 207, which emphasizes the "resurgence of hacendado control" in the 1891-1920 period, and Gil, p. 50.
21. *Political Brokers*, pp. 210-214.
22. Ibid., p. 194n.
23. Brian Loveman, *Chile: The Legacy of Hispanic Capitalism* (New York, 1979), p. 218 states that "government remained largely in the hands of a small clique of 'political families' with aristocratic pretensions and a political base in the countryside."
24. Comparisons between the tax roll values presented in Espinoza, 5th ed. and Chile, *Indice de propietarios* indicate that while the tax appraisals of some rural estates rose between 1902 and 1908, others declined. For example, Juana Ross de Edwards' estate, "Nancagua," was valued at $477,179 pesos in 1902 but only $386,543 pesos in 1908. In the same commune José Domingo Jaramillo's estate, "El Cardal," increased in value between 1902 and 1908. Changes in tax appraisals in other communes were also characterized by little consistency. In Requinoa, for example, the tax roll values of estates such as "Maiten" and "Las Cabras" remained constant between 1902 and 1908. In contrast, the appraised

value of Emilio Valdés' estate, "San José de Requinoa," increased almost 40 percent.

25. Since individuals often owned more than one estate, the total number of estate owners was somewhat smaller. In 1902, for example, 446 individuals owned the 527 most valuable private estates in Chile.

26. According to the Oficina Central de Estadística, *Estadística del avalúo de la propiedad raíz de la República de Chile* (Santiago, 1920), convents, charities, municipalities, the state, and the church together controlled only 5.1 percent of the total value of rural property in Chile.

27. This estimate is based on Chile, *Anuario estadístico*, 1917-1918, Vol. VII: *Agricultura*, p. 21.

28. See Bauer, pp. 196-197.

29. This estimate is based on Valenzuela's *Album*, which presents statistics on agricultural land totals for each of the central valley provinces as well as information on the size of individual estates.

30. See Bauer, p. 216. Private communications with Bauer indicate that the discrepancies are partially explained by the fact that Bauer included congressmen owning two or more smaller estates totalling $200,000 pesos in value in his calculations. It should also be noted that Bauer's figures for 1918 are for the 31st congress elected in 1915.

31. The 1967 land reform law defined a BIH as a unit of land equivalent to one hectare of prime quality land in the Maipo Valley of central Chile and assigned BIH conversion coefficients to each zone in the country. These coefficients took into account factors such as soil productivity, climate, market distance, and transportation links. In Santiago the conversion coefficients ranged from .013 for cordillera land to 1.0 for irrigated central flat lands. The conversion coefficients are presented in Chile, Instituto de Capacitación e Investigación en Reforma Agraria, Departamento de Derecho y Legislación Agrarios, *Exposición metódica y coordinada de la Ley de Reforma Agraria de Chile* (Santiago, 1968), pp. 273-282.

32. Even in the 1960s, when transportation links were much more highly developed than in the 1920s, the value of irrigated land in different parts of the central valley varied significantly. Under the 1967 land reform law, for example, one hectare of prime irrigated land in Santiago or O'Higgins was worth two hectares of irrigated land in Nuble. The value placed on unirrigated lands in different regions of the country varied even more significantly. As a result, a single hectare of irrigated land might be worth 2 to 154 hectares of unirrigated land.

33. The most striking difference is that the 1923 list includes a far larger proportion of large estate owners from the southern parts of the central valley, particularly the Province of Nuble, which has the least productive land of any of the central valley provinces. Estate subdivision, consolidation, turnover, and name changes all make it difficult to compare the

1923 list with those drawn from earlier tax rolls, but over 90 percent of the estates in Valparaíso on the 1923 list that could be identified in earlier tax rolls were valued at over $200,000 pesos. Because of the discrepancy between estate size and value, the percentage in the case of the Province of Talca was only 30 percent. In short, the 1923 list probably includes a large number of estates in Curicó, Talca, Linares, and Nuble that did not measure up to the $200,000 tax roll standard and excludes others, notably in the Province of Santiago, that did.

Further questions about the comparability of data on large estate ownership over time are raised by the larger size of the 1923 list of estate owners and its geographical base, which is limited to the central valley. These two characteristics of the 1923 list, however, tend to cancel each other out, and neither accounts fully for the trends reported in Table 22. Only 10 to 15 percent of large estates in the years 1894-97, 1902, and 1908 were located outside the central valley, and usually only one large estate owner in congress was identified on the basis of noncentral valley landownership.

34. Although the 1908 tax roll was used to identify large estate owners during the 1912-1924 period, landowners typically sat in congress before, rather than after, they acquired their properties. Hence very few large estate owners could be identified in congress during the latter years of the parliamentary period on the basis of the 1908 list. In 1924, for example, the figure was only four. The 1903-1906 congress, which fell between two tax rolls, illustrates the importance of multiple lists. Thirteen members of the Chamber of Deputies in the 1903-1906 congress were identified as large estate owners on the basis of the 1902 tax roll; the 1908 tax roll allowed for the identification of another seven.

35. *Diccionario histórico, biográfico y bibliográfico de Chile*, 5 vols. (Santiago, 1925-1931). As Valenzuela, *Political Brokers*, p. 255 notes, "It is reasonable to assume that if an individual does not appear in Figueroa, he was probably not considered to be a member of the higher class in the small and restricted Chilean society." Names of congressmen drawn from Valencia Avaria, II.

36. Espinoza, 4th ed. provides the tax roll information.

37. Names of legislators drawn from Valencia Avaria, II.

38. Chile, *Indice de propietarios*.

39. Names of legislators drawn from Valencia Avaria, II.

40. Ibid.

41. Cantón, *Parlamento*, pp. 196-204 provides an alphabetical list of names for the 1916 legislature.

42. On this point see Heise González, *Historia de Chile*, II, 270-272.

Chapter VI

1. As Richard I. Hofferbert has persuasively argued, the revenue base provided by economic affluence is only one government resource. The number of technically skilled and educated people and the means of communication available to political authorities, for example, condition the types of policies that may be adopted. "Ecological Development and Policy Change," in *Policy Analysis in Political Science*, ed. Ira Sharkansky (Chicago, 1970), p. 150.
2. Ibid.; Mamalakis, *Growth and Structure of the Chilean Economy*, pp. 4-6.
3. Díaz Alejandro, p. 6; Argentina, *Tercer censo*, 1914, X, 389.
4. Díaz Alejandro, p. 6; Guaresti, p. 223.
5. Chile, *Sinópsis estadística*, 1919, p. 69.
6. Chile, *Anuario estadístico*, 1925, VI, 19.
7. Ibid.
8. Chile, Congreso Nacional, *Lei de presupuestos de los gastos jenerales de la administración pública de Chile para el año de 1886* (Santiago, 1886); Chile, *Anuario estadístico*, 1915, VI, 36-51.
9. Ibid., 1922, VI, 16-17.
10. Chile, *Lei de presupuestos . . . 1896*.
11. Indeed, expenditures on wages and salaries may even have been higher during the parliamentary period than later. For example, salaries accounted for 43.1 percent of the total budget in 1936: less than in 1913 or 1918. Chile, Congreso Nacional, *Ley de presupuestos de entradas y gastos ordinarios de la administración pública de Chile* (Santiago, 1936).
12. Chile, *Sinópsis estadística*, 1919, p. 68.
13. Ibid., p. 69; *Anuario estadístico*, 1925, VI, p. 19.
14. Ibid., 1918, VI, 14.
15. Of the $890,925,035 pesos of 18d paid in export duties between 1901 and 1914, $884,183,047 pesos were derived from nitrate duties. Chilean Legation, *Resumen de la hacienda pública*, p. 5.
16. Chile, *Anuario estadístico*, VI, 1918, 14; ibid., 1925, VI, 15.
17. Law No. 2982 of 5 February 1915 imposed the inheritance tax; law No. 3091 of 5 April 1916 dealt with property taxes. Chile, Consejo de Estado, *Recopilación*, VIII, 167-172, 471-484. See also Chilean Legation, *Resumen de la hacienda pública*, pp. 26-41.
18. Chile, *Anuario estadístico*, VI, 1918, 14, 62-63; ibid., 1925, VI, 15.
19. Ibid., 1918, VI, 62-63.
20. Ibid., 1925, VI, 14.
21. Ibid., 14, 66.
22. Law No. 980 promulgated 31 December 1897, Anguita, III, 400-407. For historical background on this shift in commercial policy see William F. Sater, "Chile and the World Depression of the 1870s," *Journal of Latin American Studies*, II (May 1979):67-99; Carmagnani, pp. 97-118.

23. Law No. 3066 of 10 April 1916, Chile, Consejo de Estado, *Recopilación*, VIII, 327-424.
24. L. Domeratzky, *Customs Tariff of Chile*, U.S. Dept. of Commerce Tariff Series No. 36 (Washington, D.C., 1917), p. 6.
25. Frank R. Rutter, *Tariff Systems of South American Countries*, U.S. Dept. of Commerce Tariff Series No. 34 (Washington, D.C., 1916), p. 144. This study includes a full discussion of the evolution of customs policy in Chile during the 1897-1916 period (pp. 143-181) as well as a comparison of the average ad valorem duties collected on imports in seven Latin American countries in 1913. Bearing in mind that this index is extremely crude inasmuch as imports were valued differently in the seven countries, it is interesting that Chilean commercial policy appears to have been the most protectionist. The average ad valorem duties collected on imports were (in percentages): Chile=23.2, Argentina= 20.8, Ecuador=16.0, Paraguay=11.5, Bolivia=5.8, Uruguay=4.8, Peru= 0.6 (p. 26).
26. "La mesa de tres patas," *Desarrollo económico*, III (April-September 1963): 231-247.
27. Díaz Alejandro, p. 285.
28. Chile, *Anuario estadístico*, 1925, VI, 14, 66.
29. See, for example, Chile, Cámara de Senadores, *Sesiones extraordinarias*, 12 November 1897, pp. 524-526 for the comments of Alejandro Vial, a Conservative.
30. On the formation of the SFF as well as its role in the formulation of the 1897 tariff law, see Juan Eduardo Vargas Cariola, "La Sociedad de Fomento Fabril, 1883-1928," *Historia* (Santiago), XIII (1976):5-53. See also Rutter, p. 143.
31. Thomas C. Wright, "Agriculture and Protectionism in Chile, 1880-1930," *Journal of Latin American Studies*, VII (May 1975):45-58.
32. On the program of the Democrats, see Chapter III. The position of the Socialists is outlined in Barría Serón, *Los movimientos sociales*, p. 375.
33. T. Wright, "Politics of Inflation," pp. 239-259; idem, *Landowners and Reform*, pp. 100-109. Laws No. 2914 of 3 August 1914 and 2965 of 31 December 1914 permitted the president to suspend food exports as well as duties on imported food. Chile, *Recopilación*, VIII, pp. 75, 153.
34. See Table 32.
35. To explain very briefly, when the value of an inconvertible paper currency falls because of, say, an unfavorable balance of payments, the domestic price level rises. Exports are stimulated because exporters' costs theoretically lag behind fluctuations in the exchange rate. Exporters receive more paper currency for their goods and their profits increase. Concomitantly, the price of imports rises, hitting importers, but encouraging import-competing activities. Profits remitted abroad are squeezed because a unit of paper currency can buy less gold or foreign currency. To mention two other side effects: (1) assuming debts are payable in paper, the

rising price level benefits debtors, and (2) assuming wages are less flexible than prices and exchange rates, real wages tend to fall. Under a gold standard the process is just the reverse. An unfavorable trade balance leads to deflation, the contraction of credit, falling prices, and thus to the stimulation of exports.

36. The seminal work on the subject is Frank W. Fetter, *Monetary Inflation in Chile*, Publications of the International Finance Section of the Department of Economics and Social Institutions, Princeton University, Vol. III (Princeton, 1931). See also McBride, p. 174; Venegas, *Sinceridad*, passim; and idem, *Cartas*, passim.

37. See Chile, Cámara de Diputados, *Sesiones ordinarias*, 14 July 1897, particularly the comments of Jorge Huneeus and Fernando Alamos, pp. 493-494.

38. Cost-of-living indices were not compiled before 1913, but the composite price index Ballesteros and Davis used to deflate their value-product series suggests that the average rate of inflation between 1908 and 1924 was less than 7 percent. The price of food probably rose somewhat faster. DeShazo, *Urban Workers and Labor Unions*, pp. 64-67. The rate of inflation before 1900 remains obscure, but the rate of devaluation suggests inflation was no more rapid than in later years.

39. Chile, Cámara de Diputados, *Sesiones ordinarias*, 1898, pp. 317ff.

40. On the increase in property values see Thomas C. Wright, "The Sociedad Nacional de Agricultura in Chilean Politics, 1869-1938," (Ph.D. dissertation, University of California, Berkeley, 1971), p. 96. Bauer (pp. 87-111, 155-156) explores the advantages enjoyed by large estate owners in the credit market as well as the relationship between food prices and peon wages. See also Fetter, who emphasizes the benefits of inflation for indebted estate owners.

41. See, for example, Jobet, p. 61, who has urged that the date of the first law of emission of paper money "be recorded as one of the most sinister in our historical evolution."

42. Ten of these laws were passed in 1912 alone. Anguita, Vol. IV, passim.

43. Albert O. Hirschman, *Journeys Toward Progress: Studies of Economic Policy-Making in Latin America* (New York, 1968), pp. 160-175.

44. According to Guillermo Subercaseaux, *Monetary and Banking Policy in Chile* (Oxford, 1922), Chile almost returned to the gold standard at an earlier date, but the war intervened. In view of the number of times congress postponed a return to the gold standard, this assertion remains open to question.

45. Guaresti, p. 223; Federico Julio Herschel and Samuel Itzcovich, "Fiscal Policy in Argentina," *Public Finance*, XII (1957): 103; Carlos F. Soares, *Economía y finanzas de la Nación Argentina*, 3 vols. (Buenos Aires, 1916-1932), II, 178 and III, 229; Argentina, Cámara de Diputados, "Cuadro demostrativo de las rentas recaudadas y los gastos totales de la Nación por presupuesto, por leyes especiales y acuerdos de gobierno, por

año, déficit o superávit anual de 1864 a 1927," *Diario de sesiones*, 1928, V, 454; and Argentina, Dirección General de Estadística de la Nación, *Los gastos públicos*, Informe No. 7, Serie F, No. 3, 1923, p. 4 all provide statistics on total national government expenditures between 1910 and 1930. Figures presented by these sources for individual years diverge considerably. For example, whereas according to both Guaresti and Soares national government expenditures totalled $671.2 million paper pesos in 1924, Argentina, Cámara de Diputados, "Cuadro demostrativo," *Diario de sesiones*, 1928, V, 454 presents a figure of only $580.0 million paper pesos. The estimate of Herschel and Itzcovich for 1924 is $589.5 million paper pesos. For 1916, on the other hand, the estimates of Guaresti differ from those of Soares and agree with the figures in the 1928 *Diario de Sesiones*. In short, the differences among the various sources fail to conform to any single pattern. Similar inconsistencies characterize estimates of national government revenues. See Guaresti, p. 223; Argentina, Cámara de Diputados, "Cuadro demostrativo," *Diario de sesiones*, 1928, V, 454; Argentina, Contaduría General de la Nación, *Memoria de la Contaduría General de la Nación correspondiente al año 1931: Anexo de la memoria del Ministerio de Hacienda*, I, 53 (cuadro 23); Argentina, Dirección General de Estadística, *La deuda pública*, Informe No. 6, Serie F, No. 2, 1923, p. 9.

46. In discussing Argentine fiscal policy, it should be noted that in contrast to the Chilean case, where the value of the paper peso fluctuated considerably over time, it makes little difference whether figures are presented in gold or paper pesos. After 1899 Argentina had a dual currency system consisting of a gold and a paper peso, exchangeable at a fixed rate of forty-four centavos gold to one paper peso. Although the war led to a period of inconvertibility that lasted until August 1927, throughout the 1914-1927 period the ratio of the gold and paper peso remained constant. *Both* fluctuated against other currencies, and there was no significant monetary inflation except that incidental to the depreciation of gold. Harold E. Peters, *The Foreign Debt of the Argentine Republic* (Baltimore, 1934), pp. 53-67.

47. The distribution of the personnel of the autonomous institutions in 1922, excluding teachers, was as follows: Ferrocarriles del Estado—20,834, Banco de la Nación—4,960, Obras Sanitarias—935, Banco Hipotecario Nacional—1,046, other—230.

48. Argentina, *Los gastos públicos*, p. 9.

49. This estimate allows for the fact that 8,673 of the personnel in teaching in 1922 were secondary-school teachers and hence paid by the national treasury rather than the Consejo Nacional de Educación.

50. Hobart A. Spalding, Jr. "Education in Argentina, 1890-1914: The Limits of Oligarchical Reform," *Journal of Interdisciplinary History*, III (Summer 1972):49; Díaz Alejandro, pp. 28, 64.

51. It should be noted that Table 35 fails to account for a substantial amount of government spending in the years 1924 and 1926. In addition the accuracy of many individual figures is open to question. Nevertheless, the rate and direction of change is the same as that indicated by Argentina, *Los gastos públicos*, on which Table 33 is based. With the exception of spending on pensions, there is also substantial agreement with Herschel and Itzcovich, pp. 102-103.

52. The actual figure was probably in the region of $78 million pesos.

53. See Table 24 supra.

54. Carl Solberg, "Rural Unrest and Agrarian Policy," p. 31 analyzes budgetary data and reaches a similar conclusion.

55. Banco de la Nación, *Economic Review*, November 1930, as cited in Peters, p. 110.

56. Argentina, Cámara de Diputados, "Cuadro demostrativo," *Diario de Sesiones*, 1928, V, 460-461.

57. Whereas in 1916 the budget accounted for 91 percent of total national expenditures, in 1927 and 1928 that proportion dropped to only 66 percent. Special laws, resolutions, and transfer from previous years accounted for the remainder. Soares, *Economía y finanzas* (1916-1932), II, 178; III, 229.

58. Peters, p. 110.

59. Argentina, Dirección General de Estadística, *La deuda pública*, p. 9.

60. The text of the proposed law is reprinted in Soares, *Economía y finanzas* (1916-1932), II, 135-145.

61. Law No. 10,349, Argentina, Cámara de Senadores, *Diario de sesiones*, 1917, III, 1874-1876.

62. Law No. 11,033 of February 1920 lowered the duties on chilled meat and wheat flour 50 percent. See Soares, *Economía y finanzas* (1916-1932), II, 133.

63. Total national revenues, including the special tax revenues mentioned above, equalled $317,995,000 paper pesos in 1910 and $629,902,000 in 1924. Argentina, Dirección General de Estadística de la Nación, *Los impuestos y otros recursos fiscales de la nación y las provincias en los años 1910 y 1924-1925*, Informe No. 17, Serie F, No. 4, 1926, p. 4.

64. Ibid.

65. Argentina, Ministerio de Hacienda, "Nivel general de precios al por mayor en el período 1913-1927" (unpublished paper; Buenos Aires, 1928), pp. 4, 12.

66. Díaz Alejandro, p. 43; Argentina, Dirección General de Estadística, *El costa de la vida y el poder de comprar de la moneda*, Informe No. 9, Serie E, No. 1, 1924, pp. 7-8.

67. Peters, pp. 67, 160-163.

68. The eminent Argentine economist, Alejandro E. Bunge, provided the classical statement of this view. Writing at the end of the 1920s, Bunge argued that Argentina had made little economic progress after 1908 in

comparison with nations such as Canada because of its liberal tariff policy. *La economía argentina*, 2 vols. (Buenos Aires, 1928), II, 42. Roberto Cortés Conde, "Problemas del crecimiento industrial de la Argentina (1870-1914)," *Desarrollo económico*, III (April-September 1963): 153 has taken this argument one step further and alleged that government policy actually discriminated against industrial development by supporting "protectionism in reverse."

69. Cornblit, p. 231.
70. On this and earlier protective legislation see Donna J. Guy, "Carlos Pellegrini and the Politics of Early Argentine Industrialization, 1873-1906," *Journal of Latin American Studies*, II (May 1979):123-144; and Marcos Giménez Zapiola, "El interior argentina y el ≪desarrollo hacia afuera≫: El caso de Tucumán," in *El régimen oligárquico*, ed. Giménez Zapiola, pp. 72-115.
71. League of Nations, *Tariff Level Indices* (Geneva, 1927), p. 17.
72. See Díaz Alejandro, pp. 285-295 for a more detailed discussion of this issue.
73. Argentina, *Tercer censo*, X, 361-371 and VIII, 16; Peters, p. 70; Dirección General de Estadística, *La deuda pública*, pp. 8-9; idem, *Noticia sumaria del comercio exterior argentino en el decenio 1910-19* (Buenos Aires, 1920), p. 5; idem, *Anuario del comercio exterior de la República Argentina* (Buenos Aires, 1916-1931).
74. Statistics on the real as opposed to the nominal or tariff value of imports are not available for the years 1905-1909, but since tariff values were fixed in 1906 it can be assumed that the difference between real and nominal values was minimal in 1909.
75. Díaz Alejandro, pp. 285-295.
76. Carl Solberg, "The Tariff and Politics in Argentina, 1916-1930," *Hispanic American Historical Review* (May 1973):266-284.
77. Panettieri, p. 63.

Chapter VII

1. "American Business, Public Policy, Case Studies, and Political Theory," *World Politics*, XVI (July 1964):677-715. For a subsequent revision of this typology, see Theodore J. Lowi, "Four Systems of Policy, Politics, and Choice," *Public Administration Review*, XXXII (July-August, 1972): 298-310.
2. See George D. Greenberg et al., "Developing Public Policy Theory: Perspectives from Empirical Research," *American Political Science Review*, LXXI (December 1977):1532-1543.
3. V.O. Key developed an argument along these lines in his analysis of southern politics in the United States. He suggested that factional fluidity makes a government especially vulnerable to individual pressures and disposed toward favoritism, whereas strong party organization creates conditions favorable to government according to general rules (p. 305).

4. See, for example, the speech presented by Manuel Rivas Vicuña to the Centro de la Juventud Liberal of Santiago entitled "El seguro obrero en Alemania," reprinted in Rivas Vicuña, III, 542-557. See also Morris, pp. 37-42, who points out that more than seventy theses on social and labor topics were completed in Chile between 1898 and 1924. Most of them dealt with legislation in the "advanced" countries.

5. G. Feliú Cruz, p. 137.

6. *Sinceridad*, p. 209.

7. DeShazo, *Urban Workers*, p. 63.

8. See Jorge Gustavo Silva, *La cuestión social y la legislación social en Chile*, 2nd ed. (Santiago, 1927), p. 19.

9. See DeShazo, *Urban Workers*, pp. 40-41, 222-223; see also Jorge Gustavo Silva, *Cuestión social*, pp. 17-20.

10. Ibid., pp. 11-17.

11. Fernando Campos Harriet, *Desarrollo educacional, 1810-1960* (Santiago, 1960), p. 35.

12. Many of these proposals were included in a bill sponsored by Conservative Senators in 1919. In slightly different form they were also linked together in Alessandri's 1921 legislative program (*Mensaje*, 1921).

13. Laws 4053-4059. For a summary of social policies introduced in 1924 and 1925, see Jorge Gustavo Silva, *Cuestión social*, pp. 17-20.

14. U.S. Department of Health, Education, and Welfare, *Social Security Programs Throughout the World, 1975* (Washington, D.C., 1975).

15. Soares, *Economía y finanzas* (1916-1932), II, 62-64, 68-69, 106-113; H. Irigoyen, *Hipólito Yrigoyen: Documentación histórica de 55 años de actuación por la democracia y las instituciones*, ed. Luis Rodríguez (Buenos Aires, 1934), pp. 233-237; Irigoyen, *Ley 12839*, pp. 247-249. See also Solberg, "Tariff and Politics," pp. 267-270 for a summary of the controversy relating to sugar prices.

16. Irigoyen, *Hipólito Yrigoyen: Pueblo y gobierno*, IV, 143, 154-155; Soares, *Economía y finanzas* (1916-1932), II, 116.

17. "Notes on News," 6 January 1922, p. 21. On the broader issue of relations between the Argentine state and the British railway companies see Paul B. Goodwin, Jr., "The Politics of Rate-making: The British-owned Railways and the Unión Cívica Radical, 1921-1928," *Journal of Latin American Studies*, VI (May 1974):257-287; Winthrop R. Wright, *British-Owned Railways in Argentina: Their Effect on the Growth of Economic Nationalism, 1854-1948*, Latin American Monographs, no. 34 (Austin, 1974), pp. 110-135.

18. Soares, *Economía y finanzas* (1916-1932), II, 117-118.

19. For a critique of the Argentine educational system at this time see Spalding, "Education in Argentina," pp. 31-61.

20. Messages to congress of 30 June 1917 (Irigoyen, *Hipólito Yrigoyen: Pueblo y gobierno*, IV, 99-100); 31 July 1918 (Irigoyen, *Ley 12839*, pp. 205-209); and 9 September 1919 (ibid., pp. 224-225). See also Ar-

gentina, Cámara de Diputados, *Diario de sesiones*, 25 September 1923, VI, 397-427.

21. See Del Mazo, I, 234-257.
22. Argentina, Cámara de Senadores, *Diario de sesiones*, 20 September 1925, II, 329.
23. Irigoyen, *Ley 12839*, pp. 175-180; idem, *Hipólito Yrigoyen: Documentación*, pp. 271-280; Argentina, Cámara de Diputados, *Proyecto de Código del Trabajo presentado por el Poder Ejecutiva en la sesión de 8 de junio de 1921* (Buenos Aires, 1921); idem, *Diario de sesiones*, 20 September 1922, IV, 148-149.
24. Inaugural message of 1922 in Irigoyen, *Yrigoyen: Pueblo y gobierno*, IV, 265-266.
25. Between 1916 and 1919 there was a tremendous upsurge in strike action, so a decline existed only in comparison to 1919, not the beginning of Irigoyen's term. See Argentina, Cámara de Senadores, Comisión de Legislación, *Asociaciones gremiales de trabajadores* (Buenos Aires, 1926), p. 6.
26. As quoted by Ricardo Caballero in Argentina, Cámara de Senadores, *Diario de sesiones*, 20 September 1925, II, 328.
27. David Rock, *Politics in Argentina*, passim; idem, "Machine Politics," p. 254.
28. For an explicit statement of this view see "Nota del Ministerio del Interior que expresa el pensamiento del Presidente Yrigoyen sobre conflictos del trabajo," 16 June 1919 in Irigoyen, *Ley 12839*, pp. 102-103. See also the comments of Ricardo Caballero in Argentina, Cámara de Senadores, *Diario de sesiones*, 20 September 1925, II, 320.
29. Sandra McGee, "The Liga Patriótica Argentina and Its 'Practical Humanitarianism:' A Right-Wing Response to Social Change," paper presented at the 8th national meeting of the Latin American Studies Association, Pittsburgh, April 5-7, 1979. See also Rock, *Politics in Argentina*, pp. 180-182.
30. Olguín; Celso Rodríguez, "Cantonismo," pp. 170-201; idem, *Lencinas y Cantoni*, passim.
31. According to DeShazo, "Valparaíso Maritime Strike," p. 162, only a handful of individuals were ever deported under the Chilean law.
32. Rock, *Politics in Argentina*, p. 194.
33. Letter of 24 August 1931, Irigoyen, *Ley 12839*, p. 310.
34. Poppino, p. 59.
35. Rock, "Machine Politics," p. 254 employs the term "benign neglect" to describe Irigoyen's attitude towards the immigrant labor community. DeShazo, "Valparaíso Maritime Strike," p. 147 characterizes Chilean policy as "malign neglect."
36. Poppino, pp. 68-69.
37. Until the end of the parliamentary period, only the relatively uninfluential Democrats and a few social critics took much interest in the problem of rural inequalities. See Malaquías Concha, *Memoria presentada a la*

convención del partido democrático reunida en Chillán el 14 de julio de
1901 a la agrupación electoral que representa, por el diputado de Con-
cepción i Talcahuano don Malaquías Concha (Santiago, 1901), p. 8. See
also Venegas, *Sinceridad*, p. 265 who emphasized the need for agrarian
reform. After 1919 the idea of redressing rural inequalities became more
widespread, and several bills were introduced into the legislature that
were designed to encourage estate subdivision and improve the position
of rural workers. None of them, however, received serious attention. See
T. Wright, *Landowners and Reform*, passim.

38. Irigoyen, *Ley 12839*, p. 216.
39. Ibid., pp. 179-180, 217, 226-229; Argentina, Cámara de Diputados,
    Diario de sesiones extraordinarias, 1921, V, 20-21. See also Irigoyen,
    Hipólito Irigoyen: Pueblo y gobierno, IV, 107-109.
40. See letters to the Governor of Santiago del Estero of 17 September 1920
    and 7 January 1930, Irigoyen, *Ley 12839*, pp. 257-259.
41. Ibid., pp. 186-188.
42. Argentina, Cámara de Diputados, *Diario de sesiones*, 21 August 1924,
    III, 475-481; ibid., 28 September 1928, V, 559-560.
43. Solberg, "Rural Unrest and Agrarian Policy," pp. 49, 52.
44. For a variety of reasons, including the political strength of the left and
    the rural sector's lack of economic dynamism, Chile represents another
    exception. By the end of the parliamentary period, agrarian reform had
    become a serious issue. Efforts to encourage the redistribution of rural
    property date back to the late 1920s (see T. Wright, *Landowners and Re-*
    form, pp. 122-134). Yet even by the standards of Chile, where inequalities
    in the rural sector were far more palpable than in Argentina and the
    economic rationale for rural reform far stronger, Argentine policy makers
    addressed rural reform issues comparatively early.
45. Malaquías Concha, *La lucha económica* (Santiago, 1910), pp. 55-58.
    See also Pike's discussion of the growth of economic nationalism, pp.
    162-163.
46. Alcira Leiserson, *Notes on the Process of Industrialization in Argentina,*
    Chile, and Peru, Politics of Modernization Series, no. 3 (Berkeley, 1966),
    pp. 20-22.
47. See Claudio Véliz, *Historia de la marina mercante de Chile* (Santiago,
    1961).
48. For a description of the inadequacy of banking arrangements, see the
    speech of the Minister of Finance proposing a central bank of 20 August
    1923, Chile, Cámara de Diputados, *Sesiones ordinarias*, 1923, I, 1017-
    1022. See also G. Subercaseaux, *Monetary and Banking Policy*, passim.
49. Ricardo Pillado, "The Meat Industry in the Argentine Republic: Histori-
    cal Note on Its Past and Actual Progress," in Argentine Republic, *Agri-*
    cultural and Pastoral Census of the Nation: Stock-breeding and Agricul-
    ture in 1908, III (Buenos Aires, 1909), 346-353.

50. Smith, *Politics and Beef*, p. 103; Lebedinsky, p. 74.
51. Roger Gravit, "Anglo-U.S. Trade Rivalry and the D'Abernon Mission of 1929," in *Argentina in the Twentieth Century*, ed. David Rock (Pittsburgh, 1975), pp. 41-65.
52. Two of the twelve volumes of *Hipólito Yrigoyen: Pueblo y gobierno* (XI and XII) deal with petroleum policy. For Irigoyen's various proposals and decrees on the issue see XII, 7-52, 251-258.
53. Message to congress of 30 June 1917, ibid., IV, 116-117; Irigoyen, *Ley 12839*, pp. 124-126, 235-259, 239-240; Goodwin, 257-287; W. Wright, *British-Owned Railways*, pp. 110-135.
54. Message of 30 June 1917, Irigoyen, *Hipólito Yrigoyen: Pueblo y gobierno*, IV, 114.
55. See Soares, *Economía y finanzas* (1916-1932), II, 85-96.
56. DeShazo, *Urban Workers*, p. xxiii.

Chapter VIII

1. Régis Debray, *The Chilean Revolution: Conversations with Allende* (New York, 1971), p. 30.
2. See, for example, Kalman H. Silvert, "The Costs of Anti-Nationalism: Argentina," in *Latin American Politics: Studies of the Contemporary Scene*, 2nd ed., edited by Robert D. Tomasek (Garden City, N.Y., 1970); O'Donnell; Gilbert W. Merkx, "Sectoral Clashes and Political Change: The Argentine Experience," in *Latin American Research Review*, IV (Fall 1969):89-114; J. Samuel Valenzuela and Arturo Valenzuela, "Chile and the Breakdown of Democracy," in *Latin American Politics and Development*, ed. Howard J. Wiarda and Harvey F. Kline, (Boston, 1979), pp. 233-261. See also the seriously flawed but oft-cited essay of Maurice Zeitlin, "The Social Determinants of Political Democracy in Chile," in *Latin America: Reform or Revolution?*, ed. Petras and Zeitlin, pp. 220-234.
3. Edwards Vives, *La fronda aristocrática*, p. 177.
4. See, for example, Smith, *Politics and Beef*, passim; Solberg, "Tariff and Politics;" idem, "Rural Unrest and Agrarian Policy;" and Potter, pp. 89-90.
5. Rock, *Politics in Argentina*, especially pp. 288-298.
6. Rock, *Politics in Argentina*, p. 97 uses this phrase to describe the impact of the first Irigoyen government.
7. Gaston V. Rimlinger, *Welfare Policy and Industrialization in Europe, America, and Russia* (New York, 1971), p. 9.
8. Ibid., p. 8.
9. In particular, the contrasting experiences of Chile and Argentina tend to support Eric Nordlinger's arguments about the impact of variations in both the rate and sequence of political change. See Nordlinger, pp. 494-520.

SELECTED BIBLIOGRAPHY

Public Documents

Alessandri Palma, Arturo. *Mensaje leído por S.E. el Presidente de la República en la apertura de las sesiones ordinarias del congreso nacional.* Santiago, 1921-1924.

Argentine Republic. *Agricultural and Pastoral Census of the Nation: Stock-breeding and Agriculture in 1908.* Buenos Aires, 1909.

——. Comisión Directiva. *Segundo censo de la República Argentina, mayo 10 de 1895.* 3 vols. Buenos Aires, 1898.

——. Comisión Nacional. *Tercer censo nacional levantado el 1 de junio de 1914.* 10 vols. Buenos Aires, 1916-1919.

——. Congreso Nacional. Cámara de Diputados. *Diario de sesiones.* Buenos Aires, 1905-1930.

——. *Investigación parlamentaria sobre agricultura, ganadería y colonización.* Anexo B. Buenos Aires, 1898.

——. *Proyecto de código del trabajo presentado por el Poder Ejecutivo en la sesión del 8 de junio de 1921.* Buenos Aires, 1921.

——. Cámara de Senadores. Comisión de Legislación. *Asociaciones gremiales de trabajadores.* Buenos Aires, 1926.

——. *Diario de sesiones.* Buenos Aires, 1905-1930.

——. Contaduría General de la Nación. *Memoria de la Contaduría General de la Nación correspondiente al año 1931: Anexo de la memoria del Ministerio de Hacienda,* Vol. I. Buenos Aires, 1933.

——. Departamento Nacional del Trabajo. *Boletín del Departamento Nacional del Trabajo.* Buenos Aires, 1914-1921.

——. *Leyes: De descanso dominical, reglamentaria del trabajo de mujeres y menores y orgánica del Departamento Nacional del Trabajo.* Buenos Aires, 1913.

——. Dirección General de Estadística. *Anuario del comercio exterior de la República Argentina.* Buenos Aires, 1916-1931.

——. *El costo de la vida y el poder de comprar de la moneda.* Informe 9, serie E., no. 1. Buenos Aires, 1924.

——. *La deuda pública.* Informe 6, serie F, no. 2. Buenos Aires, 1923.

——. Dirección General de Estadística. *Los gastos públicas.* Informe 7, serie F, no. 3. Buenos Aires, 1923.

——. *Los impuestos y otros recursos fiscales de la nación y las provincias en los años 1910 y 1924-1925.* Informe 17, serie F, no. 4. Buenos Aires, 1926.

——. *Noticia sumaria del comercio exterior argentino en el decenio 1910-1919.* Buenos Aires, 1920.

——. *Personal de los servicios públicos desde 1903 hasta 1923.* Informe 3, serie A, no. 1. Buenos Aires, 1923.

——. *La población y el movimiento demográfico de la República Argentina en el período 1910-1925.* Buenos Aires, 1926.

——. Ministerio de Hacienda. "Nivel general de precios al por mayor en el período 1913-1927." Unpublished paper, Buenos Aires, 1928.

Argentine Republic. Ministerio del Interior. Subsecretaría de Informaciones. *Las fuerzas armadas restituyen el imperio de la soberanía popular*. 2 vols. Buenos Aires, 1946.

Avellaneda, Nicolás. *Mensaje del Presidente de la República al abrir las sesiones del congreso argentino en mayo de 1877*. Buenos Aires, 1877.

Chile. Comisión Central del Censo. *Censo de la República de Chile levantado el 28 de noviembre de 1907*. Santiago, 1908.

——. Congreso Nacional. *Boletín de sesiones de la Comisión Conservadora, 1902-1912*. Santiago, 1916.

——. *Boletín i actas de las sesiones celebradas por el congreso nacional en 1906 con motivo de la elección de Presidente de la República*. Santiago, 1906.

——. Cámara de Diputados. *Boletín de las sesiones extraordinarias de la Cámara de Diputados*. Santiago, 1885-1924.

——. *Boletín de las sesiones ordinarias de la Cámara de Diputados*. Santiago, 1885-1924.

——. Cámara de Senadores. *Boletín de las sesiones extraordinarias de la Cámara de Senadores*. Santiago, 1885-1924.

——. *Boletín de las sesiones ordinarias de la Cámara de Senadores*. Santiago, 1885-1924.

——. *Lei de presupuestos de los gastos jenerales de la administración pública de Chile para el año de 1886*. Santiago, 1886.

——. *Lei de presupuestos de los gastos jenerales de la administración pública de Chile para el año de 1910*. Santiago, 1910.

——. Congreso Nacional. *Lei de presupuestos jenerales de la administración pública de Chile para el año de 1918*. Santiago, 1918.

——. *Ley de presupuestos de entradas y gastos ordinarios de la administración pública de Chile*. Santiago, 1936.

——. Consejo de Estado. *Recopilación de leyes por orden numérico arreglada por la secretaría del Consejo de Estado*. Santiago, 1914-1925.

——. Controlaría General de la República. Dirrección General de Estadística. *Síntesis estadística*. Santiago, 1929.

——. Departamento de la Estadística Comercial. *Estadística comercial de la República de Chile correspondiente a los años de 1890 y 1891*. Valparaíso, 1893.

——. Dirección General de Estadística. *Anuario estadístico de la República de Chile, 1929-1930*. Santiago, 1931.

——. *Censo agropecuario, 1929-1930*. Santiago, 1933.

——. *Censo de población de la República de Chile levantado el 15 de diciembre de 1920*. Santiago, 1925.

——. *Estadística anual*. Santiago, 1929-1930.

——. *Resultados del X censo de la población efectuado el 27 de noviembre de 1930*. 3 vols. Santiago, 1931-1935.

——. *Sinopsis estadística de la República de Chile, 1926-1927*. Santiago, 1929.

Chile. Instituto de Capacitación e Investigación en Reforma Agraria. Departamento de Derecho y Legislación Agrarios. *Exposición metódica y coordinada de la Ley de Reforma Agraria de Chile.* Santiago, 1968.

——. Ministerio de Industrias y Obras Públicas. Dirección Jeneral de los Servicios Agrícolos. *Reseña sumaria del estado actual de la agricultura en Chile.* Santiago, 1919.

——. Oficina Central de Estadística. *Anuario estadístico de la República de Chile.* Santiago, 1909-1926.

——. *Censo electoral: Elecciones ordinarias de Senadores, Diputados y Municipales, verificadas el 3 de marzo de 1912.* Santiago, 1912.

——. *Censo electoral: Elecciones ordinarias de Senadores, Diputados, Municipales y Electores de la República, 1915.* Santiago, 1915.

——. *Chile económico, 1914.* Santiago, 1914.

——. Oficina Central de Estadística. *Estadística del avalúo de la propiedad raíz de la República de Chile.* Santiago, 1920.

——. *Importación, exportación y consumo de trigo en Chile, en los últimos 20 años.* Santiago, 1915.

——. *Sétimo censo jeneral de la población de Chile levantado el 28 de noviembre de 1895.* 4 vols. Santiago, 1900.

——. *Sinopsis estadística y geográfica de la República de Chile.* Santiago, 1894.

——. *Sinopsis estadística de la República de Chile.* Santiago, 1915-1921.

——. Oficina de Estadística e Informaciones Agrícolas. *Indice de propietarios rurales i valor de la propiedad rural según los roles de avalúos comunales.* Santiago, 1908.

Chilean Legation (London). *Resumen de la hacienda pública de Chile desde 1833 hasta 1914.* [London], 1915.

Domeratzky, L. *Customs Tariff of Chile.* U.S. Dept. of Commerce Tariff Series No. 36. Washington, D.C.: U.S. Government Printing Office, 1917.

Inter-American Development Bank. *Economic and Social Progress in Latin America: 1983 Report.* Washington, D.C.: Inter-American Development Bank, 1983.

Juárez Celman, Miguel. *Message of the President of the Republic on Opening the Session of the Argentine Congress, May 1888.* Buenos Aires, [1888].

League of Nations. Economic and Financial Section. *Tariff Level Indices.* Geneva: International Economic Conference, 1927.

Roca, Julio A. *Message of the President of the Republic on Opening the Argentine Congress, May 1888.* Buenos Aires, 1881.

——. *Mensaje del Presidente de la República al abrir las sesiones del Congreso Argentino en mayo de 1884.* Buenos Aires, 1884.

Rutter, Frank R. *Tariff Systems of South American Countries.* U.S. Dept. of Commerce Tariff Series No. 34. Washington, D.C.: U.S. Government Printing Office, 1916.

Sweden. *Historisk Statistik för Sverige: Statistiska Översiktstabeller.* Stockholm: Statistiska Centralbyrån, 1960.

United Nations. Economic Commission for Latin America. *El desarrollo económico de la Argentina.* Vol. V: *Análisis y proyecciones del desarrollo económico.* Mexico, 1959.
——. *El proceso de industrialización en América Latina.* New York, 1965.
United States. Department of Health, Education, and Welfare. *Social Security Programs throughout the World, 1975.* Washington, D.C.: U.S. Government Printing Office, 1975.

Periodicals

Banco de la Nación Argentina. Bureau of Economic Research. *Economic Review* (Buenos Aires), 1928-1930.
Ernesto Tornquist & Cía, Limitada. *Business Conditions in Argentina* (Buenos Aires), 1919-1927.
El Mercurio (Santiago), 1914-1924.
La Nación (Buenos Aires), 1917-1919.
La Prensa (Buenos Aires), 1908-1930.
Review of the River Plate (Buenos Aires), 1911-1930.

Other Sources

Aguirre Cerda, Pedro. *El problema agrario.* Paris: n.p., 1929.
Alem, Leandro N. *Alem: Su vida, su obra, tragedia de su muerte, las doctrinas democráticas del fundador de la Unión Cívica Radical a través de documentos, discursos y escritos.* Buenos Aires: Editorial Alem, 1928.
——. *Leandro Alem: Mensaje y destino.* 8 vols. Buenos Aires: Editorial Raigal, 1955-1957.
Alem, Roberto. *Alem y la democracia argentina.* Buenos Aires: Editorial Guillermo Kraft, 1957.
Angell, Alan. *Politics and the Labour Movement in Chile.* London: Oxford University Press, 1972.
Alessandri Palma, Arturo. *Parlementarisme et régime presidentiel.* Translated by Jacqueline Ch. Rousseau. Paris: Librairie du Recueil Sirey, 1930.
——. *Recuerdos de gobierno,* Vol. I. Santiago: Editorial Universitaria, 1952.
Alfonso, José Antonio. *El parlamentarismo i la reforma política en Chile.* Santiago: Cabeza i Cía, Impresores, 1909.
——. *Los partidos políticos de Chile.* Santiago: Imprenta i Litografía Esmeralda, [1902?].
Alvear, Marcelo T. de. *Democracia.* Buenos Aires: M. Gleizer, 1936.
Amunátegui y Solar, Domingo. *La democracia en Chile.* Santiago: Universidad de Chile, 1946.
——. *Pipiolos y pelucones.* Santiago: Imprenta y Litografía Universo, 1939.
——. *El progreso intelectual y político de Chile.* Santiago: Editorial Nascimento, 1936.

Anguita, Ricardo, comp. *Leyes promulgadas en Chile desde 1810 hasta el 1 de junio de 1913.* 5 vols. Santiago: Encuadernación Barcelona, 1913.

Arana, Enrique, (h.) et al. *Juan Manuel de Rosas en la historia argentina: Creador y sostén de la unidad nacional.* 3 vols. Buenos Aires: n.p., 1954.

Arce, José. *Marcelino Ugarte: El hombre, el político, el gobernante.* Buenos Aires: n.p., 1959.

Argentina Commercially Considered. London: Syren and Shipping, [1918].

Baily, Samuel L. *Labor, Nationalism, and Politics in Argentina.* New Brunswick, N.J.: Rutgers University Press, 1967.

Balestra, Juan. *El noventa: Una evolución política argentina.* 3rd ed. Buenos Aires: Farina Editores, 1959.

Ballesteros, Marto A. and Davis, Tom E. "The Growth of Output and Employment in Basic Sectors of the Chilean Economy, 1908-1959." *Economic Development and Cultural Change,* II (January 1963):152-176.

Banco de la Nación Argentina. *El Banco de la Nación Argentina en su cincuentario.* Buenos Aires: n.p., [1941].

Bauer, Arnold J. *Chilean Rural Society from the Spanish Conquest to 1930.* New York: Cambridge University Press, 1975.

Becerra, Olegario. "Interpretación radical de la revolución del 90." *Revista de historia,* no. 1 (primer trimestre 1957):52-55.

Bello Codesido, Emilio. *Recuerdos políticos.* Santiago: Editorial Nascimento, 1954.

Belloni, Alberto. "Las luchas obreras durante el apogeo oligárquico." In *El régimen oligárquico: Materiales para el estudio de la realidad argentina (hasta 1930),* pp. 217-231. Edited by Marcos Giménez Zapiola. Buenos Aires: Amorrortu Editores, 1975.

Bermúdez Miral, Oscar. *Historia del salitre desde sus origenes hasta la Guerra del Pacífico.* Santiago: Universidad de Chile, 1963.

Blakemore, Harold. *British Nitrates and Chilean Politics, 1886-1896: Balmaceda and North.* London: Althone Press, 1974.

———. "The Chilean Revolution of 1891 and Its Historiography." *Hispanic American Historical Review,* XLV (August 1965):393-421.

Borón, Atilio A. "La evolución del régimen electoral y sus efectos en la representación de los intereses populares." *Revista latinoamericana de ciencia política,* II (December 1971):395-431.

Bosch, Mariano G. *Historia del partido radical.* Buenos Aires: n.p., 1931.

Botana, Natalio R. *El orden conservador: La política argentina entre 1880 y 1916.* Buenos Aires: Editorial Sudamericana, 1971.

Bryce, James. *South America: Observations and Impressions.* London: Macmillan and Co., 1912.

Bucich Escobar, Ismael. *Historia de los presidentes argentinos.* 2nd ed. Buenos Aires: Juan Roldán Cía, 1934.

Bunge, Alejandro E. *La economía argentina.* 2 vols. Buenos Aires: Agencia General de Librerías y Publicaciones, 1928.

———. *Las industrias del norte.* Vol. I. Buenos Aires: n.p., 1922.

Bunge, Alejandro E. *Los problemas económicos del presente*, Vol. I. Buenos Aires: n.p., 1920.

——. *Riqueza y renta de la argentina: Su distribución y su capacidad contributiva.* Buenos Aires: Agencia General de Librerías y Publicaciones, 1917.

Burgin, Miron. *The Economic Aspects of Argentine Federalism, 1820-1852.* Cambridge, Mass.: Harvard University Press, 1946.

Burnham, Walter Dean. *Critical Elections and the Mainsprings of American Politics.* New York: W.W. Norton and Co., 1970.

Burrowes, Robert. "Theory Sí, Data No! A Decade of Cross-National Research." *World Politics*, XXV (October 1972):120-144.

Caballero, Ricardo. *Irigoyen: La conspiración civil y militar del 4 de 1905.* Buenos Aires: Editorial Raigal, 1951.

Campos Harriet, Fernando. *Desarrollo educacional, 1810-1960.* Santiago: Editorial Andrés Bello, 1960.

——. *Historia constitucional de Chile.* Santiago: Editorial Jurídica de Chile, 1956.

Cantón, Darío. *Materiales para el estudio de la sociología política en la argentina.* 2 vols. Buenos Aires: Editorial del Instituto Torcuato di Tella, 1968.

——. *El parlamento argentino en épocas de cambio: 1890, 1916 y 1946.* Buenos Aires: Editorial del Instituto Torcuato di Tella, 1966.

Cárcano, Miguel Angel. *Evolución histórica del régimen de la tierra pública, 1810-1916.* Buenos Aires: Libería Mendesky, 1917.

——. *Saenz Peña: La revolución por los comicios.* Buenos Aires: Talleres Gráficos CEPEDA, 1963.

Cárcano, Ramón J. *Mis primeros 80 años.* Buenos Aires: Editorial Sudamericana, 1943.

Carrasco, Angel. *Lo que yo ví desde el 80: Hombres y episodios de la transformación nacional.* Buenos Aires: n.p., 1947.

Carmagnani, Marcello. *Sviluppo industriale e sottosviluppo economico: Il caso cileno (1860-1920).* Turin: Fondazione Luigi Einaudi, 1971.

Castles, Francis G., ed. *The Impact of Parties: Politics and Policies in Democratic Capitalist States.* Beverly Hills, Calif.: Sage Publications, 1982.

Chambers, William Nisbet. "Party Development and Party Action: The American Origins." *History and Theory*, III (1963):91-120.

——. *Political Parties in a New Nation: The American Experience, 1776-1809.* New York: Oxford University Press, 1963.

Chambers, William Nisbet and Burnham, Walter Dean, eds. *The American Party Systems: Stages of Political Development.* New York: Oxford University Press, 1967.

Chandler, Marsha; Chandler, William; and Vogler, David. "Policy Analysis and the Search for Theory." *American Politics Quarterly*, II (January 1974): 107-118.

Cifuentes, Abdón. *Memorias.* 2 vols. Santiago: Editorial Nascimento, 1936.

Collier, David, ed. *The New Authoritarianism in Latin America.* Princeton: Princeton University Press, 1979.

Collier, David and Messick, Richard E. "Prerequisites versus Diffusion: Testing Alternative Explanations of Social Security Adoption." *American Political Science Review,* LXIX (December 1975):1299-1315.

Collier, Simon. *Ideas and Politics of Chilean Independence, 1808-1833.* Cambridge, England: Cambridge University Press, 1967.

——. "Conservatismo chileno, 1830-1860. Temas e imagenes." *Nueva historia,* II, no. 7 (1983):143-163.

Concha, Malaquías. *La lucha económica.* Santiago: Imprenta Cervantes, 1910.

——. *Memoria presentada a la convención del partido democrático reunida en Chillán el 14 de julio de 1901 a la agrupación electoral que representa por el diputado de Concepción i Talcahuano don Malaquías Concha.* Santiago: Editorial la Prensa, 1901.

El congreso nacional de Chile de 1909 a 1912. Santiago: Beaugency i Barcells, 1909.

Convención Conservadora: Ideas para la convención, programa y estatutos preséntalos a la convención un grupo de conservadores de Valparaíso. Valparaíso: Babra y Ca., 1901.

Comblit, Oscar. "European Immigrants in Argentine Industry and Politics." In *The Politics of Conformity in Latin America,* pp. 221-248. Edited by Claudio Véliz. London: Oxford University Press, 1967.

Correa Bravo, Agustín. *Comentarios y concordancias de la Ley de Organización y atribuciones de las municipalidades de 22 de diciembre de 1891.* 3rd ed. Santiago: Librería Tornero, 1914.

Cortés Conde, Roberto. "Problemas del crecimiento industrial de la Argentina (1870-1914)." *Desarrollo económico,* III (1963):143-171.

——. "El sector agrícola en el desarrollo económico argentino." Unpublished paper, Centro de Investigaciones Económicas, Instituto Torcuato di Tella, 1969.

Cortés Conde, Roberto and Gallo, Ezequiel. *La formación de la argentina moderna.* Buenos Aires: Editorial Paidos, 1967.

Couyoumdjian, Ricardo. "El mercado del salitre durante la primera guerra mundial y la postguerra, 1914-1921." *Historia,* XII (1974-1975):13-55.

Cruz-Coke, Ricardo. *Geografía electoral de Chile.* Santiago: Editorial del Pacífico, 1952.

Cuneo, Dardo. *Juan B. Justo y las luchas sociales en la Argentina.* 2nd ed. Buenos Aires: Editorial ALPE, 1956.

Da Rocha, Augusto, comp. *Leyes nacionales clasificadas y sus decretos reglamentarios.* 18 vols. Buenos Aires: La Facultad, 1935-1938.

Dahl, Robert A. *A Preface to Democratic Theory.* Chicago: University of Chicago Press, 1956; Phoenix Books, 1963.

——. *Polyarchy: Participation and Opposition.* New Haven: Yale University Press, 1971.

Defrance, F.L. "Recent Political Evolution in Argentina." *The Quarterly Review,* CCV (January 1916):38-52.

De la Torre, Lisandro. *Obras de Lisandro de la Torre*. Edited by Raúl Larra. 6 vols. Vols. I-III, 3rd ed. 1957-1958. Vols. IV-VI, 2nd ed. 1960. Buenos Aires: Editorial Hemisferio.

Del Mazo, Gabriel. *El Radicalismo: Ensayo sobre su historia y doctrina.* 2 vols. Buenos Aires: Ediciones Gure, 1957-1959.

Del Valle, Aristóbulo. *La política argentina en la década del 80.* Edited by Luis V. Sommi. Buenos Aires: Editorial Raigal, 1955.

Desarrollo de Chile en la primera mitad del siglo XX. 2 vols. Santiago: Ediciones de la Universidad de Chile, n.d.

DeShazo, Peter. *Urban Workers and Labor Unions in Chile, 1902-1927.* Madison: University of Wisconsin Press, 1983.

———. "The Valparaíso Maritime Strike of 1903 and the Development of a Revolutionary Labor Movement in Chile." *Journal of Latin American Studies,* II (May 1979):145-168.

Díaz Alejandro, Carlos F. *Essays on the Economic History of the Argentine Republic.* New Haven: Yale University Press, 1970.

Di Tella, Guido and Zymelman, Manuel. *Las etapas del desarrollo económico argentino.* Buenos Aires: EUDEBA, 1967.

Di Tella, Torcuato S. et al. *Argentina, sociedad de masas.* 3rd ed. Buenos Aires: Editorial Universitaria de Buenos Aires, 1966.

Donoso, Armando. *Recuerdos de cincuenta años.* Santiago: Editorial Nascimento, 1947.

Donoso, Ricardo. *Alessandri: Agitador y demoledor.* 2 vols. Mexico: Fondo de Cultura Económica, 1952.

———. *Las ideas políticas en Chile.* Mexico: Fondo de Cultura Económica, 1946.

Duverger, Maurice. *Political Parties: Their Organization and Activity in the Modern State.* Translated by Barbara and Robert North. 2nd ed. London: Menthuen and Co., 1959.

Edinger, Lewis J. and Searing, Donald D. "Social Background in Elite Analysis: A Methodological Inquiry," *American Political Science Review,* LXI (June 1967):428-445.

Edwards MacClure, Agustín. *Cuatro presidentes de Chile (1841-1876).* 2 vols. Valparaíso: Sociedad Imprenta y Litografía Universo, 1932.

———. *The Dawn.* London: E. Benn, 1931.

Edwards Vives, Alberto. *La fronda aristocrática.* 6th ed. Santiago: Editorial del Pacífico, 1966.

———. *El gobierno de don Manuel Montt, 1851-1861.* Santiago: Editorial Nascimento, 1932.

———. *La organización política de Chile (1810-1833).* Santiago: Editorial Difusión Chilena, 1943.

Edwards Vives, Alberto and Frei Montalva, Eduardo. *Historia de los partidos políticos chilenos.* Santiago: Editorial del Pacífico, 1949.

Encina, Francisco Antonio. *Historia de Chile.* 20 vols. Santiago: Editorial Nascimento, 1922.

Encina, Francisco Antonio. *Nuestra inferioridad económica.* Santiago: Editorial Universitaria, 1955.

Espinoza, Enrique. *Jeografía descriptiva de la República de Chile.* 4th ed. Santiago: Imprenta i Encuadernación Barcelona, 1897.

——. *Jeografía descriptiva de la República de Chile.* 5th ed. Santiago: Imprenta i Encuadernación Barcelona, 1903.

Etchepareborda, Roberto. *La revolución argentina del 90.* Buenos Aires: Editorial Universitaria de Buenos Aires, 1966.

Eyestone, Robert. "Confusion, Diffusion, and Innovation." *American Political Science Review,* LXXI (June 1977):441-447.

Eyzaguirre, Jaime. *Chile durante el gobierno de Errázuriz Echaurren, 1896-1901.* Santiago: Empresa Editora Zig-Zag, 1956.

——. *Fisonomía histórica de Chile.* 3rd ed. Santiago: Editorial del Pacífico, 1965.

——. *Historia de Chile: Génesis de la nacionalidad.* Santiago: Empresa Editora Zig-Zag, 1964.

——. *Historia de las instituciones políticas y sociales de Chile.* Santiago: Editorial Universitaria, 1967.

Feliú Cruz, Guillermo. *Chile visto a través de Agustín Ross.* Santiago: Imprenta Encuadernación Piño, 1950.

Feliú Cruz, René, comp. *Indice general sinóptico de leyes, decretos leyes y decretos con fuerza de ley dictados desde el 2 de enero de 1913 hasta el 13 de abril de 1936, con los decretos supremos que les fijan textos definitivos y reglamentarios.* 3 vols. Santiago: Editorial Nascimento, 1937-1940.

Fenton, John H. and Chamberlayne, Donald W. "The Literature Dealing with the Relationships between Political Processes, Socioeconomic Conditions and Public Policies in the American States: A Bibliographic Essay." *Polity,* I (Spring 1969):388-404.

Ferns, H.S. *Britain and Argentina in the Nineteenth Century.* London: Oxford University Press, 1960.

Ferrer, Aldo. *The Argentine Economy.* Translated by Marjory M. Urquidi. Berkeley: University of California Press, 1967.

Fetter, Frank Whitson. *Monetary Inflation in Chile.* Publications of the International Finance Section of the Department of Economics and Social Institutions in Princeton University, Vol. III. Princeton: Princeton University Press, 1931.

Figueroa, Virgilio. *Diccionario histórico, biográfico y bibliográfico de Chile.* 5 vols. Santiago: Barcells and Co., 1925-1931.

Fiorina, Morris P. *Representatives, Roll Calls, and Constituencies.* Lexington: D.C. Heath, 1974.

Frers, Emilio. *En la administración pública.* 2 vols. Buenos Aires: Gadola, 1921.

Fuentes, Jordi and Cortés, Lía. *Diccionario político de Chile.* Santiago: Editorial ORBE, 1967.

Fuenzalida Villegas, Humberto et al. *Chile.* Buenos Aires: Editorial Losado, 1946.

Galdames, Luis. *A History of Chile.* Translated by Isaac Joslin Cox. Chapel Hill, N.C.: University of North Carolina Press, 1941.

———. *Valetín Letelier y su obra, 1852-1919.* Santiago: Imprenta Universitaria, 1937.

Gallardo Nieto, Galvarino. *La Liga de Acción Cívica i los partidos políticos.* Santiago: Imprenta Universitaria, 1912.

Gallo, Ezequiel. "Agrarian Expansion and Industrial Development in Argentina, 1880-1930." In *Latin American Affairs,* pp. 45-61. St. Antony's Papers, no. 22. Oxford: Oxford University Press, 1970.

———. *Farmers in Revolt: The Revolutions of 1893 in the Province of Santa Fe, Argentina.* University of London, Institute of Latin American Studies Monographs, no. 7. London: Athlone Press, 1976.

Gallo, Ezequiel and Cortés Conde, Roberto. *Argentina: La República Conservadora.* Buenos Aires: Editorial Paidos, 1972.

Gallo, Vicente C. *Por la democracia y las instituciones: Propaganda cívica, 1891-1921.* Buenos Aires: n.p., 1921.

Germani, Gino. "Estrategia para estimular la movilidad social." In *La industrialización en América Latina,* pp. 274-306. Edited by Joseph A. Kahl. Mexico: Fondo de Cultura Económica, 1965.

———. *Política y sociedad en una época de transición.* Buenos Aires: Editorial Paidos, 1962.

Gerschenkron, Alexander. *Economic Backwardness in Historical Perspective.* Cambridge, Mass: Harvard University Press, 1962.

Gil, Federico G. *The Political System of Chile.* Boston: Houghton Mifflin Company, 1966.

Giménez Zapiola, Marcos. "El interior argentino y el «desarrollo hacia afuera»: El caso de Tucumán." In *El régimen oligárquico: Materiales para el estudio de la realidad argentina (hasta 1930),* pp. 72-115. Edited by idem. Buenos Aires: Amorrortu Editores, 1975.

Giuffra, Eduardo F. *Hipólito Yrigoyen en la historia de las instituciones argentinas.* Buenos Aires: Editorial de la Fundación, 1969.

Godwin, R. Kenneth and Shepard, W. Bruce. "Political Processes and Public Expenditures: A Re-examination Based on Theories of Representative Government." *American Political Science Review,* LXX (December 1976):1127-1135.

Goldwert, Marvin. "The Argentine Revolution of 1930; the Rise of Modern Militarism and Ultra-nationalism in Argentina." Unpublished Ph.D. thesis, University of Texas, 1962.

———. *Democracy, Militarism and Nationalism in Argentina, 1930-1966.* Austin, Texas: University of Texas Press, 1972.

González, Pedro Luis. *Chile industrial, 1919.* Santiago: Sociedad Imprenta i Litografía Universo, 1919.

Goodwin, Paul B., Jr. "The Politics of Rate-making: The British-owned Railways and the Unión Cívica Radical, 1921-1928." *Journal of Latin American Studies*, VI (May 1974):257-287.

Gran convención liberal celebrado en Valparaíso en abril de 1881. Valparaíso: Imprenta del Mercurio, 1881.

Gray, Virginia. "Innovation in the States: A Diffusion Study." *American Political Science Review*, LXVII (December 1973):1174-1185.

———. "Models of Comparative Politics: A Comparison of Cross-Sectional and Time Series Analysis." *American Journal of Political Science*, XX (May 1976):235-256.

Greenberg, George D.; Miller, Jeffrey A.; Mohr, Lawrence B.; and Vladeck, Bruce C. "Developing Public Policy Theory: Perspectives from Empirical Research." *American Political Science Review*, LXXI (December 1977): 1532-1543.

Guadagni, Alieto A. "La estructura ocupacional y el desarrollo económico de Chile." Unpublished paper, Centro de Investigaciones Económicas, Instituto Torcuato di Tella, 1965.

Guaresti, Juan José (h.). *Economía y finanzas de la Nación Argentina*. Buenos Aires: Editorial Poblet, 1933.

Guilisasti Tagle, Sergio. *Partidos políticos chilenos*. 2nd ed. Santiago: Editorial Nascimento, 1964.

Gumucio, Rafael Luis. *El partido conservador*. Santiago: Imprenta y Encuadernación Lourdes, 1911.

Gunther, Richard. *Public Policy in a No-Party State: Spanish Planning and Budgeting in the Twilight of the Franquist Era*. Berkeley: University of California Press, 1980.

Guy, Donna J. "Carlos Pellegrini and the Politics of Early Argentine Industrialization, 1873-1906." *Journal of Latin American Studies*, II (May 1979):123-144.

Hammerton, J.A. *The Argentine through English Eyes*. London: Hodder and Stoughton, [1916].

Hanson, Simon G. *Argentine Meat and the British Market*. Stanford, Calif.: Stanford University Press, 1938.

Haring, Clarence H. "Chilean Politics, 1920-1928." *Hispanic American Historical Review*, XI (February 1931):1-26.

Hartz, Louis, ed. *The Founding of New Societies*. New York: Harcourt, Brace & World, 1964.

Hawley, Willis D. *Nonpartisan Elections and the Case for Party Politics*. New York: John Wiley and Sons, 1973.

Hayes, Margaret Daly. "Policy Consequences of Military Participation in Politics: An Analysis of Tradeoffs in Brazilian Federal Expenditures." In *Comparative Public Policy: Issues, Theories, and Methods*, edited by Craig Liske, William Loehr, and John McCamant, 21-52. Beverly Hills and London: Sage Publications, 1975.

Heise González, Julio. "El caciquismo político en el período parlamentario

(1891-1925)." In *Homenaje a Guillermo Feliú Cruz*, pp. 537-575. Santiago: Editorial Andrés Bello, 1973.

Heise González, Julio. *La constitución de 1925 y las nuevas tendencias político-sociales*. Santiago: Editorial Universitaria, 1951.

——. *Historia de Chile: El período parlamentario, 1861-1925*. 2 vols. Santiago: Editorial Andrés Bello, 1974-1982.

Herschel, Federico Julio and Itzcovich, Samuel. "Fiscal Policy in Argentina." *Public Finance*, XII (1957):97-115.

Hervey, Maurice H. *Dark Days in Chile: An Account of the Revolution of 1891*. London: Edward Arnold, 1891.

Hirschman, Albert O. *Journeys Toward Progress: Studies of Economic Policy-Making in Latin America*. New York: Greenwood Press, 1968.

Hofferbert, Richard I. "State and Community Policy Studies: A Review of Comparative Input-Output Analysis." In *Political Science Annual*, III, 3-72. Edited by James A. Robinson. Indianapolis: Bobbs-Merrill Co., 1972.

Hoffman, W.G. *The Growth of Industrial Economies*. Translated by W.O Henderson and W.H. Chaloner. Manchester, England: Manchester University Press, 1958.

Irigoyen, Hipólito. *Hipólito Yrigoyen: Documentación histórica de 55 años de actuación por la democracia y las instituciones*. Edited by Luis Rodríguez. Buenos Aires: n.p., 1934.

——. *Hipólito Yrigoyen: Pueblo y gobierno*. Edited by Instituto Yrigoyeneano. 12 vols. Buenos Aires: Editorial Raigal, 1956.

——. *Ley 12839; documentos de Hipólito Yrigoyen: Apostolado cívico, obra de gobierno, defensa ante la corte*. Buenos Aires: Comisión de la Ley de Homenaje a Don Hipólito Yrigoyen, 1949.

——. *Mi vida y mi doctrina*. Buenos Aires: Editorial Raigal, 1957.

——. *La palabra de Yrigoyen*. Buenos Aires: Editorial La Voz Radical, 1932.

——. *El pensamiento escrito de Yrigoyen*. Edited by Gabriel del Mazo. 2nd ed. Buenos Aires: n.p., 1945.

Irigoyen: Proceso a su gobierno, los diplomas de San Juan, la oposición, cesantías, unicato. Buenos Aires: Atilio Moro, 1929.

Izquierdo, Luis. *Nuestro sistema político ante el senado*. Valparaíso: Sociedad Imprenta y Litografía Universo, 1916.

Izquierdo A., Guillermo. *El gobierno representativo*. Vol. I. Santiago: Escuela Tipográfica La Gratitud Nacional, 1916.

Izquierdo Fernández, Gonzalo. "Octubre de 1905: Un episodio en la historia social chilena." *Historia*, XIII (1976):55-96.

Jackman, Robert W. "Politicians in Uniform: Military Governments and Social Change in the Third World." *American Political Science Review*, LXX (December 1976):1078-1097.

Jacob, Herbert and Lipsky, Michael. "Outputs, Structure, and Power: An Assessment of Changes in the Study of State and Local Politics." *Journal of Politics*, XXX (May 1968):510-538.

Jennings, Edward T., Jr. "Competition, Constituencies, and Welfare Policies in American States" *American Political Science Review*, LXXIII (June 1979):414-429.

Jèze, Gaston. *Las finanzas públicas de la República Argentina.* Buenos Aires: n.p., 1923.

Jobet, Julio César. *Ensayo crítico del desarrollo económico-social de Chile.* Santiago: Editorial Universitaria, 1955.

———. *Luis Emilio Recabarren: Los orígenes del movimiento obrero y del socialismo en Chile.* Santiago: Prensa Latinoamericana, 1955.

Johnson, John J. *Political Change in Latin America: The Emergence of the Middle Sectors.* Stanford, Calif.: Stanford University Press, 1958.

The July Revolution 1890 in Buenos Aires. 2nd ed. Buenos Aires: n.p., [1890].

Justo, Juan B. *El impuesto sobre el privilegio.* 2nd ed. Buenos Aires: La Vanguardia, 1928.

———. *Obras completos.* Vol. I: *La moneda.* Buenos Aires: La Vanguardia, 1937.

———. *Obras completos.* Vol. VI: *La realización del socialismo.* Edited by Dardo Cuneo. Buenos Aires: La Vanguardia, 1947.

———. *El programa socialista del campo.* 2nd ed. Buenos Aires: La Vanguardia, 1915.

———. *El socialismo.* Buenos Aires: La Vanguardia, 1902.

Keller, Suzanne. *Beyond the Ruling Class: Strategic Elites in Modern Society.* New York: Random House, 1963.

Keller R., Carlos. *La eterna crisis chilena.* Santiago: Editorial Nascimento, 1931.

Key, V.O., Jr. *Southern Politics.* New York: Random House, Vintage Books, 1949.

Kirsch, Henry W. *Industrial Development in a Traditional Society: The Conflict of Entrepreneurship and Modernization in Chile.* Gainesville: University Presses of Florida, 1977.

Klingman, David. "Temporal and Spatial Diffusion in the Comparative Analysis of Social Change." *American Political Science Review*, LXXIV (March 1980):123-137.

Koebel, W.H. *Modern Argentina: The El Dorado of To-Day.* London: Francis Griffiths, 1907.

König, Abraham. *La constitución de 1833 en 1913.* Santiago: Imprenta Santiago, 1913.

———. *A través de la República Arjentina: Diario de viaje.* Santiago: Imprenta Cervantes, 1890.

Kuklinski, James H. "Representativeness and Elections: A Policy Analysis." *American Political Science Review*, LXXII (March 1978):165-177.

Kurth, James R. "Patrimonial Authority, Delayed Development, and Mediterranean Politics." Paper prepared for Annual Meeting of the American Political Science Association, New Orleans, September 1973.

Lagos, Lauro. *Doctrina y acción radical*. Buenos Aires: n.p., 1930.

Lagos Escobar, Ricardo. *La industria en Chile: Antecedentes estructurales*. Santiago: Universidad de Chile, 1966.

Landenberger, Jorge W. and Conte, Francisco M., eds. *Unión Cívica: Su origen, organización y tendencias*. Buenos Aires: n.p., 1890.

La Palombara, Joseph and Weiner, Myron, eds. *Political Parties and Political Development*. Princeton, N.J.: Princeton University Press, 1966.

Lavín Matta, Benjamín. *Organización racional del gobierno representativo*. Santiago: Imprenta Gutenberg, 1878.

Lebedinsky, Mauricio. *Estructura de la ganadería*. Buenos Aires: Editorial Quipo, 1967.

Leichter, Howard. "Comparative Public Policy: Problems and Prospects." In *Policy Studies Review Annual*, I (1977), 138-150. Edited by Stuart S. Nagel. Beverly Hills, Calif.: Sage Publications, 1977.

Leiserson, Alcira. *Notes on the Process of Industrialization in Argentina, Chile, and Peru*. Politics of Modernization Series, no. 3. Berkeley: University of California, 1966.

Letelier, Valentín. *La lucha por la cultura*. Santiago: Imprenta i Encuadernación Barcelona, 1895.

Lewis-Beck, Michael S. "The Relative Importance of Socioeconomic and Political Variables for Public Policy." *American Political Science Review*, LXXI (June 1977):559-566.

Lipset, Seymour Martin. "Party Systems and the Representation of Social Groups." In *Political Parties: Contemporary Trends and Ideas*, pp. 49-74. Edited by Roy C. Macridis. New York: Harper & Row, Harper Torchbooks, 1967.

——. *Political Man*. Garden City, New York: Doubleday and Co., 1960; Anchor Books, 1962.

Loveman, Brian. *Chile: The Legacy of Hispanic Capitalism*. New York: Oxford University Press, 1979.

Lowi, Theodore J. "American Business, Public Policy, Case Studies, and Political Theory." *World Politics*, XVI (July 1964):677-715.

——. "Four Systems of Policy, Politics, and Choice." *Public Administration Review*, XXXII (July-August 1972):298-310.

Luna, Félix. *Yrigoyen*. Buenos Aires: Editorial Desarrollo, [1964].

Mabragaña, H. *Los mensajes*. 6 vols. Buenos Aires: Comisión Nacional del Centenario, 1910.

McBride, George McCutchen. *Chile: Land and Society*. New York: American Geographical Society, 1936.

McGann, Thomas F. *Argentina, the United States, and the Inter-American System, 1880-1914*. Cambridge, Mass.: Harvard University Press, 1957.

McGee, Sandra. "The Liga Patriótica Argentina and Its 'Practical Humanitarianism:' A Right-Wing Response to Social Change." Paper prepared for 8th National Meeting of the Latin American Studies Association, Pittsburgh, April 1979.

McKinlay, R.D. and Cohan, A.S. "A Comparative Analysis of the Political and Economic Performance of Military and Civilian Regimes." *Comparative Politics*, VIII (October 1975):1-30.

——. "Performance and Instability in Military and Nonmilitary Regime Systems." *American Political Science Review*, LXX (September 1976): 850-864.

Mamalakis, Markos J. *The Growth and Structure of the Chilean Economy: From Independence to Allende.* New Haven: Yale University Press, 1976.

Mansfield, Robert E. *Progressive Chile.* New York: Neale Publishing Co., 1913.

Marcella, Gabriel. "The Structure of Politics in Nineteenth-Century Spanish America: The Chilean Oligarchy, 1833-1891." Ph.D. dissertation, University of Notre Dame, 1973.

Margolis, Michael. "From Confusion to Confusion: Issues and the American Voter (1956-1972)." *American Political Science Review*, LXXI (March 1977):31-43.

Martinez, Albert B. and Lewandowski, Maurice. *The Argentine in the Twentieth Century.* Translated by Bernard Miall. 3rd ed. London: T. Fisher Unwin, 1911.

Matienzo, José Nicolás. *El gobierno representativo federal en la República Argentina.* 2nd ed. Madrid: Editorial América, [1917].

——. *La práctica del sufrajio popular.* Buenos Aires: Imprenta, Litografía y Encuadernación de Stiller y Laass, 1886.

Mecham, J. Lloyd. *Church and State in Latin America: A History of Politico-Ecclesiastical Relations.* Rev. ed. Chapel Hill, N.C.: University of North Carolina Press, 1966.

Melo, Carlos R. *Los partidos políticos argentinos.* Córdoba: Universidad Nacional de Córdoba, 1964.

Merkx, Gilbert W. "Sectoral Clashes and Political Change: The Argentine Experience." *Latin American Research Review*, IV (Fall 1969):89-114.

Millar Carvacho, René. *Significado y antecedentes del movimiento militar de 1924.* Santiago: Universidad Católica de Chile, Instituto de Historia, 1974.

——. *La elección presidencial de 1920.* Santiago: Editorial Universitaria, 1981.

Mitre, Bartolomé. *Correspondencia literaria, histórica y política del General Bartolomé Mitre.* 3 vols. Buenos Aires: Museo Mitre, 1912.

Mohr, Luis A. *Mis setenta años.* Buenos Aires: Gadola, 1914.

Molina, Evaristo. *Bosquejo de la hacienda pública de Chile.* Santiago: Imprenta Nacional, 1898.

Monteón, Michael. *Chile in the Nitrate Era: The Evolution of Economic Dependence, 1880-1930.* Madison: University of Wisconsin Press, 1982.

Montt, Pedro. *Exposition of the Illegal Acts of Ex-President Balmaceda, which Caused the Civil War in Chile.* Washington, D.C.: Gibson Bros., 1891.

Morgan, David R. and Pelissero, John P. "Urban Policy: Does Political Structure Matter?" *American Political Science Review*, LXXIV (December 1980):999-1006.

Morris, James O. *Elites, Intellectuals, and Consensus: A Study of the Social Question and the Industrial Relations System in Chile.* Cornell International Industrial and Labor Relations Report, no. 7. Ithaca, N.Y.: Cornell University, New York State School of Industrial and Labor Relations, 1966.

Most, Benjamin. "Authoritarianism and the Growth of the State in Latin America: An Assessment of Their Impacts on Argentine Public Policy, 1930-1970." *Comparative Political Studies*, XIII, 2(1980):173-203.

Muñoz Gomá, Oscar. *Crecimiento industrial de Chile, 1914-1965.* Publicaciones del Instituto de Economía y Planificación, no. 105. Santiago: Universidad de Chile, 1968.

Nagle, John D. *System and Succession: The Social Bases of Political Elite Recruitment.* Austin: University of Texas Press, 1977.

Nordlinger, Eric A. "Political Development: Time Sequences and Rates of Change." *World Politics*, XX (April 1968):494-520.

———. "Soldiers in Mufti: The Impact of Military Rule upon Economic and Social Change in the Non-Western States." *American Political Science Review*, LXIV (December 1970):1131-1148.

Nunn, Frederick M. *Chilean Politics, 1920-1931: The Honorable Mission of the Armed Forces.* Albuquerque, N.M.: University of New Mexico Press, 1970.

O'Brien, Thomas F., Jr. "Chilean Elites and Foreign Investors: Chilean Nitrate Policy, 1880-1882." *Journal of Latin American Studies*, II (May 1979):101-121.

Oddone, Jacinto. *La burguesia terrateniente argentina.* 3rd ed. Buenos Aires: Ediciones Populares Argentinas, 1956.

O'Donnell, Guillermo. *Modernization and Bureaucratic-Authoritarianism: Studies in South American Politics.* Berkeley: University of California at Berkeley, Institute of International Studies, 1973; reprint ed., 1979.

Olavarría Bravo, Arturo. *Chile entre dos Alessandri: Memorias políticas.* 4 vols. Santiago: Editorial Nascimento, 1962-1965.

Olguín, Dardo. *Lencinas: El caudillo radical, historia y mito.* Buenos Aires: Ediciones Vendimiador, 1961.

Orrego Luco, Luis. *Chile contemporáneo.* Santiago: Imprenta Cervantes, 1904.

Ortega, Ezequiel. *"Quiera el pueblo votar?" Historia electoral argentina, desde la Revolución de Mayo a la Ley Saenz Peña, 1810-1912.* Bahia Blanca: V.M. Giner Editor, 1963.

Palma, J. Gabriel. "Chile 1914-1935: De economía exportadora a sustitutiva de importaciones." *Nueva historia*, II, no. 7 (1983):165-192.

Palma Zuñiga, Luis. *Historia del partido radical.* Santiago: Editorial Andrés Bello, 1967.

Panettieri, José. *Los trabajadores en tiempos de la inmigración masiva en Argentina, 1870-1910.* Facultad de Humanidades y Ciencias de la Educación, Departamento de Historia, Universidad Nacional de la Plata, Monografías y Tesis, Vol. VIII. La Plata: Universidad Nacional de la Plata, 1966.

Parker, William Belmont. *Argentines of To-Day.* 2 vols. Buenos Aires: Hispanic Society of America, 1920.

Los parlamentarios radicales: Senadores y diputados al congreso nacional, 1919. Buenos Aires: Juan A. Herrera y Cía, [1919].

Parry, Geraint. *Political Elites.* London: George Allen and Unwin, 1969.

Partido Liberal-Democrático. *Carta política del Señor Ismael Pérez Montt.* Santiago: Imprenta Cervantes, 1903.

Partido Socialista de la Argentina. *El partido socialista en el parlamento nacional, 1912-1916.* Buenos Aires: n.p., 1916.

Paso, Leonardo. *Historia del origen de los partidos políticos en la Argentina (1810-1918).* Buenos Aires: Ediciones Centro de Estudios, 1972.

Pellegrini, Carlos. *Pellegrini 1846-1906: Obras.* Edited by Agustín Rivero Astengo. 5 vols. Buenos Aires: Imprenta y Casa Editora Coni, 1941.

Peters, Harold Edwin. *The Foreign Debt of the Argentine Republic.* Baltimore: Johns Hopkins Press, 1934.

Pike, Fredrick B. *Chile and the United States, 1880-1962.* Notre Dame, Indiana: University of Notre Dame Press, 1963.

Poblete Troncoso, Moisés. *El balance de nuestro suedo régimen parlamentario.* Santiago: Talleres de Numen, 1920.

——. *El problema de la producción agrícola y la política agraria nacional.* Santiago: Imprenta Universitaria, 1919.

Poirier, Eduardo. *Chile en 1910.* Santiago: Imprenta, Litografía y Encuadernación Barcelona, 1910.

Poppino, Rollie. *International Communism in Latin America: A History of the Movement, 1917-1963.* Glencoe, Ill.: Free Press, 1964.

Potash, Robert A. *The Army and Politics in Argentina, 1928-1945.* Stanford, Calif.: Stanford University Press, 1969.

Potter, Anne L. "The Failure of Democracy in Argentina 1916-1930: An Institutional Perspective." *Journal of Latin American Studies,* XIII (May 1981):83-109.

Prewitt, Kenneth. *The Recruitment of Political Leaders: A Study of Citizen-Politicians.* Indianapolis: Bobbs-Merrill Co., 1970.

Prewitt, Kenneth and Stone, Alan. *The Ruling Elites: Elite Theory, Power, and American Democracy.* New York: Harper & Row, 1973.

Pryor, Frederic L. *Public Expenditures in Communist and Capitalist Nations.* Homewood, Ill.: Richard D. Irwin, 1968.

Puiggros, Rodolfo. *El yrigoyenismo.* Buenos Aires: Jorge Alvarez, 1965.

Putnam, Robert D. *The Comparative Study of Political Elites.* Englewood Cliffs, N.J.: Prentice-Hall, 1976.

Ramírez Necochea, Hernán. *Balmaceda y la contrarrevolución de 1891.* 3rd ed. Santiago: Editorial Universitaria, 1972.

——. *La guerra civil de 1891: Antecedentes económicos.* Santiago: n.p., 1943.

Ramírez Necochea, Hernán. *Historia del movimiento obrero en Chile*. Santiago: n.p., 1956.

Ramos, Jorge Abelardo. *Revolución y contrarrevolución en la Argentina*. 2nd ed. Buenos Aires: La Reja, 1961.

Ramos Mexía, Ezequiel. *Mis memorias, 1853-1935*. 2nd ed. Buenos Aires: La Facultad, 1936.

Ranis, Gustav, ed. *Government and Economic Development*. New Haven: Yale University Press, 1971.

Reinsch, Paul S. "Parliamentary Government in Chile." *American Political Science Review*, III (November 1910):507-538.

Remmer, Karen L. "Evaluating the Policy Impact of Military Regimes in Latin America." *Latin American Research Review*, XIII (1978):39-54.

Remorino, Jerónimo, et al., comps. *Anales de legislación argentina: Complemento años 1889-1919*. Buenos Aires: Editorial La Ley, 1954.

——. *Anales de legislación argentina: Complemento años 1920-1940*. Buenos Aires: Editorial La Ley, 1953.

Repetto, Nicolás. *Juan B. Justo y el movimiento político social argentino*. Buenos Aires: Ediciones Monserrat, 1964.

——. *Mis noventa años: Escritos e intervenciones parlamentarias*. Buenos Aires: Editorial Bases, 1962.

——. *Mi paso por la política: De Uriburu a Perón*. Buenos Aires: Santiago Rueda, n.d.

Riesco, Germán. *Presidencia de Riesco, 1901-1906*. Santiago: Imprenta Nascimento, 1950.

Rimlinger, Gaston V. *Welfare Policy and Industrialization in Europe, America, and Russia*. New York: John Wiley & Sons, 1971.

Rivarola, Horacio C. *Las transformaciones de la sociedad argentina*. Buenos Aires: Imprenta de Coni Hermanos, 1911.

Rivas Vicuña, Manuel. *Historia política y parlamentaria de Chile*. Edited by Guillermo Feliú Cruz. 3 vols. Santiago: Ediciones de la Biblioteca Nacional, 1964.

Robertson, David. *A Theory of Party Competition*. London: John Wiley and Sons, 1976.

Roca, Julio Argentino. *Julio A. Roca: Discursos, escritos, homenajes*. Buenos Aires: n.p., 1943.

Rock, David. "Machine Politics in Buenos Aires and the Argentine Radical Party, 1912-1930." *Journal of Latin American Studies*, IV (November 1972):233-256.

——. *Politics in Argentina 1890-1930: The Rise and Fall of Radicalism*. London: Cambridge University Press, 1975.

——, ed. *Argentina in the Twentieth Century*. Pittsburgh: University of Pittsburgh Press, 1975.

Rodríguez, Carlos J. *Irigoyen: Su revolución política y social*. Buenos Aires: Librería y Editorial La Facultad, 1943.

Rodríguez, Celso. "Cantonismo: A Regional Harbinger of Peronism in Argentina." *Americas*, XXXIV (October 1977):170-201.

———. *Lencinas y Cantoni: El populismo cuyano en tiempos de Yrigoyen.* Buenos Aires: Editorial de Belgrano, 1979.

Romero, José Luis. *A History of Argentine Political Thought.* Translated by Thomas F. McGann. Stanford, Calif.: Stanford University Press, 1963.

Romero, Luis Alberto et al. *El radicalismo.* Buenos Aires: Carlos Pérez Editor, 1968.

Ross, Marc Howard and Homer, Elizabeth. "Galton's Problem in Cross-National Research." *World Politics*, XXIV (October 1976):1-28.

Rowe, Leo Stanton. "The Early Effects of the European War upon the Finance, Commerce, and Industry of Chile." In *Preliminary Economic Studies of the War*, pp. 33-101. Edited by David Kinley. New York: Oxford University Press, 1918.

Saenz Peña, Roque. *Escritos y discursos.* 2 vols. Buenos Aires: Casa Jacobo Peuser, 1914-1915.

Salas Edwards, Ricardo. *Balmaceda y el parlamentarismo en Chile.* 2 vols. Santiago: Sociedad Imprenta y Litografía Universo, 1925.

Sanucci, Lía E.M. *La renovación presidencial de 1880.* Facultad de Humanidades y Ciencias de la Educación, Departmento de Historia, Universidad de la Plata, Monografías y Tesis, Vol. IV. La Plata: Universidad Nacional de la Plata, 1959.

Sarobe, José María. *Memorias sobre la revolución del 6 de septiembre de 1930.* Buenos Aires: Ediciones Gure, 1957.

Sater, William F. "Chile and the World Depression of the 1870s." *Journal of Latin American Studies*, II (May 1979):67-99.

Schmitter, Philippe C. "Military Intervention, Political Competitiveness and Public Policy in Latin America: 1950-1967." In *On Military Intervention*, edited by Morris Janowitz and J. van Doorn, 425-506. Rotterdam: Rotterdam University Press, 1971.

———. "Paths to Political Development in Latin America." In *Changing Latin America: New Interpretations of Its Politics and Society*, pp. 83-105. Edited by Douglas A. Chalmers. Proceedings of the Academy of Political Science, XXX, no. 4. New York: Academy of Political Science, 1972.

Schultz, Barry M. "The Concept of Fragment in Comparative Political Analysis." *Comparative Politics*, I (October 1968):111-125.

Schumpeter, Joseph A. *Capitalism, Socialism and Democracy.* 3rd ed. New York: Harper & Row, 1950; Harper Torchbooks, 1962.

Schweinitz, Karl de, Jr. "Growth, Development, and Political Modernization." *World Politics*, XXII (July 1970):518-540.

Scobie, James R. *Revolution on the Pampas: A Social History of Argentine Wheat, 1860-1910.* Austin, Texas: University of Texas Press, 1964.

Segall, Marcelo. *Desarrollo del capitalismo en Chile: Cinco ensayos dialecticos.* Santiago: Editorial del Pacífico, 1953.

Seligman, Lester E. "Political Parties and the Recruitment of Political Leaders." In *Political Leadership in Industrialized Societies*, pp. 294-315. Edited by Lewis J. Edinger and Donald D. Searing. New York: John Wiley & Sons, 1967.

Seligman, Lester G.; King, Michael R.; Lim Kim, Chong; and Smith, Roland E. *Patterns of Recruitment: A State Chooses Its Lawmakers.* Chicago: Rand McNally, 1974.

Sharkansky, Ira, ed. *Policy Analysis in Political Science.* Chicago: Markham Publishing Co., 1970.

Siegfried, André. *Impressions of South America.* Translated by H.H. Hemming and Doris Hemming. London: Jonathon Cape, 1933.

Silva, Jorge Gustavo. *La cuestión social y la legislación social en Chile.* 2nd ed. Santiago: Imprenta Nacional, 1927.

——. *Nuestra evolución político-social (1900-1930).* Santiago: Imprenta Nascimento, 1931.

Silvert, Kalman H. "The Costs of Anti-Nationalism: Argentina." *Latin American Politics: Studies of the Contemporary Scene.* 2nd ed. Edited by Robert D. Tomasek. Garden City, N.Y.: Doubleday & Co.; Anchor Books, 1970.

Smith, Peter H. *Argentina and the Failure of Democracy: Conflict among Political Elites, 1904-1955.* Madison, Wisc.: University of Wisconsin Press, 1974.

——. "The Breakdown of Democracy in Argentina, 1916-30." In *The Breakdown of Democratic Regimes: Latin America*, pp. 3-27. Edited by Juan J. Linz and Alfred Stepan. Baltimore: Johns Hopkins University Press, 1978.

——. *Politics and Beef in Argentina: Patterns of Conflict and Change.* New York: Columbia University Press, 1969.

Snow, Peter G. *Radicalismo chileno: Historia y doctrina del partido radical.* Buenos Aires: Editorial Francisco de Aguirre, 1972.

Soares, Carlos F. *Economía y finanzas de la Nación Argentina, 1903-1913.* Buenos Aires: Est. Gráfico Grau y Soules, 1913.

——. *Economía y finanzas de la Nación Argentina.* 3 vols. Buenos Aires: n.p., 1916-1932.

Soares, Glaucio Ary Dillon. "The New Industrialization and the Brazilian Political System." In *Latin America: Reform or Revolution?*, pp. 186-201. Edited by James Petras and Maurice Zeitlin. Political Perspectives Series. Greenwich, Conn.: Fawcett Publications, 1968.

Sociedad de Fomento Fabril. Sección de Estadística. *Boletín de la estadística industrial de la República de Chile.* Santiago, 1895-1897.

Sociedad Inteligencia Sud Americana. *Hombres del día: El diccionario biográfico argentino.* Buenos Aires: n.p., 1917.

Solberg, Carl. *Immigration and Nationalism: Argentina and Chile, 1890-1914.* Austin: University of Texas Press, 1970.

——. "Rural Unrest and Agrarian Policy in Argentina, 1912-1930." *Journal of Inter-American Studies and World Affairs*, XIII (January 1971):18-52.

Solberg, Carl. "The Tariff and Politics in Argentina 1916-1930." *Hispanic American Historical Review*, LIII (May 1973):260-284.

Sommi, Luis V. "La estructura económico-social de la Argentina en 1890." *Revista de historia*, no. 1 (primer trimestre 1957):18-35.

Soto V., Feliciano. *Los dos candidatos: Don Pedro Montt y Don Jermán Riesco*. Valparaíso: Lit. F. Peters, 1901.

Spalding, Hobart. *La clase trabajadora argentina (documentos para su historia—1890/1912)*. Buenos Aires: Editorial Galerna, 1970.

——. "Education in Argentina, 1890-1914: The Limits of Oligarchical Reform." *Journal of Interdisciplinary History*, III (Summer 1972):31-61.

Subercaseaux, Guillermo. *Estudios políticos de actualidad*. Santiago: Imprenta Universitaria, 1914.

——. *Monetary and Banking Policy of Chile*. Oxford: Clarendon Press, 1922.

Subercaseaux, Ramón. *Memorias de ochenta años*. 2 vols. 2nd ed. Santiago: Editorial Nascimento, 1936.

Subercaseaux Browne, Julio. "Reminiscencias." *Boletín de la Academia Chilena de la Historia*, XXVII (primer semestre 1960):108-154.

——. "Reminiscencias." Ibid., XXVIII (primer semestre 1961):134-203.

——. "Reminiscencias." Ibid., XXVIII (segundo semestre 1961):192-264.

Tagle Rodríguez, Enrique. *Liberales y conservadores: Conferencias dictadas en el Centro Conservador de Chillán*. Santiago: Imprenta Universitaria, 1917.

Therborn, Göran. "The Travail of Latin American Democracy." *New Left Review*, no. 113-114 (January-April 1979):71-109.

Udaondo, Enrique. *Diccionario biográfico argentino*. Buenos Aires: Imprenta y Casa Editor Coni, 1938.

Urzua Valenzuela, Germán. *Los partidos políticos chilenos*. Santiago: Editorial Jurídica de Chile, 1968.

Uslaner, Eric M. "Comparative State Policy Formation, Interparty Competition, and Malapportionment: A New Look at 'V.O. Key's Hypothesis.'" *Journal of Politics*, XL (May 1978):409-432.

Valderrama Pérez, Alfredo. *Album político: El Gobierno, el Parlamento y el Consejo de Estado en la República de Chile (1912-1915)*. Santiago: Empresa Zig-Zag, 1914.

Valencia Avaria, Luis, ed. *Anales de la República*. 2 vols. Santiago: Imprenta Universitaria, 1951.

Valenzuela, Arturo. *The Breakdown of Democratic Regimes: Chile*. Baltimore: Johns Hopkins University Press, 1978.

——. *Political Brokers in Chile: Local Government in a Centralized Polity*. Durham, N.C.: Duke University Press, 1977.

Valenzuela, J. Samuel and Valenzuela, Arturo. "Chile and the Breakdown of Democracy." In *Latin American Politics and Development*, edited by Howard J. Wiarda and Harvey F. Kline, 233-261. Boston: Houghton Mifflin Co., 1979.

Valenzuela O., Juvenal. *Album de informaciones agrícolas: Zona central de Chile*. Santiago: n.p., 1923.

Vargas Cariola, Juan Eduardo. "La Sociedad de Fomento Fabril." *Historia*, XIII (1976), 5-53.

Véliz, Claudio. *Historia de la marina mercante de Chile.* Santiago: University of Chile, 1961.

Venegas, Alejandro [Dr. J. Valdés Cange]. *Cartas al Excelentísimo Señor Don Pedro Montt sobre la crisis moral de Chile en sus relaciones con el problema económico de la conversión metálica.* Valparaíso: Sociedad Imprenta y Litografía Universo, 1909.

———. *Sinceridad: Chile íntimo en 1910.* 2nd ed. Santiago: Imprenta Universitaria, 1910.

Verner, Joel G. "Socioeconomic Environment, Political System, and Educational Policy Outcomes: A Comparative Analysis of 102 Countries." *Comparative Politics*, XI (January 1979):165-187.

Vicuña Mackenna, Benjamín. *Historia de los diez años de la administración de don Manuel Montt.* 5 vols. Santiago: Imprenta Chilena, 1862-1863.

Villafañe, Benjamín. *Irigoyen, el último dictador.* 6th ed. Buenos Aires: Moro, Tello y Cía, 1922.

Vitale, Luis. *Interpretación marxista de la historia de Chile.* 3 vols. Santiago: Prensa Latinoamericana, 1967-1971.

———. *Las guerras civiles de 1851 y 1859 en Chile.* Concepción: Universidad de Concepción, 1971.

Walker, Jack L. "The Diffusion of Innovations among the American States." *American Political Science Review*, LXIII (September 1969):880-899.

Walker, Richard J. "Elections in the City of Buenos Aires during the First Yrigoyen Administration: Social Class and Political Preferences." *Hispanic American Historical Review*, LVIII (November 1978):595-624.

———. *The Socialist Party of Argentina, 1890-1930.* Latin American Monographs, no. 42. Austin, Texas: University of Texas Press, 1977.

Wilensky, Harold L. *The Welfare State and Equality: Structural and Ideological Roots of Public Expenditures.* Berkeley: University of California Press, 1975.

Williams, John H. *Argentine International Trade Under Inconvertible Paper Money, 1880-1900.* Harvard Economic Studies, Vol. XXII. Cambridge, Mass.: Harvard University Press, 1920.

Winters, Richard. "Party Control and Policy Change." *American Journal of Political Science*, XX (November 1976):597-636.

Wright, Thomas C. "Agriculture and Protectionism in Chile, 1880-1930." *Journal of Latin American Studies*, VII (May 1975):45-58.

———. *Landowners and Reform in Chile: The Sociedad Nacional de Agricultura, 1919-40.* Urbana, Ill.: University of Illinois Press, 1982.

———. "Origins of the Politics of Inflation in Chile, 1888-1918." *Hispanic American Historical Review*, LIII (May 1973):239-259.

———. "The Sociedad Nacional de Agricultura in Chilean Politics, 1869-1938." Ph.D. dissertation, University of California at Berkeley, 1971.

Wright, Winthrop R. *British-Owned Railways in Argentina: Their Effect on*

the Growth of Economic Nationalism, 1854-1948. Latin American Monographs, no. 34. Austin, Texas: University of Texas Press, 1974.

Yeager, Gertrude M. "The Club de la Unión and Kinship: Social Aspects of
Political Obstructionism in the Chilean Senate, 1920-1924." *Americas,*
XXXV (April 1979):539-572.

Yrarrázaval Larraín, José Miguel. "Las elecciones de 1888." *Boletín de la
Academia Chilena de la Historia,* XXI (primer semestre 1954):71-87.

———. *La política económica del Presidente Balmaceda.* Santiago: Academia
Chilena de la Historia, 1963.

Zegers Ariztia, Cristian. "Historia política del gobierno de Aníbal Pinto."
Historia, VI (1967):7-126.

Zeitlin, Maurice. "The Social Determinants of Political Democracy in Chile."
In *Latin America: Reform or Revolution?,* pp. 220-234. Edited by James
Petras and Maurice Zeitlin. Political Perspectives Series. Greenwich,
Conn.: Fawcett Publications, 1968.

Zorraquín Becú, Horacio et al. *Cuatro revoluciones argentinas.* Buenos Aires:
Ediciones del Club Nicolás Avellaneda, 1960.

INDEX

Agriculture: as basis for personal wealth in Chile, 40; as distinguished from stock-raising, 237n. 42; expansion in Argentina, 45–46; and government policy, 158–159, 194–198, 202; importance to Chilean economy, 35, 40. *See also* Labor, rural; Landowners; Legislation, rural; Rural sector
Agrarian reform, 194–195, 197–198, 212, 264nn.37, 44. *See also* Legislation, rural
Alem, Leandro: and formation of UCR, 32, 88; and Republican party, 26; and revolt of 1890, 33; suicide, 89; support for PAN, 28
Alessandri Palma, Arturo: election to Senate, 85; electoral intervention of, 134; family of, 125; presidential election, 85–86; reform proposals, 86, 206, 245n. 94, 246n. 96
Allende, Salvador, 221
Alsina, Adolfo, 25, 26
Alvear, Marcelo T. de: administration of, 159, 192, 195, 197; election of, 102; and petroleum issue, 204
Anarchism, 69, 108. *See also* Labor, organizations
Anarcho-syndicalism, 70. *See also* Labor, organizations
Antipersonalist Radicals: electoral support, 96, 99; social backgrounds, 121–122; and UCR schism, 101–103. *See also* Unión Cívica Radical
Araucanians, 35
Aristocracy. *See* Landowners; Legislators; Upper class
Asambleas, of Chilean Radical party, 17, 64, 67, 74
Autonomist party, 25, 26, 27, 32
Autonomous institutions, 157–158, 160–161
Avellaneda, Nicolás, 25, 26

Balmaceda, José Manuel: and banking, 22, 199, 201, 231n. 45; and civil war, 22–24; electoral intervention of, 21–22, 230n. 38; interpretation of overthrow, 214; organization of government party, 18–19, 22, 27
Balmacedists. *See* Liberal Democratic party
Banking legislation, 199, 201
Bauer, Arnold J., 43, 126, 128, 254n. 30
Besa, Arturo, 75
Besa Infantes, José, 75
Bribery, 67, 81–82, 106, 110. *See also* Electoral fraud
Buenos Aires, City of: and elections, 92, 96, 97, 191; growth, 56; immigrant population, 45, 56; and industrialization, 47; and labor legislation, 184; political status, 27; and railway network, 45; and Socialists, 95, 96, 97, 99, 187; and worker unrest, 107–108
Buenos Aires, Province of: and agriculture, 51, 52; Conservative party base, 99; immigrant settlement, 52; and industrialization, 47; in nineteenth-century politics, 10, 24–27
Bulnes, Manuel, 12, 199
Bureaucracy, 173–174, 216; expansion in Argentina, 156–159; expansion in Chile, 144–145, 155, 256n. 11

Caballero, Ricardo, 189, 190
Cabinet instability, 63, 239n. 6, 245n. 93; causes, 80–82, 219; consequences, 81, 83–85, 111, 194, 212
Cabinet responsibility, 22, 62, 63, 82

Economic growth: Argentine, 44, 47; Chilean, 35–36, 234nn. 9, 10; Chile and Argentina compared, 46
Education: in Argentina, 156, 158, 188–189; Argentina and Chile compared, 173, 174, 216; in Chile, 141–144, 155; 181–182, 183; and political recruitment, 113–114, 124; as political issue, 78–79, 229n. 12
Edwards Ross, Agustín, 23
Edwards Vives, Alberto, 13, 71, 74, 211
Elections: Argentine of 1912, 1914, and 1916, 92; Chilean of 1891–1924, 66–67, 77–78, 81; of deputies (Argentina), 95; in nineteenth-century Argentina, 25–27, 30–31; in nineteenth-century Chile, 18–22, 229n. 22; participation in Argentina and Chile, 58, 82–84, 91, 104–106; presidential in Argentina, 94, 232n. 68. See also Participation, political; Electoral fraud; Electoral system
Electoral fraud: in Argentina, 106; in Chile, 20, 66–67, 81–82, 106, 134. See also Bribery
Electoral system: Argentine, 91–92; Argentina and Chilean compared, 94; Chilean, 71–72, 81, 83; and Chilean electoral law, 20–21, 62, 85, 242n. 41, 243n. 43. See also Elections; Electoral fraud; Participation, electoral; Saenz Peña law
Encina, Francisco Antonio, 17
Entrepreneurs, 117–120
Errázuriz Echaurren, Federico, 75
Errázuriz Zañartu, Federico, 14, 16
Estate ownership. See Landowners; Rural sector
Exchange policy: Argentine, 166, 171–173, 259n. 46; Chilean, 153–155, 258n. 44. See also Monetary policy

Expenditures, governmental, 137–146, 155–161, 173–174
Exports: expansion of, 34, 44–46, 139–140; taxation of, 35, 147–148, 163–164, 166. See also Agriculture; Nitrates

Factionalism (Chile), 17–18, 82
Federación Agraria Argentina (FAA), 109, 195
Federación Obrera de Chile (FOCH), 69
Federalists, 10, 24
Figueroa, Virgilio, 130
Figueroa Alcorta, José, 90, 91, 203
Focus, of policy, 176–177, 205–206
Foreign investment: in Argentina, 44–45, 47–48, 236n. 36; in Argentina and Chile compared, 46; in Chile, 35, 37–38; and policy, 166, 169
Frente Unico, 99
Fusionists, 13, 14

Gallo, Ezequiel, 123, 135
Gallo, Vicente, 28
GDP. See Income
Germani, Gino, 107

Housing, worker: in Argentina, 187, 188; Chilean legislation on, 178, 180, 181; and Chilean public spending, 144, 155
Huneeus, Francisco, 178
Huneeus, Jorge, 79

Ibáñez, Carlos, 209
Immigrants: in Chile, 41, 42, 54; impact (Argentina), 45, 47, 50, 56; and political participation (Argentina), 106–109; role in commerce and industry (Argentina) 47, 49–50; in rural sector (Argentina), 51–52, 109
Imports: 36, 150, 173. See also

within, 90-91, 100; opposition to, 32-33; organization, 27-28; structure and program, 28, 30, 31
Partido Demócrata Progresista (PDP), 94-95, 97-99, 117
Party competition: definition, 7-9, previous research on impact, 6-7, 220; theoretical perspectives on, 4-6
Party development: Argentina and Chile compared, 11, 80, 87, 221-222; impact, 1; as index of political development, 224nn. 2, 3; and socioeconomic change, 58-59; timing of, 61-62
Pastoral interests. See Rural sector
Paternalism, 216, 217
Patronage, 174; in Argentina, 104, 156; in Chile, 81, 145
Patronato, 12-13
Pellegrini, Carlos, 26, 33, 89-91
Pelucones, 10, 12-13
Pensions, 156-157
Pérez, José Joaquín, 13, 14
Perón, Juan, 102
Personalist Radicals, 101, 122. *See also* Antipersonalist Radicals; Unión Cívica Radical
Petroleum, 202-204
Piñero, Norberto, 99
Pipiolos, 10
Popular-sector groups: and policy, 165, 169-171, 213; representation of, 114, 218-219. *See also* Labor; Lower class; Middle class
Population, movement of, 41-42
Presidency: Argentina and Chile compared, 29, 94; importance in Argentina, 29, 189, 232nn. 61, 63; in nineteenth-century Chile, 12, 13, 20; in parliamentary period, 63. *See also* Elections
Professionals, 114-120
Progressive Democrats. *See* Partido Demócrata Progresista

Proportional representation, 81. *See also* Cumulative vote; Electoral system
Protoparties, 14-19, 221
Provinces, policies of, 192
Public sector. *See* Bureaucracy
Public works: Argentine, 156-157, 158, 159, 161; Chilean, 145-146

Quintana, Manuel, 89, 90, 91
Radical party, Argentine. *See* Unión Cívica Radical
Radical party, Chilean: anticlericalism, 14, 16, 77, 79; base of support, 67; and elections, 85, 86; leadership, 66; legislators, 66, 118-120, in nineteenth century, 14-17, 23, 63-64, 228n. 10, 229n. 15; organization, 64, 67, 74, 244n. 60; and policy issues, 79-80, 244n. 69; and political coalitions, 74, 77, 230n. 29; programs, 64-66, 79, 111, 229n. 21; rising influence, 66; and working class, 64
Railway: network in Argentina, 29, 45; policy, 204-205; workers, 182, 184, 187-188
Recabarren, Luis Emilio, 68
Recruitment, political: in Argentina, 216; in Chile, 19-20, 212, Chile and Argentina compared, 110, 134-135, 174, 211, 218; theoretical perspectives on, 4-6. *See also* Legislators
Regime type: research on, 223n. 1, 225n. 9, 226n. 15; theoretical importance of, 1, 4-6. *See also* party competition
Religion. *See* Church
Rent control. *See* Housing, worker
Republican party, 26, 27, 28, 88
Residence, Law of, 192
Revenues, public: Argentina, 161-166; Chilean, 146-149. *See also*

Taxation

Revolts: Argentine, 25, 27, 33, 34, 89, 90; Chilean, 12. *See also* Civil war

Reyes, Vicente, 19

Riesco, Germán, 74

Rimlinger, Gaston, 215–216

Roca, Julio: *acuerdo* with Mitre, 88; and PAN, 27–29, 90–91; presidential candidacy, 26, 231n. 53; and revolt of 1890, 33; rift with Pelligrini, 89

Rocha, Dardo, 26

Rock, David, 104, 107, 191, 211

Rosas, Juan Manuel de, 24

Rural sector: expansion, 35, 45–46, 51; and immigrants, 47, 51–52; inequalities in, 53–55; and land values, 254nn. 31, 32; linkages with urban sector, 40, 59; and policy, 51, 166, 169, 170, 171; political impact, 43, 60, 110; structure of, 43, 51–54; reform of, 212, 216; and tariff, 151; value added by, 48. *See also* Agriculture; Labor, rural; Landowners; Legislation

Saenz Peña, Luis, 88, 91, 247n. 3

Saenz Peña, Roque, 26, 91, 92, 107, 247n. 3

Saenz Peña law, 3, 91–93, 103, 104, 107

Sanfuentes, Enrique Salvador, 23, 74

Sanfuentes, Juan Luis, 74–75, 243n. 51

Santa María, Domingo: conflict with church, 16; election of, 230n. 29; elections under, 21; and liberals, 18, 27; opposition to, 23

Sarmiento, Domingo, 25, 26, 27, 28, 231n. 53

Scope, of policy, 175–176, 205–206, 217

Secret ballot. *See* Electoral system

Semana Trágica, 191, 193–194

Sigal, Silvia, 123, 135

Smith, Peter H., 120, 122–123, 128, 248n. 28

Social Defense, Law of, 108

Socialist party, 61, 92, 94–97; and immigrant community, 107, 109; legislators, 117; and tariff policy, 169–170. *See also* Labor, organizations

Socialist Worker party (POS), 69, 70, 152

Social policy, 86, 178–192, 206–207, 213–218. *See also* Labor; "Social question"

"Social question," 80

Sociedad de Fomento Fabril, 151

Sociedad de Igualdad, 12, 228n. 4

Sociedad Nacional de Agricultura (SNA), 130

Sociedad Rural, 122, 123, 169, 170, 202

Solberg, Carl, 169–170

Spending. *See* Expenditures

Strikes. *See* Labor, unrest

Subercaseaux, Ramón, 80, 81

Suffrage. *See* Electoral system

Syndicalism, 108, 109. *See also* Labor, organizations

Tariff. *See* Commercial policy

Taxation: in Argentina, 161–166, 173, 217; in Chile, 35, 146–149, 154, 212, 213. *See also* Commercial policy; Revenues, public

Tejedor, Carlos, 26, 27, 231n. 53

Tocornal, Ismael, 75

Trade unions. *See* Labor

Ugarte, Marcelino, 89, 91, 98

Unión Cívica, 32–33, 87–88

Unión Cívica Nacional, 88, 89

Unión Cívica Radical: divisions within, 197; elections of 1912, 1914, 1916, 92; formation, 87–90; and